Basic Concepts in Data Structures

Basic Concepts in Data Structures acquaints the reader with the theoretical side of the art of writing computer programs. Instead of concentrating on the technical aspects of how to instruct a computer to perform a certain task, the book switches to the more challenging question of what in fact should be done to solve a given problem.

The volume is the result of several decades of teaching experience in data structures and algorithms. It is self-contained and does not assume any prior knowledge other than of some basic programming and mathematical tools. Klein reproduces his oral teaching style in writing, with one topic leading to another, related one. Most of the classic data structures are covered, though not in a comprehensive manner. Alternatively, some more advanced topics, related to pattern matching and coding, are mentioned.

SHMUEL TOMI KLEIN started teaching in high school, repeating to his classmates almost daily the lectures of their mathematics teacher. As a computer science undergraduate at the Hebrew University of Jerusalem, he acted as teaching assistant in the Statistics Department and has since given courses and lectures on data structures, algorithms, and related topics in English, French, German, and Hebrew.

Klein's research focuses on data compression and text-processing algorithms. He is a full professor and former chair of the Computer Science Department at Bar-Ilan University and a coauthor of more than 100 academic publications and 10 patents.

Basic Concepts in Data Structures

SHMUEL TOMI KLEIN
Bar-Ilan University, Israel

CAMBRIDGE
UNIVERSITY PRESS

CAMBRIDGE
UNIVERSITY PRESS

Shaftesbury Road, Cambridge CB2 8EA, United Kingdom

One Liberty Plaza, 20th Floor, New York, NY 10006, USA

477 Williamstown Road, Port Melbourne, VIC 3207, Australia

314–321, 3rd Floor, Plot 3, Splendor Forum, Jasola District Centre, New Delhi – 110025, India

103 Penang Road, #05–06/07, Visioncrest Commercial, Singapore 238467

Cambridge University Press is part of Cambridge University Press & Assessment,
a department of the University of Cambridge.

We share the University's mission to contribute to society through the pursuit of
education, learning and research at the highest international levels of excellence.

www.cambridge.org
Information on this title: www.cambridge.org/9781107161276

10.1017/9781316676226

First published 2016

A catalogue record for this publication is available from the British Library

Library of Congress Cataloging-in-Publication data
Names: Klein, Shmuel T., author.
Title: Basic concepts in data structures / Shmuel Tomi Klein,
Bar-Ilan University, Israel.
Description: Cambridge, United Kingdom ; New York, NY : Cambridge University Press,
[2016] | Includes bibliographical references and index.
Identifiers: LCCN 2016026212 | ISBN 9781107161276 (hardback : alk. paper)
Subjects: LCSH: Data structures (Computer science)
Classification: LCC QA76.9.D35 K558 2016 | DDC 005.7/3–dc23
LC record available at https://lccn.loc.gov/2016026212

ISBN   978-1-107-16127-6   Hardback
ISBN   978-1-316-61384-9   Paperback

Contents

List of Background Concepts

Preface

After having mastered some high-level programming language and acquired knowledge in basic mathematics, it is time for a shift of attention. Instead of concentrating on the technical aspects of *how* to instruct a computer to perform a certain task, we switch to the more challenging question of *what* in fact should be done to solve a given problem. The aim of this book on data structures is to start acquainting the reader with the theoretical side of the art of writing computer programs. This may be considered as a first step in getting familiar with a series of similar fields, such as algorithms, complexity, and computability, that should be learned in parallel to improve practical programming skills.

The book is the result of several decades of teaching experience in data structures and algorithms. In particular, I have taught a course on Data Structures more than 30 times. The book is self-contained and does not assume any prior knowledge of data structures, just a comprehension of basic programming and mathematics tools generally learned at the very beginning of computer science or other related studies. In my university, the course is given in the second semester of the first year of the BSc program, with a prerequisite of Discrete Mathematics and Introduction to Programming, which are first-semester courses. The format is two hours of lecture plus two hours of exercises, led by a teaching assistant, per week.

I have tried to reproduce my oral teaching style in writing. I believe in associative learning, in which one topic leads to another, related one. Although this may divert attention from the central, currently treated subject, it is the cumulative impact of an entire section or chapter that matters. There was no intention to produce a comprehensive compendium of all there is to know about data structures but rather to provide a collection of what many could agree to be its basic ingredients and major building blocks, on which subsequent courses on algorithms could rely. In addition, many more advanced topics are mentioned.

Each chapter comes with its own set of exercises, many of which have appeared in written exams. Solutions to selected exercises appear in the appendix. There are short inserts treating some background concepts: they are slightly indented, set in another font, and separated from the main text by rules. Though each chapter could be understood on its own, even if it has pointers to earlier material, the book has been written with the intent of being read sequentially.

There is of course a long list of people to whom I am indebted for this project, and it is not possible to mention them all. Foremost, I owe all I know to the continuous efforts of my late father to offer me, from childhood on, the best possible education in every domain. This included also private lessons, and I am grateful to my teacher R. Gedalya Stein, who interspersed his Talmud lessons with short flashes to notions of grammar, history, and more, and thereby planted the seeds of the associative learning techniques I adopted later. There is no doubt that my high school mathematics teacher Fernand Biendel was one of the best; he taught us rigor and deep understanding, and the fact that more than half of our class ended up with a PhD in mathematics should be credited to him.

I wish to thank all my teachers at the Hebrew University of Jerusalem and at the Weizmann Institute of Science in Rehovot as well as my colleagues at Bar-Ilan University and elsewhere. Many of them had an impact on my academic career, especially the advisors for my theses, Eli Shamir and Aviezri Fraenkel. Amihood Amir is directly responsible for this book because he asked me, when he was department chair, to teach the course on Data Structures. Thanks also to Franya Franek for providing a contact at Cambridge University Press.

Last, but not least, I wish to thank my spouse and children, to whom this book is dedicated, for their ongoing encouragement and constructive comments during the whole writing period. As to my grandchildren, they have no idea what this is all about, so I thank them for just being there and lighting up my days with their love.

1

Why Data Structures?
A Motivating Example

To begin the study of data structures, I demonstrate the usefulness of even quite simple structures by working through a detailed motivating example. We shall afterward come back to the basics and build up our body of knowledge incrementally.

The algorithm presented in this introduction is due to R. S. Boyer and J S. Moore and solves the *string matching problem* in a surprisingly efficient way. The techniques, although sophisticated, do not require any advanced mathematical tools for their understanding. It is precisely because of this simplicity that the algorithm is a good example of the usefulness of *data structures*, even the simplest ones. In fact, all that is needed to make the algorithm work are two small arrays storing integers.

There are two sorts of algorithms that, when first encountered, inspire both perplexity and admiration. The first is an algorithm so complicated that one can hardly imagine how its inventors came up with the idea, triggering a reaction of the kind, "How could they think of that?" The other possibility is just the opposite – some flash of ingeniousity that gives an utterly simple solution, leaving us with the question, "How didn't I think of that?" The Boyer–Moore algorithm is of this second kind.

We encounter on a daily basis instances of the string matching problem, defined generically as follows: given a text $T = T[1]T[2] \cdots T[n]$ of length n characters and a string $S = S[1]S[2] \cdots S[m]$ of length m, find the (first, or all) location(s) of S in T, if one appears there at all. In the example of Figure 1.1, the string $S = $ TRYME is indeed found in T, starting at position 22.

To solve the problem, we imagine that the string is aligned underneath the text, starting with both text and string left justified. One can then compare corresponding characters, until a mismatch is found, which enables us to move the string forward to a new potential matching position. We call this the *naive* approach. It should be emphasized that our discourse of moving the pattern

1

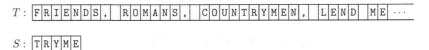

$T:$ | F | R | I | E | N | D | S | , | | R | O | M | A | N | S | , | | C | O | U | N | T | R | Y | M | E | N | , | | L | E | N | D | | M | E | $\cdots$

$S:$ | T | R | Y | M | E

Figure 1.1. Schematic of the string matching problem.

along an imaginary sliding path is just for facilitating understanding. Actually, text and string remain, of course, in the same location in memory during the entire search process, and their moving is simulated by the changing values of pointers. A *pointer* is a special kind of a variable, defined in many programming languages, holding the address of some data item within computer memory. A pointer may often be simulated by a simple integer variable representing an index in an array.

The number of necessary character comparisons is obviously dependent on the location of S in T, if it appears there at all, so to enable a unified discussion, let us assume that we scan the entire text, searching for all occurrences of S. In the worst case (that is, the worst possible choice of both text T and string S), the naive approach requires approximately $n \times m$ comparisons, as can be seen by considering a text of the form $T = \text{AAA} \cdots \text{AB}$ and a string of similar form $S = \text{A} \cdots \text{AB}$, where the length of the string of As is $2n$ in the text T and n in the string S; only after $(n + 1)^2$ comparisons will we find out that S occurs once in T, as a suffix.

The truth is that, actually, this simple algorithm is not so bad under more realistic assumptions, and the worst-case behavior of the previous paragraph occurs just for a rather artificial input of the kind shown. On the average, the number of comparisons in the naive approach will be approximately

$$c \cdot n, \qquad (1.1)$$

where c is some constant larger than 1 but generally quite close to 1. It is larger than 1, as every character of the text is compared at least once with some character of the string, and some characters are compared more than once.

In 1977, D. Knuth, J. H. Morris, and V. Pratt published an algorithm that inspects every character of the text and the string exactly once, yielding a complexity of $n + m$ rather than $n \times m$ comparisons. The *complexity* of an algorithm is the time or space it requires, as a function of the size of its input. In particular, the Knuth–Morris–Pratt algorithm also yields $c = 1$ in eq. (1.1). We shall not give here the details of this algorithm, simply because in the same year, Boyer and Moore found an even better algorithm, for which $c < 1$! At first sight, this might look impossible, as $c < 1$ means that the number of characters involved in comparisons is less than the length of the text, or in other words, the algorithm does not inspect all the characters. How could this be possible? We shall see that it all derives from clever use of simple data structures.

1.1 Boyer and Moore's Algorithm

A nice feature of the Boyer–Moore algorithm is that its main idea can be expressed in just four words:

Start from the end.

By repeatedly applying these words as a mantra, we will see how they may help to improve the search.

Let us first try to interpret them correctly. It should be clear that the intention is not just to reverse the process and start by aligning the string S at the end of the text T, and then scanning both from right to left. That would be symmetric to the more natural forward scan from left to right, and the expected search time would be the same. We must therefore conclude that it is only for the string that the scanning will *start at the end* and proceed right to left, whereas the text is scanned in the usual way, from left to right, although with the required minor adaptations.

Figure 1.2 depicts the initial positions of the pointers i and j, showing the current indices in text and string, respectively, for an imaginary text T and the name of my university $S = $ BAR-ILAN as a running example for the string. The pointer j is set to the end of the string, that is, $j = m$, 8 in our example, but the initial position of the pointer i is quite unusual – it is neither at the leftmost nor at the rightmost character but rather at that indexed m, corresponding to the last character of the string S.

So what do we gain by this curious setting? The first comparison, in the example of Figure 1.2, would be of character N in S against a W in T, yielding a mismatch. This disqualifies the current position of S, so the string has to be

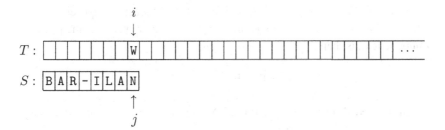

Figure 1.2. Initialization of the Boyer–Moore algorithm.

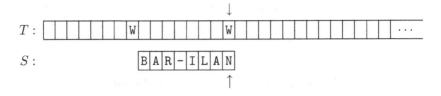

Figure 1.3. After first shift in the Boyer–Moore algorithm.

moved. Does it make sense to move it by $1, 2, \ldots, 7$ positions to the right? That would still leave the W in position 8 of T over one of the characters of S and necessarily lead to some mismatch, because W does not appear at all in S. We may therefore move S at once beyond the W, that is, to be aligned with position 9. Yet the next comparison, according to our mantra, will again be at the end of S, corresponding now to position $i = 16$ in T, as in Figure 1.3. Note that we have not looked at all at any of the first seven characters in T; nevertheless, we can be sure that no match of S in T has been missed.

The careful reader might feel cheated at this point. The previous paragraph showed an example in which the string could be moved at a step of size m, but this depended critically on the fact that W did not appear in S. The natural question is, then, "How do we know that?" An evident approach would be to check it, but this requires m comparisons, exactly counterbalancing the m comparisons we claimed to have saved! To answer these concerns, suppose that in the position of the second comparison, indexed 16, there is again a W, as in Figure 1.3. Obviously, there is no need to check again if there is a W in S, if we can remember what has already been checked.

1.2 The Bad-Character Heuristic

This leads to the idea of maintaining a Boolean table Δ_0, defining, for each given string S, a function from Σ, the set of all the characters (called also the *alphabet*), to $\{\mathsf{T}, \mathsf{F}\}$: $\Delta_0[x] = \mathsf{T}$, if and only if the character x appears in the string S. The main step of the scanning algorithm, which increases the pointer i into the text, is then

$$\text{if } \Delta_0[T[i]] = \mathsf{F} \qquad i \longleftarrow i + m.$$

The time needed for the construction of Δ_0 is just $m + |\Sigma|$, which is independent of the size n of the text.

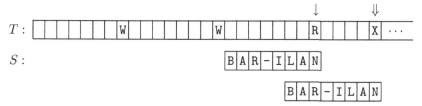

Figure 1.4. Mismatching character appears in S.

And if the mismatching character does appear in S, as in Figure 1.4? Again, one may argue that nothing can be gained from shifting the string one to four positions, so we should, for the given example, shift it by five to align the two Rs, as seen in the lower part of Figure 1.4. The next comparison, however, will be at the end, as usual, indicated by the double arrow. The last ideas may be unified if one redefines the auxiliary table to hold integers rather than Boolean values and to store directly the size of the possible jump of the pointer. More formally, define a table Δ_1, for a given string S, as a function from Σ to the integers, $\Delta_1[x] = r$, if the string can safely be moved by r positions forward in the case of a mismatch at its last character. This reduces the main step of the scanning algorithm to

$$i \longleftarrow i + \Delta_1[T[i]]. \tag{1.2}$$

For our example string $S = \text{BAR-ILAN}$, the Δ_1 table is given in Figure 1.5. It can be built by initializing each entry with m, 8 in our example, and then processing the string left to right, setting

$$\text{for } j \leftarrow 1 \text{ to } m \qquad \Delta_1[S[j]] \leftarrow m - j.$$

This leaves the index for the rightmost appearance, should a character appear more than once in S, like A in our example. The complexity is, as for Δ, $m + |\Sigma|$.

-	A	B	C	D	E	F	G	H	I	J	K	L	M
4	1	7	8	8	8	8	8	8	3	8	8	2	8
N	O	P	Q	R	S	T	U	V	W	X	Y	Z	
0	8	8	8	5	8	8	8	8	8	8	8	8	

Figure 1.5. Table Δ_1 for example string $S = \text{BAR-ILAN}$ and $\Sigma = \{\text{A, B}, \ldots, \text{Z, -}\}$. The upper lines are the characters, and the lower lines are the corresponding Δ_1 values. The entries for characters not appearing in S are in smaller font.

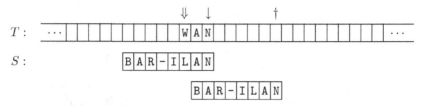

Figure 1.6. Mismatch after a few matches.

So far, only the case of a mismatch at the last character of S has been dealt with. Consider now the possibility of a match, as in Figure 1.6, where the single arrow shows the position of the first comparison for the current location of S, as usual, at the end. In that case, we decrement both i and j and repeat the process. One possibility for exiting this loop is when j reaches zero, that is, the entire string is matching and a success is declared:

$$\text{if } j = 0 \qquad \text{return } i + 1.$$

Another possibility is that, after k steps backward, we again encounter a mismatch, as indicated by the double arrow in Figure 1.6, where the mismatch occurs for $k = 2$. The string can then only be shifted beyond the current position, by six positions in our example, and more generally, by $\Delta_1[T[i]] - k$, as in the lower part of Figure 1.6. But we are interested in moving the current position of the pointer i, not in shifting the string, and one has to remember that i has been moved backward by k positions since we started comparing from the end of the string. As the following comparison should again be according to $j = m$, we have to compensate for the decrement by adding k back. The correct updated value of i is therefore

$$i + (\Delta_1[T[i]] - k) + k = i + \Delta_1[T[i]],$$

just as before, so that the assignment in line (1.2) is valid not only for the case of a mismatch at the first trial (at the end of the string) but also for every value of $k > 0$. In our example of Figure 1.6, the current position of i points to W, which does not appear in S, hence i is incremented by $\Delta_1[\text{W}] = 8$, bringing us to the position indicated by the dagger sign.

There is possibly a slight complication in the case when the mismatching character of T appears in S to the right of the current position, as would be the case if, in Figure 1.6, there would be an A or N instead of W at the position indicated by the double arrow (there are two As in our example, but recall that the value in Δ_1 refers to the rightmost occurrence of a character in S). This is the case in which $\Delta_1[T[i]] < k$, so to get an alignment, we would actually shift the string *backward*, which is useless, because we took care to move the string only over positions for which one could be certain that no match is missed. Incrementing i by k would bring us back to the beginning position of the current iteration; therefore the minimal increment should be at least $k + 1$. The corrected update is therefore

$$i \longleftarrow i + \max(k + 1, \Delta_1[T[i]]). \tag{1.3}$$

1.3 The Good-Suffix Heuristic

Actually, this idea of moving the pointer i into the text forward according only to the mismatching character $T[i]$ is already efficient enough to be known as one of the variants of the Boyer–Moore algorithm. But one can do better. Consider the case in which the first mismatch occurs after k steps backward, for $k > 0$, as in Figures 1.6 and 1.7. Instead of concentrating on what went wrong, let us rather insist on the fact that if the first mismatch is at the $k + 1$st trial, this means that there was a success in the k first comparisons. But this implies that when the mismatch occurs, we know what characters appear in the text at positions $i + 1, \ldots, i + k$: these must be the characters of the suffix of length k of S. We can therefore check where there is a reoccurrence of this suffix in the string S, if at all. In Figure 1.7, the suffix AN does not appear again in S, so we can move the pattern beyond the position where the present iteration started, as shown in the lower part of Figure 1.7. The next comparison is at the position indicated by the dagger sign, so that i has been incremented from its current position, indicated by the double arrow, by 10. Had we used $\Delta_1[\text{I}]$, we could have added only 3 to i.

As previously, we shall not search for another copy of the current suffix during the scanning of the text. There are only m possible suffixes, and one can prepare a table of the possible increments of index i for each of them, independently of the text, in a preprocessing stage. The table Δ_2 will assign a value to each of the possible positions $j \in \{1, \ldots, m\}$ in the string S: $\Delta_2[j]$ will be defined as the number of positions one can move the pointer i in the case where

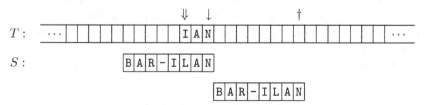

Figure 1.7. The good-suffix heuristic.

j	1	2	3	4	5	6	7	8
$S[j]$	B	A	R	-	I	L	A	N
shift	8	8	8	8	8	8	8	1
k	7	6	5	4	3	2	1	0
$\Delta_2[j]$	15	14	13	12	11	10	9	1

Figure 1.8. Table Δ_2 for example string $S = $ BAR-ILAN.

the first mismatch is at position j, still keeping in mind that we started the comparisons, as usual, from $j = m$.

The increment of i consists of two parts, the first being the number of steps we moved the pointer backward for the current position of the string, the second relating to repositioning the string itself. As we moved already $k = m - j$ steps to the left, i can be increased to point to the position corresponding to the end of the string again, by adding k to i; then we should shift the string S, so as to align the matching suffix with its earlier occurrence in S. $\Delta_2[j]$ will be the sum of k with this shift size.

So which heuristic is better, Δ_1 of the *bad character* or Δ_2 of the *good suffix*? It depends, but because both are correct, we can just choose the maximal increment at each step. The main command would thus become

$$i \longleftarrow i + \max(k + 1, \Delta_1[T[i]], \Delta_2[j]), \qquad (1.4)$$

but $\Delta_2[j]$ is k plus some shift, which has to be at least 1. Therefore, the command in line (1.4) is equivalent to

$$i \longleftarrow i + \max(\Delta_1[T[i]], \Delta_2[j]). \qquad (1.5)$$

Figure 1.8 depicts the Δ_2 table for our example string. For example, the values in columns 7, 6, and 5 correspond to the first mismatch having occurred with the characters, A, L, and I, which means that there has been a match for N, AN, and LAN, respectively. But none of these suffixes appears again in S, so in all these cases, S may be shifted by the full length of the string, which is 8. Adding the corresponding values of k, 1, 2, and 3, finally gives Δ_2 values of 9, 10, and 11, respectively. Column 8 is a special case, corresponding to a matching suffix that is empty and thus reoccurs everywhere. We can therefore only shift by 1, but in fact it does not matter, as in this case, the Δ_1 value in command (1.5) will be dominant.

The simple form of this table, with increasing values from right to left, is misleading. Let us see what happens if the string changes slightly to $S = $ BAN-ILAN. The value in column 6 corresponds to a mismatch with L after having

j	1	2	3	4	5	6	7	8
$S[j]$	B	A	N	-	I	L	A	N
shift	8	8	8	8	8	5	5	1
k	7	6	5	4	3	2	1	0
$\Delta_2[j]$	15	14	13	12	11	7	6	1

j	1	2	3	4	5	6	7	8
$S[j]$	B	A	N	-	I	L	A	N
shift	8	8	8	8	8	5	**8**	1
k	7	6	5	4	3	2	1	0
$\Delta_2[j]$	15	14	13	12	11	7	**9**	1

Figure 1.9. Table Δ_2 for example string $S = $ BAN-ILAN.

matched AN. This suffix appears again, starting in position 2 of S, so to align the two occurrences, the string must be moved by five positions. For $j = 7$, the corresponding suffix is of length 1, just N, which seems also to trigger a shift of five positions, like for column 6. For columns $j < 6$, we are looking for LAN or longer suffixes of S, none of which reoccurs in S, thus the string can be shifted by its full length, 8. This yields the table in the upper part of Figure 1.9.

The value in column 7 should, however, be reconsidered. Applying $\Delta_2[7]$ as increment corresponds to a scenario in which there has been a match with N, and a mismatch with the next, preceding, character. We thus know that there is an N in the text, which is preceded by some character that is not A. Therefore, when we look for another occurrence of N, the one found in position 3 does not qualify, because it is also preceded by A; if this lead to a mismatch at the current position, it will again yield a mismatch after the shift. Our strategy can therefore be refined: for a given suffix S' of the string S, we seek its previous occurrence in S, if there is one, but with the additional constraint that this previous occurrence should be preceded by a *different* character than the occurrence at the end of S. For $S' = $ N in our example, there is no such re-occurrence, hence the correct shift of the string is by the full length 8, and not just by 5, which yields the table in the lower part of Figure 1.9. The other entries remain correct. For example, for $j = 6$, we search for another appearance of the suffix AN that is not preceded by L, and indeed, the previous AN is preceded by B, so one may shift the string only by 5.

We are not yet done and there is need for a final slight amendment in certain cases. Consider another small change of the given string to $S = $ LAN-ILAN.

j	1	2	3	4	5	6	7	8
$S[j]$	L	A	N	-	I	L	A	N
shift	8	8	8	8	5	8	8	1
k	7	6	5	4	3	2	1	0
$\Delta_2[j]$	15	14	13	12	8	10	9	1

j	1	2	3	4	5	6	7	8
$S[j]$	L	A	N	-	I	L	A	N
shift	5	5	5	5	5	8	8	1
k	7	6	5	4	3	2	1	0
$\Delta_2[j]$	12	11	10	9	8	10	9	1

Figure 1.10. Table Δ_2 for example string $S = $ LAN-ILAN.

Treating this example in the way wé have done earlier would produce the table in the upper part of Figure 1.10. Though the suffixes N and AN appear earlier, they are preceded by the same characters A and L, respectively, in both occurrences, and are therefore regarded as if they would not re-appear, yielding a shift of 8. The suffix LAN, on the other hand, appears again as prefix of S, but is not preceded there by I, so we can shift only by 5.

Refer now to Figure 1.11 and suppose the first mismatch is for $j = 4$, comparing the character W in the text with the dash character - in S, after having matched already the suffix ILAN. Since this suffix does not re-occur, the upper Δ_2 table of Figure 1.10 suggests to shift by 8, moving the pointer i by 12, from the position indicated by the single arrow to that indicated by the double arrow. But this could have resulted in a missed occurrence, as indicated by the brace in the figure.

How could this happen? The answer is that our current string S has a special property, namely, that it contains a suffix, LAN, that is also a prefix. This allows different occurrences of S, or its suffixes, to overlap in the text. One

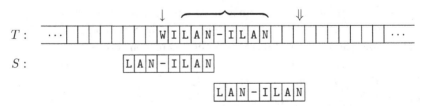

Figure 1.11. Example of a missed occurrence by the upper Δ_2 table of Figure 1.10.

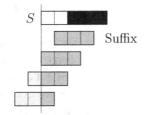

Figure 1.12. Constructing the Δ_2 table.

therefore needs some special care in this particular case, refining the definition of a plausible re-occurrence as follows:

> for a given suffix S' of S, we are looking for a previous occurrence of S' in S, not preceded by the same character; if no such previous occurrence is found, we are looking for an occurrence of some suffix S'' of the suffix S', but only if S'' appears as prefix of S.

This definition sounds admittedly terrible, but is nonetheless quite easy to implement. Referring to the string S in Figure 1.12, we wish to locate a plausible re-occurrence of the suffix S' of S that appears in black. We thus imagine that S' is shifted by one, two, etc., positions to the left and we check whether there is a match with the corresponding substring of S. In a first attempt, we would shift a copy of S' only until its left end is aligned with the beginning of S (first two lines below S in Figure 1.12). To check also the variant with the suffix of the suffix, all we need is to continue the shifting loop further, as long as there is still some overlap between S' and S (bottom two lines in the figure); for each such position, only the darker gray cells have to be checked for a match, the lighter gray cells are simply ignored.

Referring again to our example, if there is a mismatch at position $j = 4$, after having matched already the suffix $S' = \text{ILAN}$, it is true that S' does not reoccur in S. But the suffix $S'' = \text{LAN}$ of the suffix S' does reoccur as prefix of S, so the pattern can only be shifted by 5 and not by 8 positions. The same will be true for mismatches at the other positions j with $j < 4$. This yields the table in the lower part of Figure 1.10, in which the changes relative to the table in the upper part are emphasized.

Summarizing: by starting the comparisons from the end of the string S, for each potential matching position, we were able to scan the text T for an occurrence of S, inspecting only a fraction of the characters of T. It is like sifting the text characters with a comb or a rake, whose teeth are close enough so that no occurrence of S can slip through, yet distant enough to imply only a partial scan of T. The main tool was a clever use of two integer arrays as simple data structures.

Boyer and Moore evaluated that the constant c of eq. (1.1) is approximately $1/(m-1)$, implying the surprising property that: the longer the string, the faster one can locate it (or assert that it does not occur).

We shall see in the following chapters more examples of how various data structures may enhance our ability to cope with algorithmic problems.

Exercises

1.1 Run the Boyer–Moore algorithm on the example text and string that appears in their original paper:

$T =$ WHICH-FINALLY-HALTS.--AT-THAT-POINT-... and
$S =$ AT-THAT.

1.2 Build the Δ_2 tables for the strings ABRACADABRA and AABAAABAABAA.

1.3 Complete the statement of the following (probably quite useless) theorem, and prove it:

> Given is a string S of length m. Let k be the length of the longest suffix of S consisting of identical characters, $1 \le k \le m$. The last k entries of the Δ_2 array of S all contain the value . . ..

1.4 Suppose that instead of the corrected update of eq. (1.3) we would use the original incrementing step of eq. (1.2), without the maximum function. Build an example of a string of length 6 over the alphabet $\Sigma = \{$A, B, C$\}$ and a corresponding small text for which the Boyer–Moore algorithm, using only Δ_1 and not Δ_2, would then enter an infinite loop.

1.5 Suppose that by analyzing the performance of our algorithm, we realize that for strings of length $m > 50$, the part of the Δ_2 table corresponding to $j < 45$ is only rarely used. We therefore decided to keep only a partial Δ_2 table, with indices $j \ge 45$, to save space. The algorithm is of course adapted accordingly. Choose the correct statement of the following ones:

(a) The algorithm works and the time to find the string will be shorter.
(b) The algorithm works and the time to find the string will be longer.
(c) The algorithm works but we cannot know how the change will affect the time to find the string.
(d) The algorithm does not work: it may not find all the occurrences of the string.
(e) The algorithm does not work: it may announce wrong matches.

1.6 You have a nonsorted array A of n numbers. The task is to prepare a data structure in time $O(n)$ in a preprocessing stage, such that any subsequent query of the form $sum(i, j)$, for $1 \leq i \leq j \leq n$, can be answered in constant time, where $sum(i, j) = \sum_{r=i}^{j} A[r]$ is the sum of the elements in the subarray from i to j.

1.7 The definition of Δ_2 included two corrections:

C_1: We are looking for a reoccurrence of a suffix, but only if the preceding characters are different;

C_2: while searching for a reoccurrence of a suffix, we allow also only partial overlaps between suffix and string.

Consider now the following variants of the algorithm:

V_1: Use correction C_1, but not C_2;

V_2: use correction C_2, but not C_1;

V_3: do not use any of the corrections C_1 or C_2;

V_4: use Δ_1 instead of $\max(\Delta_1, \Delta_2)$.

Finally, we define the following assertions:

A_1: The algorithm is not correct;

A_2: the algorithm is correct, but will be slower;

A_3: the algorithm is correct, its speed will not change, but more space will be needed;

A_4: the algorithm is correct, its speed will not change, and less space will be needed.

Fill in the values yes or no in the entries of the following table, for each of the possible (variant, assertion) pairs:

	V_1	V_2	V_3	V_4
A_1				
A_2				
A_3				
A_4				

2

Linear Lists

2.1 Managing Data Storage

In our first steps as programmers, we often write short programs with a quite limited number of variables. Very soon, however, the programming tasks get more involved, and we need some advanced tools to manage efficiently the increasing number of elements dealt with by our programs. This is the role of what has become known as *Data Structures*, which are the subject of this book.

When coming to organize the data we are supposed to handle, we shall deal with entities called *records*, like the one in Figure 2.1, representing, in this chapter's running example, the information about a given student at some university. A record may be divided into *fields*, each standing for a data item relating to the given student, like the name, given name, address, field of study, a list of courses and their grades, etc. One of the fields is particular in that it will serve to identify the records and to distinguish between them. It is emphasized in Figure 2.1, its content is called here ID number, and the assumption will be that different records have different IDs.

Our task is to maintain a large collection of such records, allowing efficient access and updates. Maintaining means here to store the records in such a way that queries about any of their data fields may be processed quickly, but also to facilitate subsequent changes, like insertions of new records, or deletion of those that are not needed any more. Getting back to our example, a student might ask what grade she got on a specific course, a new record has to be allocated if a new student enrolls, and the records of students who finished their studies should be erased from the current list and possibly transferred to another collection, dealing with alumni.

The technical problem of processing records with variable length fields may be overcome by storing the records wherever convenient, and keeping only a list of fixed length (ID, pointer) pairs. We may then restrict our attention to

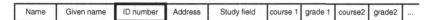

Name	Given name	ID number	Address	Study field	course 1	grade 1	course2	grade2	...

Figure 2.1. A sample record and its subfields.

processing only the list of IDs, and shall henceforth narrow our discussion to the handling of the identifying field alone.

An immediate question to be dealt with is how to store such a list. A straightforward solution would be to store the records sequentially, in the order they appear in the system. More precisely, we might allocate a certain amount of sequential memory cells, and store there new records on demand, one after the other. This is called *sequential allocation*, and it is clearly advantageous for allowing inserts, as long as the allocated space has not been exhausted, but searches could force a scan of the entire list. To avoid such worst case behavior, one could require the list to be kept in order, for example sorted by increasing ID. This would then enable an improved lookup procedure, known as *binary search*.

Background Concept: Binary Search

Binary search belongs to a family of algorithms called *Divide and Conquer*. The common feature of these algorithms is that they solve a problem by dividing it into several similar, but smaller, subproblems, which can be solved recursively. For instance, when looking for an element x within a sorted array $A[1], \ldots, A[n]$, we start by comparing x to the middle element $A[n/2]$. If it is found there, we are done, but if not, we know whether x is smaller or larger, and may restrict any further comparisons to the lower or upper part of the array A accordingly. Continuing recursively, the next comparison will be at the middle element of the subarray we deal with, i.e., either $A[n/4]$ if the array is $A[1], \ldots, A[n/2]$, or $A[3n/4]$ if the array is $A[n/2], \ldots, A[n]$. The search procedure stops either when x is found, or when the size of the array is reduced to 1 and one can say with certainty that x is not in A.

If $T(n)$ denotes the number of comparisons (in the worst case) to find an element x in an array of size n, we get that $T(1) = 1$, and for $n > 1$:

$$T(n) = 1 + T(n/2). \tag{2.1}$$

Applying equality (2.1) repeatedly yields

$$T(n) = i + T(n/2^i), \qquad \text{for} \quad i = 1, 2, \ldots. \tag{2.2}$$

To get rid of the T on the right-hand side of the equation, let us choose i large enough to get to the boundary condition, that is $n/2^i = 1$, so that $n = 2^i$, hence $i = \log_2 n$. Substituting in (2.2), we get

$$T(n) = 1 + \log_2 n.$$

We conclude that having sorted the list of records allows us to reduce the number of needed comparisons in the worst case from n to about $\log_2 n$, indeed a major improvement.

Another problem, however, has now been created: updating the list is not as simple as it used to be. If a new record has to be added, it cannot be simply adjoined at the end, as this might violate the sorted order. Inserting or deleting records may thus incur a cost of shifting a part, possibly as many as half, of the records. Overall, the reduction of the search complexity from n to about $\log n$ came at the cost of increasing the number of steps for an update from 1 to about n.

This problem may be solved by passing to a scheme known as *linked allocation*, in which the records are not necessarily stored in contiguous locations, but are rather linked together, in some order, by means of pointers. The insertion or deletion of a record in a list can then be performed by a simple update of a small number of pointers, without having to move any of the other records. Regretfully, while there is an improvement for the update operations, it is again the search time that is hurt: since we do not know where to find the middle element in the list for the linked model, the use of binary search is not possible, and we are back to a linear search with about n comparisons.

In fact, to get efficient performances for both searches and updates, more sophisticated structures than the linear ones we consider here are needed, and we shall get back to this problem in Chapter 4, dealing with *Trees*. Note also that linked lists are not necessarily built by means of pointers, which are defined in many programming languages. The left part of Figure 2.2 is a schematic of a linked list consisting of 6 elements, and the right part of the figure is an equivalent list, for which the pointers have been replaced by indices in a table. As can be seen, the pointers or indices are incorporated as a part of the records. The index -1 is an indicator of the end of the list, and is equivalent to the ground sign, representing the NIL pointer.

2.2 Queues

Probably the most natural way of organizing a set of records into a structured form is what we commonly call a *queue*. When approaching a bus stop, a bank

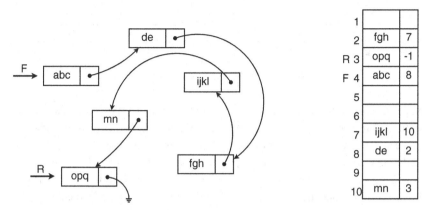

1		
2	fgh	7
R 3	opq	-1
F 4	abc	8
5		
6		
7	ijkl	10
8	de	2
9		
10	mn	3

Figure 2.2. Example of a list in linked allocation.

counter or a supermarket cash register, one may assume that the requested services will be provided on a first come, first serve basis, and if one has to wait, a queue, also known as **FIFO** (First In, First Out), will be formed.

Two pointers are kept: one, **R**, to the Rear of the queue, where new incoming records should be adjoined, the other, **F**, to the Front of the queue, indicating the next element to be extracted, that is, the next to be "served." Referring again to Figure 2.2 and considering the list as a queue Q, if an element has to be extracted from Q, it will be the one with value abc, denoted by e_{abc}. In the updated queue, **F** will then point to e_{de}, which is the successor of e_{abc}. Suppose then that we wish to insert a new element, with value rstu. This should happen at the rear of the queue, so a new element e_{rstu} is created, its successor is defined as NIL, the current rear element, e_{opq} will point to it, and **R** will also point to this new element. Figure 2.3 gives the formal definitions of (a) inserting an element with value x into a queue Q (at its rear), which shall be denoted by $Q \Longleftarrow x$, and (b) extracting (the front) element of Q and storing its value in a variable x, denoted by $x \Longleftarrow Q$. These operations are often called *enqueue* and *dequeue*, respectively.

A queue can also be kept within an array in sequential allocation. This may save the space for the pointers and simplify the update procedures, but one needs then a good estimate for the maximal number of elements that will be stored. If no reliable prediction of this size is possible, there is a risk of *overflow*.

$Q \Longleftarrow x$

allocate($node$)
value($node$) $\leftarrow x$;   succ($node$) $\leftarrow$ NIL
succ(R) $\leftarrow node$;   R $\leftarrow node$

$x \Longleftarrow Q$

$x \leftarrow$ value(F)
F $\leftarrow$ succ(F)

Figure 2.3. Insertion into and extraction from a queue in linked allocation.

Figure 2.4. A queue in sequential allocation.

Suppose then that we decide that n elements should be enough, so we may initialize an array $Q[0], \ldots, Q[n-1]$. The pointers F and R will now be indices in the array, F will be the index of the front of the queue and it will be convenient to define R as the index of the element *following* the last one in the queue, that is, the index where a new element should be inserted, as seen in the left part of Figure 2.4, in which the elements of the queue appear in gray. The small arrows indicate that updates are performed only at the extremities of the queue.

Extracting or inserting an element then involve increasing the pointers F or R by 1. The queue will thus have a tendency to "move" to the right and will eventually reach the last element indexed $n-1$. We shall therefore consider the array as if it were cyclic by simply performing all increments modulo n. At some stage, the queue may thus look as depicted in the right side of Figure 2.4. The formal update procedures are given in Figure 2.5.

2.2.1 Example: Optimal Prefix Code

We shall see several examples of the usefulness of queues later in this book, and focus here on a possible solution to the following simple problem. We are given a set of n numbers $a_1, \ldots, a_n$, and should repeatedly remove the two smallest ones and add their sum as a new element, until only one element remains. This is a part of the solution of the problem of finding an optimal prefix code, to be studied in Chapter 11.

If the set is not ordered, then $n-1$ comparisons are required to find and remove the minimal element. The total number of required comparisons is thus

$$\sum_{i=2}^{n-1}(i + (i-1)) = \left(2\sum_{i=1}^{n-1} i\right) - n. \qquad (2.3)$$

$Q \Longleftarrow x$
if R = F then overflow – STOP
$Q[R] \leftarrow x$
$R \leftarrow (R+1) \bmod n$

$x \Longleftarrow Q$
$x \leftarrow Q[F]$
$F \leftarrow (F+1) \bmod n$
if R = F then underflow

Figure 2.5. Insertion into and extraction from a queue in sequential allocation.

Background Concept: Summing the m First Integers

It might be useful to remember the summation $\sum_{i=1}^{m} i$ on the right-hand side of eq. (2.3), giving the sum of the first m integers, for some $m \geq 1$. Imagine the numbers written in order in a line:

1   2   3   4 $\cdots$ $m-1$ m

Now consider another line with the same numbers, but in reversed order:

m $m-1$ $m-2$ $m-3$ $\cdots$ 2   1

Adding by columns gives the sum $m+1$ in every column, and since there are m columns, this all adds up to $(m+1)m$. But this is twice the sum we are looking for, so

$$\sum_{i=1}^{m} i = \frac{(m+1)m}{2}.$$

Hence about n^2 comparisons are needed if the set is not ordered, and we shall see that the set can be sorted in only about $n \log n$ steps, and then be stored in a linked list. Extracting the two smallest elements takes then constant time, and the newly formed element has to be inserted in the proper place within the ordered list. The total running time for the $n-1$ iterations will be of the order of n comparisons, if we start the search where to insert a new element at the location of the previous insert.

Here is an alternative procedure, using two queues Q_1 and Q_2 rather than a linked list. The elements of Q_1 will be the original elements of the set, in nondecreasing order. The second queue Q_2 will initially be empty, and will contain only elements that are created by the algorithm, that is, an element whose value is the sum of two previously treated elements. In each iteration, the two smallest numbers in the combined set $Q_1 \cup Q_2$, x and y, are extracted. These are either the two first elements in Q_1, or those in Q_2, or the first elements of both Q_1 and Q_2. The key observation is that there is no need to search where to insert $x + y$: it cannot be smaller than any of the previously created combinations, so its place in the queue Q_2 must be at the rear end. The formal algorithm is given in Figure 2.6, where first(Q) and second(Q) refer to the first two elements of a queue Q.

The overall time to perform the task is thus linear in n, once the elements have been sorted, or of the order of $n \log n$ if the sorting has also to be accounted for.

$$\text{if first}(Q_1) > \text{second}(Q_2) \text{ then}$$
$$x \Longleftarrow Q_2 \qquad y \Longleftarrow Q_2$$
$$\text{else} \quad \text{if first}(Q_2) > \text{second}(Q_1) \text{ then}$$
$$x \Longleftarrow Q_1 \qquad y \Longleftarrow Q_1$$
$$\text{else}$$
$$x \Longleftarrow Q_1 \qquad y \Longleftarrow Q_2$$
$$Q_2 \Longleftarrow x + y$$

Figure 2.6. Iterative insertion of the sum of two smallest elements of a sorted list.

Background Concept: Asymptotic Notation

The following notation is widespread in Computer Science, and will replace the vague phrases like *of the order of* used earlier. It is generally used to describe the complexity of some algorithm as a function of the size n of its input. For two integer functions f and g, we write $f \in O(g)$, which is read as *f is in big-O of g*, if there are constants n_0 and $C > 0$ such that

$$\forall n \geq n_0 \qquad |f(n)| \leq C\,|g(n)|.$$

Roughly speaking, this means that f is bounded above by g, but the strictness of the bound is relaxed in two aspects:

(i) we are only interested in the asymptotic behavior of f, when its argument n tends to infinity, so the ratio of $f(n)$ to $g(n)$ for n smaller than some predefined constant n_0 is not relevant;

(ii) we do not require g itself to be larger than f – it suffices that some constant $C > 0$ multiplied by g be larger than f.

For example, $f(n) = n^2 + 10n \log_2 n + \frac{1000}{n} \in O(n^2)$, as can be checked using the constants $n_0 = 24$ and $C = 3$.

Though $O(g)$ is defined as a set, a prevalent abuse of notation refers to it as if it were a number, writing $f(n) = O(g(n))$. This is not really an equality, in particular, it is not transitive, as you cannot infer from $n^2 = O(n^3)$ and $n^2 = O(n^4)$ that $O(n^3) = O(n^4)$.

There is a similar notation also for lower bounds: $f \in \Omega(g)$, which is read as *f is in big-omega of g*, if there are constants n_0 and $C > 0$ such that

$$\forall n \geq n_0 \qquad |f(n)| \geq C\,|g(n)|.$$

For example, $n^2 - n \in \Omega(n^2)$.

Finally, for a more precise evaluation, we may use a combination of the bounds: $f \in \theta(g)$, which is read as f *is in theta of* g, if both $f \in O(g)$ and $f \in \Omega(g)$, obviously with different constants, that is, there are constants n_0, $C_1 > 0$ and $C_2 > 0$ such that

$$\forall n \geq n_0 \qquad C_1 \, |g(n)| \leq |f(n)| \leq C_2 \, |g(n)|.$$

For example, $\log n + \cos(n) \in \theta(\log n)$.

This symbolism can also be extended to the reals and to letting the argument tend to some constant, often 0, rather than to ∞.

2.3 Stacks

The counterpart of the First-In-First-Out paradigm of queues is known as LIFO, which stands for Last In, First Out. This might clash with our natural sense of fairness when applied to waiting in line, but is nevertheless useful in other scenarios. Possible examples are

- a pile of books, from which the elements can only be removed in the reverse of the order by which they have been added;
- a narrow, dead-ended parking lot, accommodating several cars in its length, but at most one in its width;
- luggage space in an airplane, so that the always late travelers arriving at the last moment at the check-in counter, will be the first ones to get their suitcases at destination. . .

Figure 2.7 is a schematic of a stack in both linked and sequential allocation. Insertions and deletions are now performed at the same end of the stack, identified by a pointer or index T (Top). In the upper part of Figure 2.7, the elements are numbered in order of their insertion into the stack. We shall use a similar notation as for queues, $S \Longleftarrow x$ standing for the insertion of an element with

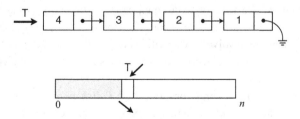

Figure 2.7. A stack in linked and sequential allocation.

$S \Longleftarrow x$ (linked) $x \Longleftarrow S$ (linked)
   allocate($node$) $x \leftarrow$ value(T)
   value($node$) $\leftarrow x$; succ($node$) $\leftarrow$ T   T $\leftarrow$ succ(T)
   T $\leftarrow node$

$S \Longleftarrow x$ (sequential) $x \Longleftarrow S$ (sequential)
   if T $= n$ then   if T $= 0$ then
      overflow $-$ STOP   underflow $-$ STOP
   $S[\text{T}] \leftarrow x$ T $\leftarrow$ T $- 1$
   T $\leftarrow$ T $+ 1$ $x \leftarrow S[\text{T}]$

Figure 2.8. Insertion into and extraction from a stack in linked and sequential allocation.

value x into the stack S, and $x \Longleftarrow S$ for the removal of the top element from the stack S and storing its value into x. These operations are often referred to as *push* and *pop*, respectively, and are formally given in Figure 2.8.

2.3.1 Example: Arithmetic Expression

Consider an arithmetic expression like those any programmer encounters on a daily basis, for example

$$4 + 3 \times 5.$$

While certain cheap pocket calculators still evaluate this to be 35 (when the $\times$ key is pressed, the display already shows 7), the more advanced ones correctly recognize that multiplication has priority over addition, so that the result should rather be 19. If the intention was indeed to add 4 to 3 before multiplying, parentheses should have been used, as in

$$(4 + 3) \times 5.$$

In fact, arithmetic expression are written the way they are probably mainly for historic reasons, as this way is not consistent with the customary form of writing functions. We usually write, e.g., $f(x)$ or $\log x$, preceding the argument x by the function name f or log, with or without parentheses. When several variables are involved, we write $f(x, y)$ rather than $x f y$. Similarly, we should have written the displayed expressions as add(4, multiply(3, 5)) or multiply(add(4, 3), 5).

This way of writing expressions is called *Polish notation*. Note that the parentheses are then redundant, so that the preceding expressions can be written unambiguously as

$$+ \ 4 \ \times \ 3 \ 5 \qquad \text{or} \qquad \times \ + \ 4 \ 3 \ 5.$$

There exists also a *Reversed Polish notation*, in which the arguments precede the function name instead of following it. This makes even more sense as once the operation to be performed is revealed, its arguments are already known. The preceding in reversed Polish notation would be

$$4 \ 3 \ 5 \ \times \ + \qquad \text{or} \qquad 4 \ 3 \ + \ 5 \ \times.$$

Because of the positions of the operators, these notations are often referred to as prefix or postfix, whereas the standard way of writing is infix.

The evaluation of a long arithmetic expression given in infix seems to be quite involved: there are priorities, parentheses to change them if necessary, and defaults, like $a - b - c$ standing for $(a - b) - c$; but using $\uparrow$ for exponentiation, $a \uparrow b = a^b$, the default of $a \uparrow b \uparrow c$ is $a \uparrow (b \uparrow c)$, because $(a \uparrow b) \uparrow c = (a^b)^c = a^{bc}$. When the expression is given in postfix, on the other hand, the following simple procedure can be used to evaluate it by means of a single scan from left to right and using a stack S.

Operands are pushed into the stack in the order of appearance; when an operator X is encountered, the two last elements, y and z are popped from the stack, $z \ X \ y$ is calculated (note that the order of the operands is reversed), and its value is pushed again into S. At the end, the result is in the only element of S. Formally,

> while end of expression has not been reached
> $X \leftarrow$ next element of the expression (operator or operand)
>   if $X \notin \{\text{Operators}\}$
> $S \Longleftarrow X$
>   else
> $y \Longleftarrow S; \qquad z \Longleftarrow S$
> $r \Longleftarrow \text{compute}(z \ X \ y)$
> $S \Longleftarrow r$

Figure 2.9 shows the stack after having read an operator, as well as at the end, when the expression to be evaluated, $(4 + 3) * (2 \uparrow (14 - 8)/2)$, has been converted into its corresponding postfix form $4 \ 3 \ + \ 2 \ 14 \ 8 \ - \ 2 \ / \ \uparrow \ *$.

The question is therefore how to convert an expression from infix to postfix. This is again done using a stack, which, in contrast to the stack in the example of Figure 2.9, holds the operators rather than the operands. We also need a table

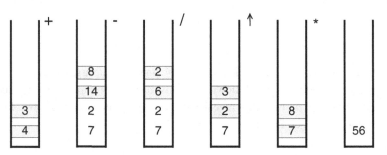

Figure 2.9. Evaluating an arithmetic expression using a stack.

of priorities, and actually, two such tables, called STACK-PRIORITY and INPUT-PRIORITY, will be used to deal with the special cases. Parentheses have highest priority in the input, since their purpose is to change the default priorities, but once in the stack, their priority should be the lowest. The two tables also enable the correct treatment of exponentiation, which associates to the right, as seen earlier. A dummy element with lowest priority is inserted into the stack as *sentinel*, to facilitate the treatment of boundary conditions.

The algorithm scans the infix expression left to right and transfers the operands directly to the output, in the order of their appearance. Operators, including left parentheses, are pushed into the stack, and are popped according to the order imposed by their priorities. The priority tables and the formal algorithm are given in Figure 2.10. The tables may be extended to deal also with

operator	sentinel	(	+ -	* /	↑	)
STACK-PRIORITY	-1	1	2	3	4	–
INPUT-PRIORITY	–	6	2	3	5	2

$S \Longleftarrow$ sentinel
while end of expression has not been reached
    $X \leftarrow$ next element of the expression
    if end of input then   while Top $\neq$ sentinel
                            $y \Longleftarrow S$;   print y
    else   if $X \notin \{$Operators$\}$ then print X
           else   while STACK-PRIORITY(Top) $\geq$ INPUT-PRIORITY(X)
                    $y \Longleftarrow S$;   print y
                if X is not right parenthesis ')' then
                    $S \Longleftarrow X$
                else   dummy $\Longleftarrow S$ // pop matching left parenthesis

Figure 2.10. Priority tables and algorithm for conversion from infix to postfix.

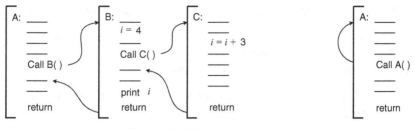

Figure 2.11. Chain of function calls.

other operators defined by the given programming language, such as assignments =, logical operations & | or shifts ≫.

2.3.2 Example: Handling Recursion

It is good programming practice to partition a given task into several small logical units, and large programs often consist of numerous procedures, creating chains of functions $f_1, f_2, f_3, \ldots$, where f_1 is calling f_2, which in turn calls f_3, etc. These functions are usually written by different programmers, and each comes with its own set of parameters and local variables. The challenge is to keep track of their correct values. Consider, for example, the function calls on the left side of Figure 2.11, we would not like the increment $i = i + 3$ in procedure C to affect the value of variable i in procedure B.

The problem is aggravated if the chain of calling functions includes more than one copy of a given function. This is called *recursion*, where, in its simplest form, a function calls itself, as depicted on the right-hand side of Figure 2.11. The commands of the recursive function appear physically only once in the memory of our computer, there is therefore a need to differentiate between the values the same variable gets at different generations of the function calls. This is done by means of a *program stack*.

Each entry of the program stack corresponds to a single function call and holds a record consisting of the following fields: the input parameters, the local variables, and an address from which to continue when returning after the execution of the current function call. The following actions are taken when a function call Call B( ) is encountered within a function A:

Call 1: Push a new entry into the stack.

Call 2: Update parameters and initialize local variables.

Call 3: In the return-address field, store the address of the command following the function call in the calling routine A.

Call 4: Continue executing commands from the beginning of B.

When exiting a function, generally via a return command, the actions are:

Ret 1: Read the return address field of the Top element into a variable adr.
Ret 2: Discard the Top element by Pop.
Ret 3: Continue executing commands from adr.

As example, we show what happens when executing a Mergesort procedure on a small input vector.

Background Concept: Mergesort

Mergesort is another example of the *Divide and Conquer* family. To sort an array $A[1], \ldots, A[n]$, we apply mergesort recursively on the left and right halves of the array, that is on $A[1], \ldots, A[\frac{n}{2}]$ and $A[\frac{n}{2} + 1], \ldots, A[n]$, and then use a function merge(i, k, j), which supposes that the subarrays $A[i], \ldots, A[k]$ and $A[k + 1], \ldots, A[j]$ are already sorted, to produce a merged array $A[i], \ldots, A[j]$. The merging may be implemented with the help of three pointers, two to the parts of the array that are to be merged, and one to an auxiliary array B, holding temporarily the sorted output, before it is moved back to the array A. The formal definition, in which the element following the last is defined by $A[j + 1] \leftarrow \infty$ to deal with the boundary condition of one of the subarrays being exhausted, is given by:

merge(i, k, j)
$\qquad p_1 \leftarrow i; \qquad p_2 \leftarrow k + 1; \qquad p_3 \leftarrow i$
$\qquad$ if $p_1 \leq k$ and $A[p_1] < A[p_2]$ then
$\qquad\qquad\qquad B[p_3] \leftarrow A[p_1]; \qquad p_1\text{++}; \qquad\qquad p_3\text{++}$
$\qquad$ else $\quad B[p_3] \leftarrow A[p_2]; \qquad p_2\text{++}; \qquad\qquad p_3\text{++}$
$\qquad A[i] \cdots A[j] \leftarrow B[i] \cdots B[j]$

The number of comparisons for the merge is clearly bounded by $j - i$. The formal definition of mergesort(i, j), which sorts the subarray of A from index i to, and including, index j, is then

mergesort(i, j)
$\qquad$ if $i < j$ then
$\qquad\qquad\qquad k \leftarrow \lfloor (i + j)/2 \rfloor$
$\qquad\qquad\qquad$ mergesort(i, k)
$\qquad$ L1: mergesort$(k + 1, j)$
$\qquad$ L2: merge(i, k, j)

The analysis is similar to the one we did earlier for binary search. Let $T(n)$ denote the number of comparisons needed to sort an array of size n by mergesort, we get that $T(1) = 0$, and for $n > 1$:

$$T(n) = 2\,T(n/2) + n. \tag{2.4}$$

Applying equality (2.4) repeatedly yields

$$T(n) = 2^i\,T(n/2^i) + i\,n, \qquad \text{for} \quad i = 1, 2, \ldots. \tag{2.5}$$

To get rid of the T on the right-hand side of the equation, let us choose i large enough to get to the boundary condition, that is $n/2^i = 1$, so that $i = \log_2 n$. Substituting in (2.5), we get

$$T(n) = n \log_2 n.$$

Suppose our input vector A, indexed 1 to 5, contains the elements 9,2,1,5,3, in the given order. Somewhere in the calling program, the sorting procedure is invoked by

$$\cdots$$

mergesort$(1, 5)$

L4: $\cdots$

When the call is executed, a new entry is created in the stack, as depicted in the lowest line of part (a) in Figure 2.12. Initially, the line contains only the parameters i and j, 1 and 5 in our case, and the return address L4 from which the program execution will continue after having finished with mergesort. The execution of the program continues from the beginning of the recursive function. Since $i = 1 < 5 = j$, the value 3 is assigned to k, and the value of k in the entry in the stack will be updated only at this stage. The next command is again a (recursive) call to mergesort. Hence a new entry is pushed onto the stack, with parameters 1 and 3, and return address L1. The process repeats twice until a fourth entry is created, with parameters 1 and 1, and return address L1.

At this point, no command is executed during the recursive call, and upon exiting from mergesort, the top entry is popped and the execution flow continues from L1. The values of k and j, 1 and 2, are taken from the entry which is now at the top of the stack. The next command is again a call to mergesort, and the program stack after this call is depicted in part (b) of Figure 2.12. When the current top element is popped, one gets to label L2, which invokes the merge procedure. This is the first access to the input vector A itself. In this case, subvectors of size 1 are merged, which is equivalent to just reordering

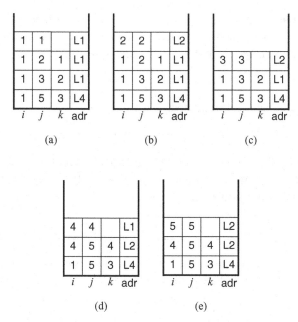

Figure 2.12. Mergesort: program stack when called on input vector 9, 2, 1, 5, 3.

the two elements involved. The vector A after the merge will thus contain the elements 2, 9, 1, 5, 3, and we have reached the end of one of the function calls. Execution thus continues at label **L1**, with the program stack containing the two lowest lines of Figure 2.12(c).

After the following call to **merge**, with parameters $(i, k, j) = (1, 2, 3)$, the vector A will contain 1, 2, 9, 5, 3, the line 1,3,2,L1 will be popped and the stack will contain only a single entry. The reader is encouraged to continue this simulation through parts (d) and (e) of the figure. The next merge, with parameters $(4, 4, 5)$, should transform the vector A into 1, 2, 9, 3, 5, and then finally into 1, 2, 3, 5, 9.

2.4 Other Linear Lists

In the general family called *linear lists*, of which queues and stacks are special cases, the records are ordered according to some criterion. This order is given either implicitly by the position of the record in a sequential allocation, or explicitly by means of pointers in a linked allocation. There are many more linear lists and we shall mention only the following. Generally, the decision whether to prefer one type over another will be guided by the details of the

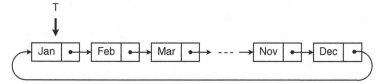

Figure 2.13. Circular list.

specific application at hand. One can then adapt the choice of the data structures to the tradeoff between the resources which best fits their purpose.

2.4.1 Circular Lists

A circular list is a linear list in which the last element points to the first one, thus exploiting the wasted space of the NIL pointer. This may be advantageous for lists that are intrinsically periodic like the months of the year. If one wishes to change the calendar year to the school or academic year, all one needs to do is to move the pointer T in Figure 2.13 to September or October.

There are, however, also applications for which it would seem natural to use a noncyclic linear list. Nevertheless, closing a cycle may permit the execution of certain operations more efficiently, for example, having the possibility to reach any record x by starting a linear search from any other record y. Another feature of a circular list is that only one pointer is needed (to the last element), which is useful to enable the efficient concatenation of lists.

The algorithms for inserting or deleting records from circular lists are straightforward , but special care should be taken when dealing with an empty list. A standard way, not only for circular lists, of facilitating the handling of special cases such as empty lists is the use of a so-called *sentinel* element: this is a record like the others of the given data structures, just that it does not carry any information. For large enough structures, the waste caused by such a dummy element can be tolerated and is generally outweighed by the benefits of the simplified processing.

2.4.2 Doubly Linked Lists

Additional flexibility may be gained by adding also a link from each record to its predecessor, in addition to the link to its successor. Whether the increased overhead can be justified will depend on the intended application: navigating through the list for searches will be facilitated, whereas updates when inserting or deleting records are becoming more involved. Figure 2.14 shows a doubly

Sentinel

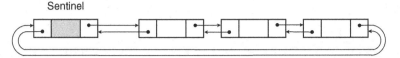

Figure 2.14. Doubly linked list with sentinel element.

linked list with three records and an additional sentinel element acting both as
the predecessor of the first element, and as the successor of the last one.

A typical application of a doubly linked list would be for the management
of dynamic allocations of memory space.

2.4.3 Deques

Unifying the properties of both queues and stacks, a *deque* allows inserts and
deletes at both ends of the list, which for symmetry reasons will now be called
Left and Right rather than Front and Rear. Like queues and stacks, deques can
be managed in sequential allocation, as shown in Figure 2.15, or in linked allocation, usually as a special case of a doubly linked list.

Think of a deque as a model simulating the use of large elevators as found
in large public facilities like hospitals, where one may enter or exit on two
opposing sides. Similarly, certain airplanes may be boarded or left through front
or rear doors.

2.4.4 Higher Order Linear Lists

All these ideas can be generalized to d dimensions, with $d \geq 2$. Even though we
usually do not consider a two-dimensional matrix as a linear object, the linearity
we refer to in this chapter relates to the fact that records can be arranged in order,
in which each element has a well-defined successor and predecessor, and this
may be true for each dimension. The number of pointers included in each record
will increase with d, but this will often be compensated for by the more efficient
algorithms.

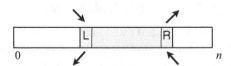

Figure 2.15. A deque in sequential allocation.

An example could be representing a sparse matrix (i.e., a matrix with a large number of elements that are 0) by linked lists of records defined only for the nonzero elements. The records will be linked together in both their rows and columns (and further dimensions, if necessary). This leads to more efficient handling of these and other special matrices, such as triangular.

Exercises

2.1 You have a linked list of n records, each consisting of a value field and a next-pointer. The length n of the list is not known, but may be assumed to be a multiple of 3. Show how to print the values of the records in the middle third of the list using only two pointers and without using a counter.

Apply the same idea to solve the following problem: given is a list like the preceding, show how to check in time $O(n)$ whether the list contains a cycle.

2.2 Let M be a matrix of dimension $n \times n$, and assume that only $O(n)$ of the n^2 elements of M are nonzero. Use a linked representation of the nonzero elements of M to calculate the *trace* of M^2 in time $O(n)$ (the trace of a matrix $A = (a_{ij})$ is the sum of the elements in its diagonal, $\sum_{i=1}^{n} a_{ii}$).

2.3 Let A be an array of n numbers. You know that there exists some index k, $1 \le k < n$, such that $A[1], \ldots, A[k]$ are all positive, and $A[k + 1], \ldots, A[n]$ are all negative. Show how to find k:

(a) in time $O(\log n)$;
(b) in time $O(\min(\log n, k))$;
(c) in time $O(\log k)$.

2.4 A column of n cars is approaching a highway from an access road. The cars are numbered 1 to n, but not necessarily in order. We would like to rearrange the cars so that they enter the highway by increasing order of their indices. The problem is that the access road is so narrow that only one car fits in its width. However, just before the road meets the highway, there is a dead-ended parking lot, long enough to accommodate all cars, but again not wide enough for two cars side by side. Can the task of rearranging the cars be completed with the help of the parking lot, for every possible input permutation? If so, prove it, if not, give a counter-example.

2.5 A known game chooses the winner among n children in the following way: the children stand in a circle and transfer clockwise, at a regular pace, some object from one to another. At irregular intervals, at the sound of some bell, the child holding the object passes it to the next one and leaves the game, so that the circle shrinks. The winner is the last child remaining in the circle.

To program the game, simulate the bell by generating a random integer t between 1 and some given upper bound K; t will be the number steps the object will be forwarded until the next sound of the bell.

(a) What is the time complexity of the process until the winner is found, as a function of n and K, if the players are represented as records in a doubly linked cyclic deque?
(b) What is the time complexity of the process until the winner is found, as a function of n and K, if the players are represented as elements of an array?
(c) Compare the two methods, in particular for the case $K > n$.

2.6 Write the algorithms for inserting and deleting elements in circular doubly linked lists with a sentinel element. Take care in particular how to deal with the empty list.

2.7 Find constants n_0 and C to complete the examples given in the description of the asymptotic notation, showing that

(a) $n^2 - n \in \Omega(n^2)$
(b) $\log n + \cos(n) \in \theta(\log n)$.

2.8 The closed form for $T(n)$ defined by the recurrence relation of eq. (2.1) was $T(n) \in O(\log n)$.

(a) Show that if the recursion is $T(n) = 1 + T(\sqrt{n})$, with the same boundary condition as earlier, then the closed form is $T(n) \in O(\log \log n)$.
(b) What is the function $f(n)$ for which the recurrence relation $T(n) = 1 + T(f(n))$, again with the same boundary condition, yields as closed form $T(n) \in O(\log \log \log n)$?
(c) What is the closed form, if the recurrence is
$T(n) = 1 + T(\log n)$?

3

Graphs

3.1 Extending the Relationships between Records

In a generalization of the linear lists of the previous chapter, we may allow the connection between any two elements, without insisting on some specific order. The resulting structure is known as a *graph*. This models quite naturally several real life situations, like networks of communicating computers, or road systems connecting the various locations of some neighborhood. We shall, however, see that a graph may be a useful tool for many other applications, some of which seeming a priori completely unconnected to a graph structure.

Mathematically, a graph G is defined as a pair of sets $G = (V, E)$. There is no restriction on the set V, called the *vertices* of the graph, and its elements are usually denoted $V = \{v_1, v_2, \ldots, v_n\}$, or simply $V = \{1, 2, \ldots, n\}$. The set of *edges* E satisfies $E \subseteq V \times V$ and actually describes whether some binary relation exists between certain pairs of vertices. We may have $E = \emptyset$ or $E = V \times V$, in which cases the graph is called *empty* or *full*, respectively. Note that this refers only to the number of edges, so a graph may be empty and yet have many vertices. The complexities of algorithms involving graphs are often given as a function of the sizes of V and E, for example $O(|V| + |E|)$, but it has become common practice to simplify this notation to $O(V + E)$ when no confusion can arise.

It is customary, and often very helpful as a visual aid, to represent a graph by a drawing in which the vertices appear as dots or circles, and an edge (a, b) as an arrow from the circle corresponding to a to that of b. Figure 3.1 is such a drawing for a graph with $V = \{1, 2, \ldots, 13, 14\}$ and $E = \{(1, 2), (1, 3), (1, 6), (2, 2), \ldots, (10, 11), (12, 13)\}$, and will serve as a running example in this chapter. It should be emphasized that this drawing is *not* the graph G itself, but rather one of its infinitely many possible *representations*. Indeed, there are almost no restrictions on the layout of the drawing: the circles

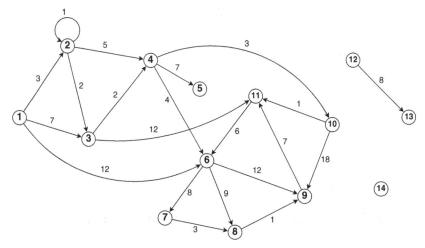

Figure 3.1. An example graph $G = (V, E)$ with $V = \{1, 2, \ldots, 13, 14\}$ and $E = \{(1, 2), (1, 3), (1, 6), (2, 2), (2, 3), (2, 4), (3, 4), (3, 11), (4, 5), (4, 6), (4, 10), (6, 7), (6, 8), (6, 9), (7, 8), (8, 9), (9, 11), (10, 9), (10, 11), (11, 6), (12, 13)\}$.

representing the vertices are generally scattered in any visually appealing way, the edges may be straight lines or arcs or have any other form, they may cross each other, etc. The formalism of not identifying a graph with its representation is thus necessary, because one can easily get completely different drawings, yet representing the same graph.

A graph in which we distinguish between edges (a, b) and (b, a) is called *directed*, and its edges are usually drawn as arrows, like in Figure 3.1. In other applications, only the fact whether there is a connection between the elements a and b is relevant, but the direction of the edge (a, b) or (b, a) is not given any importance; such graphs are called *undirected* and their edges are shown as lines rather than arrows, as in Figure 3.2. Even though in a strictly mathematical sense, we should then denote edges as sets $\{a, b\}$ instead of ordered pairs (a, b), it is common practice to use the pair notation (a, b) even for the undirected case.

An edge of the form (a, a), like the one emanating from and pointing to vertex 2, is called a *loop*. A sequence of edges

$$(v_a, v_b), (v_b, v_c), (v_c, v_d), \ldots, (v_w, v_x),$$

in which the starting point of one edge is the endpoint of the preceding edge, is called a *path* from v_a to v_x. For example, $(2, 4), (4, 6), (6, 9), (9, 11)$ is a path from 2 to 11. If $v_a = v_x$, that is, if the last edge of a path points to the beginning of the first edge, the path is called a *cycle*. For example, $(8, 9), (9, 11), (11, 6), (6, 8)$ is a cycle. If there is a path from every vertex to

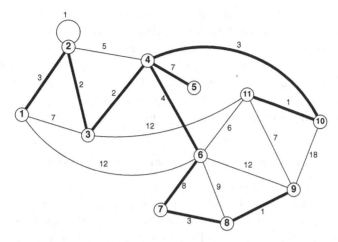

Figure 3.2. A minimum spanning tree.

any other, the graph is *connected*. Our example graph is not connected, because, e.g., vertex 13 cannot be reached from vertex 4.

The number of outgoing edges from a given vertex is called its *out-degree* and the number of incoming edges is called its *in-degree*. In undirected graphs, there is no such distinction and one simply defines the *degree* of a vertex v as the number of edges touching v. Vertex 9 has in-degree 3 and out-degree 1, and vertex 4 in Figure 3.2 has degree 5. A vertex with in-degree 0, like vertex 1, is a *source* and a vertex with out-degree 0, like vertex 5, is a *sink*, and if there is no edge touching the vertex at all, like for vertex 14, it is *isolated*.

An important special case is a *tree*, defined as a graph that is connected but has no cycles. Our graph is not a tree, because it is not connected, but even if we restrict the intention to the subgraph G' induced by the vertices $V' = \{1, 2, \ldots, 11\}$, that is, ignoring the vertices in $V - V'$ and the edges touching them, as in Figure 3.2, the graph would still not be a tree, because it contains cycles. On the other hand, the bold edges in Figure 3.2 form a tree.

Regretfully, there is another, quite different, notion in Computer Science that is also called a *tree*, as we shall see already in the following chapter. There are certain similarities between a tree as a data structure and a tree as a special kind of a graph, but there are many differences and calling both by the same name is a source of confusion. More details will be given in Chapter 4.

In many applications, it is convenient to assign a *weight* $w(a, b)$ to each edge (a, b) of a graph, as we did in Figure 3.1. The weight of a path will be defined as the sum of the weights of the edges forming it. There are many possible interpretations for these weights, and a few examples will be given in what follows.

There are entire courses devoted to the study of graph related algorithms. They are beyond the scope of this book, and we mention here only a few of the well-known problems, without presenting possible solutions. What is relevant to our topic of data structures is the way to transform a problem we might be dealing with into a related one that can be solved by means of a known graph algorithm. Such a transformation is known as a *reduction*, which is an essential tool in the study and development of algorithms.

3.1.1 The Minimum Spanning Tree Problem

Suppose the vertices of the undirected graph $G = (V, E)$ represent locations and that we wish to construct an electricity network reaching each vertex $v \in V$. The weight $w(a, b)$ may stand for the cost of building a high voltage transmission line from location a to location b. For technical or topographical reasons, there may be vertices that are not connected by an edge, so the graph is not necessarily full. The problem is to find the cheapest layout of the network of transmission lines. Alternatively, one could think of the vertices as computers in a network, of the edges as wired communication lines and of the weights as the costs to build the lines.

There must be a possibility to transfer electricity, or allow communication, from every point to each other, therefore the graph G has to be connected. On the other hand, we assume that there is no reason to build a network with more than one possibility to get from a vertex a to a vertex b. This implies that the sought network should not include any cycle, so what we are looking for is in fact a tree. A tree touching all the vertices in V is called a *spanning tree*. The challenge is that there might be many such trees.

The problem can thus be reformulated mathematically as: given an undirected connected graph $G = (V, E)$ with weights $w(a, b)$ for each $(a, b) \in E$, find a subset $T \subseteq E$ of the edges such that T is a spanning tree, and such that $\sum_{(a,b) \in T} w(a, b)$ is minimized over all possible choices of such trees T. Figure 3.2 is an undirected version of the graph of Figure 3.1, restricted to the vertices $V' = \{1, 2, \ldots, 11\}$, in which the edges of one of the possible *Minimum Spanning Trees*, with weight 34, have been boldfaced.

3.1.2 The Shortest Path Problem

Returning to the directed version of the graph in Figure 3.1, imagine that the vertices are locations and the edges represent roads connecting certain pairs of them. The weight of an edge (a, b) could be the distance between its endpoints, or the cost of getting from a to b, or the time it takes to do it, etc. Accordingly,

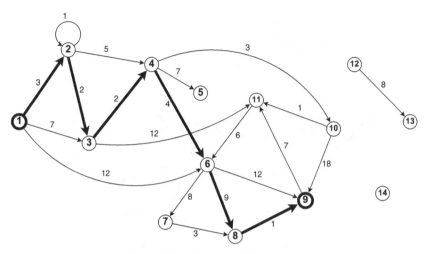

Figure 3.3. A shortest path from 1 to 9.

the problem to deal with is to find the shortest, or cheapest, or fastest path from a given point to another.

These seem at first sight as if they were different problems, but they are all equivalent to the following formulation: given a directed graph $G = (V, E)$ with weights $w(a, b)$ for each $(a, b) \in E$, and given a source vertex s and a target vertex t, find a path from s to t such that its weight is minimized over all the (possibly many) paths from s to t.

Figure 3.3 shows, in boldface, one of the possible *Shortest paths*, with weight 21, from source vertex 1 to target vertex 9.

3.1.3 The Maximum Flow Problem

In this application, the edges are considered as highways and their meeting points, the vertices, are interchanges. We assume that there is some measure to describe numerically the traffic load on a given highway at a certain moment. The weight $w(a, b)$ is the maximal possible traffic capacity on the highway from a to b. The goal is to measure the maximal possible traffic flow from a source interchange s to a target point t.

Alternatively, the edges could be pipelines and the weight $w(a, b)$ would represent the maximal quantity of some liquid that can traverse the edge (a, b) in some given time interval. The problem is then to evaluate how much of the liquid can be shipped from s to t.

Figure 3.4 shows one of the possible *Maximal Flows*, with total weight 16, from source vertex 1 to target vertex 9. Each edge is annotated with a pair a/c,

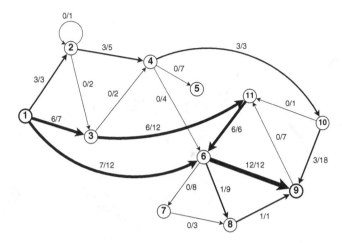

Figure 3.4. A maximal flow network.

with $a \leq c$, where c is the capacity of the edge, and a is the actual value of the flow assigned to it. Note that for certain edges $a = c$, meaning that their capacity is fully exploited, like on edge (11,6); for others, $a = 0$, that is, the edges are not used at all, like edge (3,4); finally, for certain edges, their capacity is only partially used, like edge (10,9), using only 3 of the possible 18. Note also that at each interchange, the incoming and outgoing flows must be the same, but that the whole quantity may be reshuffled. For example, the three incoming edges on vertex 6 contribute $7 + 0 + 6$, which are redistributed into the three outgoing edges as $0 + 1 + 12$.

3.2 Graph Representations

One way to represent a graph $G = (V, E)$ in a computer program is to define a two dimensional matrix $A = (a_{ij})$, with $1 \leq i, j \leq |V|$, called an *adjacency matrix*, and setting

$$a_{ij} = \begin{cases} 1 & \text{if } (i, j) \in E \\ 0 & \text{otherwise,} \end{cases}$$

as can be seen in the upper part of Figure 3.5, corresponding to this chapter's running example. Outgoing edges from vertex i can then easily be checked by inspecting the ith row, and incoming edges on vertex j are found in the jth column. Instead of using a Boolean matrix that only shows whether a certain edge exists, one may define a general matrix for a weighted graph by setting $a_{ij} = w(i, j)$ if $(i, j) \in E$, but care has to be taken to reserve a special

	1	2	3	4	5	6	7	8	9	10	11	12	13	14
1	0	1	1	0	0	1	0	0	0	0	0	0	0	0
2	0	1	1	0	1	0	0	0	0	0	0	0	0	0
3	0	0	0	1	0	0	0	0	0	0	1	0	0	0
4	0	0	0	0	1	1	0	0	0	1	0	0	0	0
5	0	0	0	0	0	0	0	0	0	0	0	0	0	0
6	0	0	0	0	0	0	1	1	1	0	0	0	0	0
7	0	0	0	0	0	0	0	1	0	0	0	0	0	0
8	0	0	0	0	0	0	0	0	1	0	0	0	0	0
9	0	0	0	0	0	0	0	0	0	0	1	0	0	0
10	0	0	0	0	0	0	0	0	1	0	1	0	0	0
11	0	0	0	0	0	1	0	0	0	0	0	0	0	0
12	0	0	0	0	0	0	0	0	0	0	0	0	1	0
13	0	0	0	0	0	0	0	0	0	0	0	0	0	0
14	0	0	0	0	0	0	0	0	0	0	0	0	0	0

Matrix

vertex	neighbors	weights
1	2,3,6	3,7,12
2	2,3,4	1,2,5
3	4,11	2,12
4	5,6,10	7,4,3
5		
6	7,8,9	8,9,12
7	8	3
8	9	1
9	11	7
10	9,11	18,1
11	6	6
12	13	8
13		
14		

List of neighbors

Figure 3.5. Graph representations.

value, which cannot be confused with a weight, to indicate the absence of an edge.

The matrix representation may be wasteful, because algorithms requiring a full scan of the graph will often imply the processing of all the V^2 elements of the matrix, even if the number of edges is significantly lower. This leads to the idea of representing the graph by an array of linked lists, as shown in the lower part of Figure 3.5. The array is indexed by the vertices, and the ith element of the array points to the list of the neighbors of i, which are in fact the endpoints of the outgoing edges from i. Another linked list may be added giving the weights on the edges in the same order, if necessary. For a full scan of the

BFS(G, v)

    mark v
    $Q \Longleftarrow v$
    while $Q \neq \emptyset$ do
        $w \Longleftarrow Q$
        visit w
        for all x such that $(w, x) \in E$
           if x is not marked then
             mark x
             $Q \Longleftarrow x$

DFS(G, v)

    mark v
    $S \Longleftarrow v$
    while $S \neq \emptyset$ do
        $w \Longleftarrow S$
        visit w
        for all x such that $(w, x) \in E$
           if x is not marked then
             mark x
             $S \Longleftarrow x$

Figure 3.6. BFS and DFS algorithms for a graph G, starting at vertex v.

graph, all these linked lists will be processed, but even for an undirected graph, no edge appears more than twice in the union of the lists, so the algorithms may be bounded by $O(E)$, which may be lower than $O(V^2)$.

3.3 Graph Exploration

One of the motivations for passing from linear lists to the more general graphs was to overcome the dependency on some order among the vertices, which is often imposed artificially and cannot be justified. Nevertheless, even in applications for which a graph representation is most natural, the need often arises to scan the vertices in some systematic way, processing each of them exactly once.

The most popular scan orders are known as *Breadth first search* (BFS) and *Depth first search* (DFS). This is most easily understood for a tree: in BFS, starting at some chosen vertex v, the vertices are explored by layers, first the direct neighbors of v, then the neighbors of the neighbors, etc.; in DFS, the order is by branches, fully exploring one branch before starting another. However, both algorithms can be applied to general graphs, not only to trees.

The formal algorithms for BFS and DFS are given in Figure 3.6. The parameters are a graph G and a chosen vertex v from which the search emanates. A function mark is used to avoid the processing of a vertex more than once. The algorithms are in a generic form, concentrating on the order in which the vertices are scanned, rather than specifying what exactly to do with them. The actions to be performed with any given vertex v may differ according to the application at hand, and they are globally referred to here as "visiting" v.

The algorithms appear side by side to show their similarity. Indeed, the only difference is the data structure in which newly encountered vertices are temporarily stored: BFS uses a queue Q, whose FIFO paradigm assures that the vertices are processed by layers, whereas DFS stores the elements in a stack S. Vertices are marked before being inserted into Q or S, and are visited immediately after being extracted. The sequences produced by visiting our example restricted graph G' of Figure 3.1, starting at vertex 1, are

$$\text{BFS}(G', 1): 1, 2, 3, 6, 4, 11, 7, 8, 9, 5, 10$$
$$\text{DFS}(G', 1): 1, 2, 4, 5, 10, 9, 11, 3, 6, 7, 8.$$

It should be noted that the order of visiting the vertices is not necessarily unique, neither for BFS nor for DFS, and depends on the order in which the neighbors of a given vertex are inserted into Q or S. In the preceding example, this insertion order has been chosen by increasing indices for BFS, and by decreasing indices for BFS, for example, the neighbors of vertex 4 have been inserted as 5,6,10 for BFS and as 10,6,5 for DFS.

The complexity of both algorithms is $O(V + E)$, because every edge is processed once. There are applications for which BFS is preferable, like finding a shortest path as in Section 3.1.2 when all weights are equal. For other applications, like dealing with a maze, DFS might be better. In many cases, however, the exact order does not matter and all we want to assure is that no vertex is skipped or processed twice, so BFS or BFS can be applied indifferently.

3.4 The Usefulness of Graphs

This section presents several examples of problems, chosen from different domains of Computer Science, that can be solved by means of a transformation into related problems involving graphs.

3.4.1 Example: Compressing a Set of Correlated Bitmaps

A *bitmap* or bit-vector is a simple data structure often used to represent a set, as we shall see later in Chapter 8. For example,

$$A = 000100110000000010000000$$

is a bitmap of length $\ell = 24$ bits, of which $m = 4$ are ones and 20 are zeros. A possible application could be to an *Information Retrieval* system, in which such bitmaps may replace the index by acting as occurrence maps for the terms in the different documents. The length ℓ of the maps will be the number of documents in the system, and there will be a bitmap B_x for each different term x. The ith bit of B_x will be set to 1 if and only if the term x appears in the document indexed i.

In the example bitmap A, the corresponding term appears in documents 4, 7, 8, and 17.

Most of the terms occur only in very few documents, thus in this application, as well as in many others, most of the bitmaps used are sparse, with an overwhelming majority of zeros. The maps can therefore be compressed efficiently, and we shall assume that the size of a compressed form of a bitmap A is an increasing function of $N(A)$, which denotes the number of 1-bits in A. A simple way to achieve this is by encoding the indices of the 1-bits, using $\lceil \log_2 \ell \rceil$ bits for each. If indeed the bitmap is sparse, its compressed size $m \lceil \log_2 \ell \rceil$ will be smaller than the original length ℓ.

Suppose now that we are given a set of n bitmaps $\mathcal{B} = \{B_1, \ldots, B_n\}$, all of the same length ℓ. One may compress this set by processing each bitmap individually. But certain bitmaps may be correlated and include similar bit-patterns, simply because the corresponding terms appear mostly together. To continue the example, consider a second bitmap

$$B = 01000011000000010000000.$$

Instead of compressing A and B, let us exploit their similarity to produce a new map C by recording only the differences between A and B. This can be done by defining $C = A$ xor B:

$$C = 01010000000000000000000.$$

The bitmap C will be sparser than both A or B, and thereby more compressible. We may thus keep A and C instead of A and B. No information is lost, because the bitmap B can be recovered by simply xoring again: $B = A$ xor C.

Generalizing this idea to n bitmaps seems to be a difficult task. How can one decide which bitmaps should be xored? There might be chains, like $A \leftarrow B \leftarrow C \leftarrow \cdots$, meaning that one should keep A on its own, and B xor A, and C xor B, etc. These chains should not contain any cycles otherwise the decoding would not be possible. The problem is thus to find a partition of the set of bitmaps $\mathcal{B}$ into two disjoint subsets: $\mathcal{B}_i$, the bitmaps that will be compressed individually, and $\mathcal{B}_x$, those that will be xored before being compressed. In addition, we seek a function f from $\mathcal{B}_x$ to $\mathcal{B}$, assigning to each bitmap $B \in \mathcal{B}_x$ a bitmap $B' \in \mathcal{B}_i \cup \mathcal{B}_x$ with which it should be xored. The additional constraints are:

(i) for all bitmaps $A \in \mathcal{B}_x$, the sequence $A, f(A), f(f(A)), \ldots$ should not contain any cycle, as long as it is defined;

(ii) the total number of 1-bits in the set of compressed bitmaps,

$$\sum_{B \in \mathcal{B}_i} N(B) + \sum_{B \in \mathcal{B}_x} N(B \text{ XOR } f(B)),$$

should be minimized over all possible partitions and choices of f.

An exhaustive search over all possible partitions and functions f would have a complexity that is exponential in n, which is clearly not feasible for larger sets of bitmaps. Here is a faster solution.

Recall that given two equal length bitmaps A and B, their *Hamming distance*, denoted by $HD(A, B)$, is the number of indices at which the bitmaps differ, so that

$$HD(A, B) = N(A \text{ XOR } B).$$

In particular, the number of 1-bits in a bitmap A can be expressed in terms of the Hamming distance as

$$N(A) = HD(A, Z),$$

where Z is defined as a bitmap consisting only of zeros.

Define an undirected weighted graph $G = (V, E)$, with

$$V = \mathcal{B} \cup Z, \quad E = V \times V - \{(a, a) \mid a \in V\}, \quad w(a, b) = HD(a, b).$$

In other words, the vertices are the given bitmaps, to which the 0-bitmap Z has been adjoined. The edges are those of a full graph without loops, and the weight on edge (a, b) is the number of 1-bits in a XOR b. We are looking for a subset $T \subseteq E$ of the edges that does not contain any cycles, touches all vertices while minimizing the sum of weights on the edges in T. This is a *minimum spanning tree* of G.

The direct neighbors of Z in T are those bitmaps that are best compressed individually, and for any other bitmap A, its best choice $f(A)$ will be the successor of A in the unique directed path from A to Z in T. For example, refer to the minimum spanning tree of Figure 3.2 as if it were the result of this procedure, and to vertex 6 as the one representing the bitmap Z. This induces a partition into two trees, as shown in Figure 3.7. We get $\mathcal{B}_i = \{4, 7\}$ and the directed edges are $(A, f(A))$, i.e., each other bitmap should be compressed by XORing it first with the bitmap it points to in Figure 3.7.

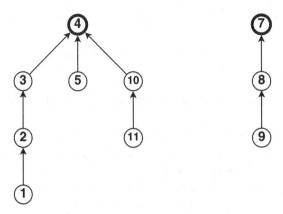

Figure 3.7. Optimal layout for compressing bitmaps.

3.4.2 Example: Optimal Parsing of a Text by means of a Dictionary

Suppose we are given a text $T = x_1 x_2 \cdots x_n$ of length n characters, which all belong to some alphabet Σ. For example, T could be the text aaabccbaaaa of length 11 and $\Sigma = \{a, b, c\}$. To encode the text, we assume the existence of a *dictionary D*. Unlike standard collections like the Oxford English Dictionary, the elements of D are not restricted to be words in some language, and can also be word fragments, of phrases, or in fact any string of characters of Σ. We shall use as an example

$$D = \{a, b, c, aa, aaaa, ab, baa, bccb, bccba\}.$$

The goal is to encode the text T by means of the dictionary D, replacing substrings of T by (shorter) pointers to elements of D, if indeed the replaced substring is one of the elements of D. We do not deal here with the (difficult) problem of building such a dictionary according to some optimization rules, and assume that D is given as a part of the description of the problem. Formally, we wish to represent the text as a sequence $T = w_1 w_2 \cdots w_k$, with $w_i \in D$, and such that the number k of elements in this sequence is minimized. The decomposition of a text into a sequence of dictionary elements is called a *parsing*.

The problem is that because the elements of D might be overlapping, the number of different possible parsings can be too large to allow an exhaustive search over all possibilities. Simple solutions do not yield an optimal parsing. For example, a greedy approach, trying to match the longest possible element of D in a left to right scan would yield

greedy: aa $-$ ab $-$ c $-$ c $-$ baa $-$ aa,

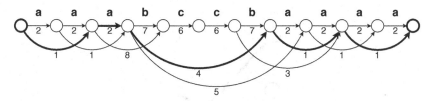

Figure 3.8. Optimal parsing of a text by means of a dictionary.

a partition into 6 elements. A better solution would be to try to locate the longest possible fragment w, and continue this heuristic recursively on the remaining text preceding w and on that following w. This gives

longest fragment: aa − a − bccba − aa − a,

a partition of only 5 elements, which is still not optimal, since one can get a sequence of only 4 elements as in

minimal number of elements: aa − a − bccb − aaaa.

However, the number of elements is only relevant if one assumes that the pointers to the dictionary will all be of the same length, which could be $\lceil \log_2 |D| \rceil$, or 4 bits in our example. If D is encoded by some *variable length code* (see Chapter 11), even if it is given and fixed in advance, the problem is even more involved.

Suppose then that in addition to T and D, there is also a given encoding function $\lambda(w)$ defined for all $w \in D$, producing binary strings of variable length. The length (in bits) of the string encoding w is denoted by $|\lambda(w)|$. The lengths of the elements in our example could be, in order, 2,7,6,1,8,8,3,4,5. The generalized problem is then to find a parsing $T = w_1 w_2 \cdots w_k$ as earlier, minimizing the total length $\sum_{i=1}^{k} |\lambda(w_i)|$ of the encoded text. For the given lengths, the preceding three solution would yield encodings of length 25, 11, and 15 bits, respectively, none of which is optimal.

To build the optimal solution, define a weighted directed graph $G = (V, E)$. The vertices $V = \{1, 2, \ldots, n, n + 1\}$ correspond, in sequence, to the characters of the string, plus an additional vertex numbered $n + 1$. The edges correspond to substrings of the text that are elements of the dictionary D, setting, for all $1 \leq i < j \leq n + 1$:

$$(i, j) \in E \qquad \text{if and only if} \qquad x_i x_{i+1} \cdots x_{j-1} \in D.$$

The weight on edge (i, j) is defined as $|\lambda(x_i x_{i+1} \cdots x_{j-1})|$.

Figure 3.8 displays the graph corresponding to our running example. The sought solution is the weight of the *shortest path* from vertex 1 to vertex $n + 1$. The edges of such a path have been emphasized in the figure, and the weight of this path, which is the length in bits of the optimal parsing of the text, is 9.

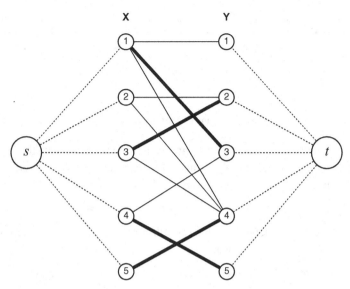

Figure 3.9. Optimal matching.

3.4.3 Example: Generating an Optimal Set of Matches

The solution of the following problem is essential for the survival of the human race. Given are two sets of the same size n, one of girls, $X = \{x_1, x_2, \ldots, x_n\}$, and one of boys, $Y = \{y_1, y_2, \ldots, y_n\}$. We further assume the existence of a collection $\mathcal{C}$ of potential matches (x_i, y_j), that is, $\mathcal{C} \subseteq X \times Y$, with $(x_i, y_j) \in \mathcal{C}$ expressing the fact that x_i would be willing to marry y_j and vice versa, with complete symmetry between the sexes. So unlike the more tragic situation that gave rise to much of the romantic literature, we assume here an idyllic world without unrequited love, in which x wants to marry y if and only if y wants to marry x. Moreover, the set of potential mates of x, $\{y_j \mid (x, y_j) \in \mathcal{C}\}$, as well as the set of potential mates of y, $\{x_i \mid (x_i, y) \in \mathcal{C}\}$, are not ordered, so there are no preferences, and each of the possibly many choices are equally acceptable for all involved parties.

For example, set $n = 5$ and $\mathcal{C} = \{(x_1, y_1), (x_1, y_4), (x_2, y_2), (x_2, y_4), (x_3, y_2), (x_3, y_4), (x_4, y_3), (x_4, y_5), (x_5, y_4)\}$. The goal is to produce as many marriages as possible. This is a problem, because there is still an additional constraint of monogamy, allowing any girl or boy to have at most one spouse.

The solution is the construction of a weighted graph $G = (V, E)$, with

$$V = X \cup Y \cup \{s, t\} \qquad E = \mathcal{C} \cup \{(s, x) \mid x \in X\} \cup \{(y, t) \mid y \in Y\},$$

and the weights on all the edges being set to 1, as shown in Figure 3.9.

Consider the edges as oriented from left to right in the figure, and interpret the graph as a flow network with equal capacity on each edge. The maximal matching is then the set of edges having nonzero flow in a *maximum flow* from s to t. For the given example, only four couples can be formed, one of the several possible solutions corresponds to the boldfaced edges, while x_2 and y_1 will stay singles.

Exercises

3.1 One of the algorithms solving the shortest path problem of Section 3.1.2 is due to *Edsger W. Dijkstra*. Its correctness, however, depends on the additional assumption that all the weights $w(a, b)$ are nonnegative. This might sound reasonable in many applications, but there are others in which negative weights should also be supported. A natural suggestion is the following reduction.

Given a graph $G = (V, E)$ with weights $w_G(a, b)$, some of which are negative, let $m = \min\{w_G(a, b) \mid (a, b) \in E\}$ be the smallest weight in the graph. By assumption, m is negative. Define a graph $G' = (V, E)$ with the same vertices and edges as G, only with different weights, by setting, for all $(a, b) \in E$,

$$w_{G'}(a, b) = w_G(a, b) - m.$$

All the weights in G' are thus nonnegative, so we can apply Dijkstra's algorithm and deduce the shortest paths also for G.

Show that this reduction does not give a correct shortest path, that is, give an example of a graph G and a shortest path in G which does not correspond to a shortest path in G'. Note that there is no need to know the details of Dijkstra's algorithm to answer this and any of the subsequent questions.

3.2 Suppose you are given a complete list of all the airports, and all the flights and their exact schedules. For simplicity, assume that the schedule is periodic, repeating itself every day. You may use the algorithm A which finds the shortest path in a weighted graph, but you cannot change A. What can be done to find:

(a) a cheapest path from a source s to a target t, under the constraint that airport T should be avoided;
(b) a cheapest path from s to t, but preferring, whenever possible, the use of airline X, because you are a frequent flyer there;

(c) a path from s to t minimizing the number of intermediate stops;

(d) a path from s to t minimizing the number of changes from one airline to another;

(e) a path from s to t minimizing the overall travel time from departure from s to landing at t.

3.3 In a communication network connecting n computers, a message may be sent from a source computer s to a target computer t via several intermediate stations. The probability of a message to get from a to b without corruption is $p(a, b)$. How can one choose a path from s to t in the network, so that the probability of receiving the correct message is maximized? Like in exercise 3.2, you may use algorithm A, but you may not change it.

3.4 Cartographers have been struggling for long with the problem of how many colors they need to be able to print any map according to the rules that

(a) there is no restriction on the number, shape or size of the countries in a given map;

(b) countries having a common border (not just a single point, like Utah and New Mexico) should be given different colors.

It has been shown in 1977 that *four colors suffice*: this is the famous 4-color problem, which has been open for many years. Show how to translate the problem of coloring a map using k colors into a graph-theoretic one, and give an algorithm for $k = 2$.

Remark: No algorithm is needed for $k = 4$, since by the mentioned theorem, every map is 4-colorable. Interestingly, for $k = 3$, the problem seems to be very difficult, and so far, no reasonable algorithm is known.

3.5 A *De Bruijn sequence* of order k is a cyclic binary string of length 2^k that includes each of the 2^k possible binary strings of length k exactly once as a substring. For example, 11010001 is a De Bruijn sequence of order 3, as each of the possible 8 strings of length 3, 000, 001, 010, 011, 100, 101, 110, 111, appears exactly once, namely, at positions 5, 6, 3, 7, 4, 2, 1, and 8, respectively. Construct a De Bruijn sequence of order 4.

The following reduction may be used to solve the problem. Consider a graph $G = (V, E)$ defined as follows. The vertices correspond to the 2^{k-1} binary strings representing the integers

$$0, 1, \ldots, 2^{k-1} - 1$$

in a standard binary encoding. There is an edge labeled b, for $b \in \{0, 1\}$, emanating from a vertex corresponding to $x_1 x_2 \cdots x_{k-1}$ to the vertex

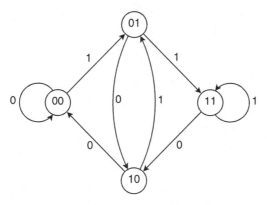

Figure 3.10. Graph for the construction of a De Bruijn sequence.

corresponding to $x_2x_3 \cdots x_{k-1}b$, that is, if the suffix of length $k - 2$ of the former is the prefix of the latter. Figure 3.10 displays this graph for $k = 3$. Every vertex has exactly two outgoing and two incoming edges. It can be shown that in this case, there exists a so-called *Euler circuit*, which is a closed path traversing each of the edges exactly once. One possible such path in our example is 01-11-11-10-01-10-00-00-01. Concatenating the labels on the edges of such a path yields the De Bruijn sequence.

4

Trees

4.1 Allowing Multiple Successors

The graphs of the previous chapter were a generalization of the linear lists to structures without order. We now turn to another generalization, still keeping some order, but a more relaxed one. The main motivation may be the fact that a linear list is ultimately not able to support both efficient searches and updates. To get the possibility to perform a binary search, the elements have to be stored sequentially, but then inserts and deletes may require $\Omega(n)$ steps. Using a linked list, on the other hand, may reduce the update time to $O(1)$, but at the price of losing the ability to locate the middle elements needed for the binary search, so the time complexity can be $\Omega(n)$.

The problem is that the constraint of every record having only a single successor, as depicted on the left-hand side of Figure 4.1, might be too restrictive. This chapter explores the structures one obtains by allowing each element to be directly followed by possibly more than one other element, as on the right-hand side of Figure 4.1. Because of the repeated branching, such structures are known as *trees*. Formally, the definition of a tree is general enough to encompass a broad family of recursive structures, and we shall deal with several such families in this and the following chapters.

Definition 4.1. A *tree* is a set of elements called *nodes* for which:

(i) there is a special element in the set, called the *root*;
(ii) the other elements can be partitioned into m subsets, each of which is a tree.

Actually, almost any set can then be considered to be a tree. Refer for example to the nodes in the left part of Figure 4.2, 5 might be chosen as the root, and the others can be partitioned into $m = 3$ subsets, as shown. The convention is

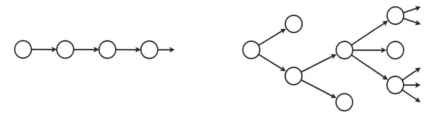

Figure 4.1. Linear lists versus tree structure.

to draw such a tree in levels top down, the root being placed on the top in level 0, and the *m* subtrees following in some order below the root, starting with the next level. This yields the equivalent tree on the right side of Figure 4.2. Accordingly, the vocabulary of genealogic trees has been adopted, for example, 3 is the *parent* of 4, and 3, 9, and 10 are *siblings* and the *children* of 5. Nodes without children, like 9 or 7, are called *leaves*, and the others, like 8 or 5, are called *internal* nodes.

A tree will be the natural choice if one has to represent a set that is intrinsically hierarchic, like a book, which can be subpartitioned into parts, and then into chapters, sections, sentences, etc.; or a university, partitioned into faculties, departments, and so on. The interesting aspect, however, of using trees, is that they might be the preferred choice even in other situations, which have *a priori* nothing to do with a recursive structure. Nonetheless, the properties of trees we shall see may turn them into the optimal solution for many problems.

Keeping the definition of a tree in its general form, with no limits imposed on the number *m* of subtrees, may be appropriate in many situations, but the processing is more complicated. As alternative, one defines a *binary tree* as follows:

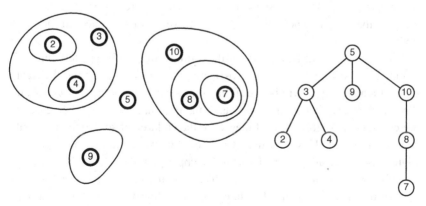

Figure 4.2. A tree structure.

general tree   binary tree

Figure 4.3. General and binary trees with two nodes.

Definition 4.2. A *binary tree* is a set of elements which is:

(i) either empty, or
(ii) consists of a special element, called the *root*, and two subsets that are them-
     selves binary trees and are called *left subtree* and *right subtree*, respectively.

Note that a binary tree is therefore *not* a special case of a general tree. First,
a general tree is never empty as it contains at least a root. Second, the subtrees
of a general tree are not ordered, while we do differentiate between a left and a
right child of a node in a binary tree. In particular, there is only a single general
tree with two nodes, as shown in Figure 4.3, but there are two different binary
trees with two nodes: both have a root, but the second node can be either a left,
or a right child, and this will be reflected in our drawings.

4.2 General versus Binary Trees

Limiting the number of children of a node to at most 2 has the advantage of
using only two pointers for each node. General trees may be handled by transforming them first into equivalent binary trees, as follows. Consider an ordered
forest $\mathcal{F}$, which is a sequence of general trees; we shall construct an equivalent binary tree $\mathcal{T}$, by using the same set of nodes, but reordering them differently, so that only two pointers, to a left and a right child, are needed for each
node.

The root of $\mathcal{T}$ will be the root of the leftmost tree in $\mathcal{F}$. The left child of
a node in $\mathcal{T}$ will be the first (leftmost) child of that node in $\mathcal{F}$, and the right
child of a node v in $\mathcal{T}$ will be the sibling immediately to the right of v in $\mathcal{F}$, if
there is such a sibling at all. The roots of the trees in $\mathcal{F}$ are special cases, and
are considered as siblings, as if they were the children of some virtual global
root of the forest. This procedure yields the binary tree in the lower part of
Figure 4.4 if we start with the forest in the upper part of the figure.

This construction process is reversible, implying that the function relating
a given forest with its equivalent binary tree is a bijection. It follows that the
number of different such forests with n nodes is equal to the number of different
binary trees with n nodes.

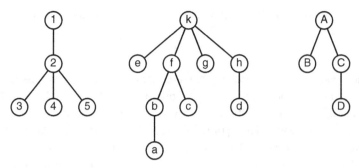

Forest of 3 general trees

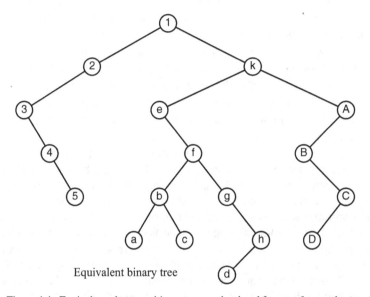

Equivalent binary tree

Figure 4.4. Equivalence between binary trees and ordered forests of general trees.

Background Concept: Number of Binary Trees

To evaluate the number of such forests or binary trees, it is convenient to use the following compact representation of trees, which is also useful when the information describing a tree has to be stored or transmitted. A tree T with root R and subtrees $T_1, T_2, \ldots, T_k$, will be represented by the recursively defined sequence (R T_1 T_2 $\cdots$ T_k). For example, the sequence corresponding to the tree of Figure 4.2 is

$$\Big(5 \; (3 \; (2) \; (4)) \; (9) \; (10 \; (8 \; (7)))\Big).$$

If one is only interested in the structure of the tree, and not in the values of its nodes, the values can be eliminated and one is left with a sequence of opening and closing parentheses, as in the preceding example:

$$((( ) ( )) ( ) ((( )))).$$

The sequence for a forest is just the concatenation of the sequences of the corresponding trees, so ( ) ( ) represents two trees, each consisting of a single node. Notice that not every sequence of parentheses is appropriate. Since every opening parenthesis has a matching closing one, their number must be equal. Denoting a sequence of x opening parentheses and y closing parentheses as a (x, y)-sequence, the sequence corresponding to a forest with n nodes has thus to be an (n, n)-sequence.

That this is not a sufficient condition can be seen when considering, e.g., the sequence $S = (( ) ( ))) (( )$, which is not properly nested. So the following nesting condition has to be added: when scanning the sequence left to right, at each point, the number of opening parentheses seen so far is not smaller than the number of closing parentheses. Let us call *good* (n, n)-sequences those satisfying the nesting condition. To evaluate their number, we consider the complementing set of *bad* (n, n)-sequences.

In any bad (n, n)-sequence, the number of closing parentheses exceeds the number of opening ones, so there must be a leftmost position in a left to right scan at which this happens for the first time. In the example of the sequence S, it is at position 7, and the violating closing parenthesis is emphasized. Consider then the function f transforming such bad (n, n)-sequences by inverting all the parentheses following this first occurrence. For our example, the resulting sequence would be $f(S) = (( ) ( )))) ($, in which all inverted parentheses are emphasized. The resulting sequence will always be an $(n - 1, n + 1)$-sequence, and since the function is reversible by applying it again, that is, $f^{-1} = f$, the function f is a bijection, implying that the number of bad (n, n)-sequences is equal to the total number of $(n - 1, n + 1)$-sequences, which is $\binom{2n}{n-1}$. We can thus conclude that

$$
\begin{array}{cccc}
\text{number of} & \text{number of} & \text{total number} & \text{number of} \\
\text{forests with} = & \text{good } (n, n)\text{-} = & \text{of } (n, n)\text{-} & - (n-1, n+1)\text{-} \\
n \text{ nodes} & \text{sequences} & \text{sequences} & \text{sequences}
\end{array}
$$

$$= \binom{2n}{n} - \binom{2n}{n-1} = \frac{1}{n+1}\binom{2n}{n}.$$

These numbers are known as *Catalan* numbers, the first of which are $1, 2, 5, 14, 42, \ldots$. Asymptotically, the nth Catalan number is $O(\frac{4^n}{n^{3/2}})$.

Returning to the equivalence between ordered forests and binary trees, it seems that we can always restrict ourselves to deal with binary trees, which are more convenient to handle, since a general tree can be transformed into an equivalent binary one. Indeed, most of our discussion on trees will assume that the trees are binary. It should however be noted that a certain price has been payed for this convenience: some direct connections that existed in the general tree have been replaced by more expensive alternatives. For example, in the forest of Figure 4.4, only two links were needed to get from node k to node d, whereas in the equivalent binary tree, this path is now of length 5.

4.3 Binary Trees: Properties and Examples

Similarly to what we saw for graphs in the previous chapter, there is a need to explore all the nodes of a tree in a systematic way. We shall use the term *visit* to describe such an exploration. Any visit consists of a well-defined order in which all the nodes are processed, and of some action to be taken at each of the nodes. In our examples, this action will be simply to print the value of the node.

By convention, given a binary tree, its left subtree is visited before the right one, but there are three possibilities for the visit of the root: in a top down processing, the root will be processed before dealing, recursively, with the subtrees, while in applications requiring a bottom up approach, the root will be visited after the visit of the subtrees has been completed. An interesting third alternative is to visit the root after the left subtree but before the right one. The orders corresponding to these three visit strategies are known, respectively, as *pre-order*, *post-order*, and *in-order*.

Consider the general binary tree depicted in the upper drawing of Figure 4.5. The recursive visit procedures and the results produced by applying them on this tree are given in Figure 4.6.

If every internal node has exactly two children, the tree is called *complete*, as the one in the left lower part of Figure 4.5. The tree in the upper part of this figure is not complete, because the internal nodes labeled B, C, G and E have only a single child each. Instead of defining a complete tree as a special case of a general binary tree, one could have given it a recursive definition of its own, only slightly different from Definition 4.2:

Definition 4.3. A *complete binary tree* is a set of elements which is:

(i) either a single element, or
(ii) consists of a special element, called the *root*, and two subsets that are themselves complete binary trees and are called *left subtree* and *right subtree*, respectively.

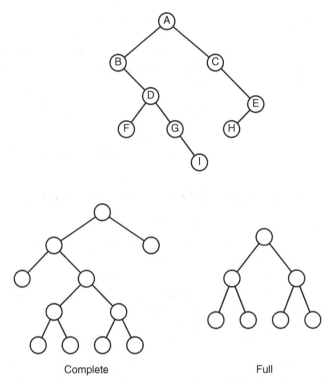

Figure 4.5. General, complete, and full binary trees.

Since this is a recursive definition, it covers actually a broad range of similar structures. Consider, for instance, the definition of an arithmetic expression including only binary operators, like $+, -, \times, /, \uparrow, \ldots$ (as before, we use the symbol $\uparrow$ for exponentiation).

Definition 4.4. An *arithmetic expression* is a string of elements which is:

(i) either a single element, called an *operand*, or
(ii) consists of a special element, called the *operator*, and two substrings that are themselves arithmetic expressions.

Pre-order(T)	In-order(T)	Post-order(T)
visit $root(T)$	In-order($left(T)$)	Post-order($left(T)$)
Pre-order($left(T)$)	visit $root(T)$	Post-order($right(T)$)
Pre-order($right(T)$)	In-order($right(T)$)	visit $root(T)$
A B D F G I C E H	B F D G I A C H E	F I G D B H E C A

Figure 4.6. Visiting a binary tree.

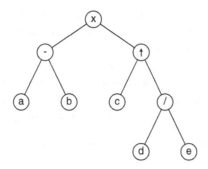

Figure 4.7. Complete binary tree of an arithmetic expression.

In fact, the conclusion is that such an expression can be considered as a complete binary tree, which may be useful for certain applications. As example, refer to the expression

$$(a - b) \times c \uparrow (d/e)$$

and to the corresponding binary tree given in Figure 4.7. Visiting this tree in the orders discussed earlier yields

For pre-order	For in-order	For post-order
$\times - a\,b \uparrow c\,/\,d\,e$	$((a - b) \times (c \uparrow (d\,/\,e)))$	$a\,b - c\,d\,e\,/ \uparrow \times$

which can be recognized as **prefix**, **infix**, and **postfix** notation, respectively, of the given expression. These notations have been discussed in Section 2.3.1 about stacks. As mentioned, parentheses are needed for in-order to change the operator priorities, when necessary.

We now turn to the problem of formally proving certain properties of trees. The proof of many properties dealt with in discrete mathematics is often based on *induction*. This works fine for mathematical identities, once they are known, like $\sum_{i=1}^{n} i^3 = \left(\sum_{i=1}^{n} i\right)^2$, but it is not trivial to extend this technique also to the more involved structure of a binary tree. Indeed, there are several options on which to base the induction: the number of nodes, the number of leaves, the depth of the tree, etc. One also has to show that every possible tree is covered by the inductive procedure. As alternative, one can exploit the recursive structure of a tree to devise a type of proof called *induction on the structure* of the tree. The following example will illustrate this approach.

The *depth* of a node in a tree is the level on which it appears, where the level of the root is defined as 0. In many applications, our interest is focused on the leaves of the tree rather than the internal nodes, and in particular on the depths of these leaves. The exact shape of the tree might be less important, and a tree is often characterized by the sequence of depths of its leaves. For example, these sequences would be $3\,3\,4$, $1\,2\,4\,4\,4\,4$, and $2\,2\,2\,2$ for the three binary trees of Figure 4.5, and each sequence is given in nondecreasing order, rather than in the order of the leaves themselves.

We would like to recognize those sequences that correspond to complete binary trees. A sequence may not correspond to any tree, like $1\,1\,1$, since no binary tree can have more than two leaves on level 1. Other sequences may correspond to binary trees, but not to complete ones, like $3\,3\,4$.

Theorem 4.1. Given is a complete binary tree with leaves on levels $\ell_1, \ell_2, \ldots, \ell_n$, respectively. Then

$$\sum_{i=1}^{n} 2^{-\ell_i} = 1.$$

Proof by induction on the structure of the tree. For $n = 1$, the only leaf must also be the root, so its depth is 0, and we have $\sum_{i=1}^{n} 2^{-\ell_1} = 2^0 = 1$.

For $n > 1$, the tree consists of a root and nonempty left and right subtrees. Without loss of generality, we may assume that there is some k, $1 \le k < n$, such that the leaves in the left subtree are indexed $1, \ldots, k$, while those in the right subtree are indexed $k + 1, \ldots, n$. Denote the depth of a leaf in one of the subtrees by d_i, we then have that $\ell_i = d_i + 1$. It follows that

$$\sum_{i=1}^{n} 2^{-\ell_i} = \sum_{i=1}^{k} 2^{-\ell_i} + \sum_{i=k+1}^{n} 2^{-\ell_i}$$

$$= \sum_{i=1}^{k} 2^{-(d_i+1)} + \sum_{i=k+1}^{n} 2^{-(d_i+1)}$$

$$= \frac{1}{2} \sum_{i=1}^{k} 2^{-d_i} + \frac{1}{2} \sum_{i=k+1}^{n} 2^{-d_i} = \frac{1}{2} + \frac{1}{2} = 1,$$

where we have used the inductive assumption for each of the two subtrees. ∎

4.4 Binary Search Trees

One of the main applications of binary trees is the processing of a set of records, as explained in the previous chapters. Operations that need to be supported are the efficient search for a given record in the set, as well as insertion and deletion. This leads to the definition of *binary search trees*, in which every record is assigned to one of the nodes of the tree, and can be identified by its value stored in the node. For the simplicity of the discussion, we shall assume

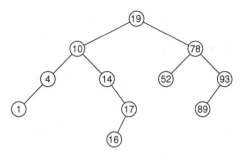

Figure 4.8. Binary search tree.

that all the values in the tree are different from each other. The special property of binary search trees is:

Definition 4.5. In a binary search tree, for every node x with value v_x, the values in the left subtree of x are smaller than v_x and the values in the right subtree of x are larger than v_x.

Here and subsequently, we shall use the convention of denoting by v_x the node containing the value x. An example of a binary search tree can be seen in Figure 4.8. Scanning the tree using inorder will list the elements ordered by increasing values. This property can also be used to induce an order in any binary tree. For example, if one considers the tree in the lower part of Figure 4.4 as a binary search tree, the implied order of its elements would be

$$3\ 4\ 5\ 2\ 1\ e\ a\ b\ c\ f\ g\ d\ h\ k\ B\ D\ C\ A.$$

4.4.1 Search

Searching for an element in a binary search tree always starts at the root. If the element is not found there, we know already if it is smaller or larger than the value stored in the root. In the former case, the search continues recursively in the left subtree, and in the latter case in the right subtree.

For example, suppose one looks for an element with value 12 in the tree of Figure 4.8. The value 12 is smaller than 19 stored in the root, so the next comparison is with the root of the left subtree, storing 10; 12 is larger, hence one continues to v_{14}; 12 is smaller than 14, so we should continue to the left child of v_{14}, but there is no such left child. We conclude that v_{12} is not in the tree.

The formal recursive procedure searching for an element v_x in the subtree rooted by T is given in Figure 4.9. It should be invoked by Search(*root*, x), and it returns a triplet (*indic*, R, *side*). If a node v_x with value x is in the tree, then

Search(T, x)

> $v \longleftarrow value(T)$
> if $x = v$ then return (found, T, 0)
> else   if $x < v$ then
>   if $left(T) =$ NIL then   return (not-found, T, left)
>   else   Search($left(T), x$)
>   else   // here $x > v$
>   if $right(T) =$ NIL then   return (not-found, T, right)
>   else   Search($right(T), x$)

Figure 4.9. Recursive search for x in tree rooted by T.

the indicator *indic* = found and R points to v_x (the third element *side* is not used in this case). Otherwise, *indic* = not-found, R is a pointer to a node w which should be the parent of v_x, and *side* = left or right, showing whether v_x should be a left or right child of w.

The number of comparisons and thus the complexity of the search procedure is clearly dependent on the level in the tree at which v_x, in case of a successful search, or w, for an unsuccessful one, are found. We have, however, no control over the depth of the tree or the level at which a certain node will appear. In the worst case, for example, if the nodes are created by increasing order of their values, the depth of the tree will be $n - 1$, which is clearly unacceptable. The best scenario would be a *full* binary tree, defined as one having all its leaves on the same level, like the right tree in the lower part of Figure 4.5. There is regretfully no consensus about the use of the terms *full* and *complete*, and some books invert their definitions.

In a full binary tree with n nodes, the depth of a node is at most $\lfloor \log_2 n \rfloor$, and this will thus be the bound on the search time. We shall see in the following chapters what actions can be taken to ensure that the depth of the binary search tree will be logarithmic in n even for the worst case.

4.4.2 Insertion

To insert an element v_x with value x into a tree rooted at T, one has first to check that there is no node with value x already in the tree. One may thus search for x using the procedure of Figure 4.9, which returns a pointer to a node R that should be the parent node of v_x, and indicates whether v_x is a left or right child of R. The formal procedure is in Figure 4.10.

Note that any newly inserted element creates a new leaf in the tree. The complexity of inserting an element depends on the depth at which the corresponding leaf will be inserted, which is at most the depth of the tree. As for the search, insertion might thus require $\Omega(n)$ steps.

Insert(T, x)
─────────────
    $(indic, R, side)$ ⟵ Search(T, x)
    if $indic =$ not-found then
        create node v_x
        $value(v_x)$ ⟵ x
        $left(v_x)$ ⟵ $right(v_x)$ ⟵ NIL
        $side(R)$ ⟵ v_x

Figure 4.10. Insertion of v_x in tree rooted by T.

4.4.3 Deletion

While insertion into and deletion from linear lists could be treated more or less symmetrically, this is not the case when dealing with search trees. Indeed, a node is always inserted as a leaf, whereas one might wish to delete any node in the tree, possibly also an internal one.

The deletion procedure gets as parameters a pointer T to the root of the tree and the value x of the element to be deleted. The process starts by checking whether there is a node v_x with value x in the tree, and where it is located. If such an element is found, the process distinguishes between three cases, according to the number of children N of v_x:

(i) If $N = 0$, v_x is a leaf, and it can be removed by changing the pointer to v_x, if it exists, into a NIL-pointer, without further action. If v_x is the root, we are in the special case of a tree with a single node, and this tree becomes empty after the deletion.

(ii) If $N = 1$, v_x is deleted by directly connecting its parent node, if it exists, to the only child of v_x. If v_x is the root, its only child becomes the new root.

(iii) If $N = 2$, we have to deal with the problem that there is a single incoming pointer to v_x, but there are two outgoing pointers. Simply eliminating the node would thus disconnect the tree. To circumvent the problem, the node v_x will not be deleted, only the value x it contains will be erased and replaced by some other value y that does not disturb any possible subsequent searching process. This value y should be the value of one of the nodes v_y of the tree, and the only possible candidates for y are thus the immediate predecessor or successor of x in the ordered sequence of all the elements stored in the tree. Let us choose the successor. After replacing x by y, the node v_y should be deleted, which can be done recursively.

The successor v_y of a node v_x which has a right child is found as follows: it has to be in the right subtree of v_x, since this subtree includes the elements with smallest values that are larger than x, and it has to be the element with smallest

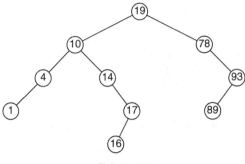

Deleting 52

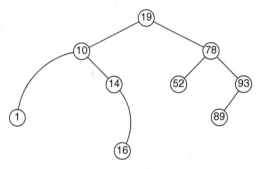

Deleting 4 and 17

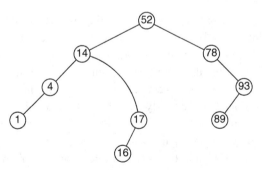

Deleting 10 and 19

Figure 4.11. Deletion from a binary search tree.

Delete(T, x)

> ($indic, R, dum$) $\longleftarrow$ Search(T, x)
> if $indic =$ found then
>
> > case 0: R is a leaf, then   // just erase the leaf
> > if R is the *root* then erase it   // case of empty tree
> > else if R is a left child then $left(parent(R))$ $\longleftarrow$ NIL
> > else $right(parent(R))$ $\longleftarrow$ NIL
> >
> > case 1: R has 1 child, then   // bypass the node, then erase
> > if $left(R) =$ NIL then $child$ $\longleftarrow$ $right(R)$
> > else $child$ $\longleftarrow$ $left(R)$
> >
> > if R is the *root* then $root$ $\longleftarrow$ $child$
> > else if R is a left child then $left(parent(R))$ $\longleftarrow$ $child$
> > else $right(parent(R))$ $\longleftarrow$ $child$
> >
> > case 2: R has 2 children, then   // search for successor C to replace R
> > C $\longleftarrow$ $right(R)$
> > while $left(C) \neq$ NIL C $\longleftarrow$ $left(C)$
> > $value(R)$ $\longleftarrow$ $value(C)$
> > Delete($C, value(C)$)

Figure 4.12. Deletion of v_x from tree rooted by T.

value within this subtree. The way to get from v_x to v_y is thus to take one step to the right, and then repeatedly steps to the left, as long as possible. Refer, for example, to the tree in the lower part of Figure 4.4, assuming that the order of its elements' values is indeed given by an inorder traversal, then the successor of v_e in this order is v_a, and the successor of v_k is v_B. Note that the successor is not necessarily a leaf, as can be seen in the latter example, but it cannot have a left child. This is the reason that deleting v_y instead of v_x will not cause a loop of recursive calls, since it is invoked in the case $N = 2$, but the deletion of the successor involves one of the cases $N = 0$ or $N = 1$.

Figure 4.11 brings examples of all the cases for the deletion process. For each of them, the starting point is the tree of Figure 4.8. In the upper example in Figure 4.11, the element to be deleted is the one with value 52, which is a leaf. The examples in the middle part of Figure 4.11 correspond to $N = 1$: deleting v_4 is a case in which two *left* pointers are combined, while the deletion of v_{17} replaces a *right* and a *left* pointer by a single *right* pointer. Finally, the tree in the lower part of Figure 4.11 shows two instances of the case $N = 2$: the successor of v_{10} is the root v_{14} of its right subtree, and v_{14} itself has only one child; and the successor of v_{19} is v_{52}, which is a leaf.

The formal algorithm for deleting an element v_x from a tree rooted at T is given in Figure 4.12. A technical remark: one could save the special treatment involving the *root* by the addition of a sentinel element carrying no value, as already mentioned earlier in Sections 2.4.1 and 2.4.2. Instead of reserving a *root* pointer to access the tree, there would be a root node v_{root} without value, but having the entire tree as, say, its right subtree. For large enough trees, the relative overhead of such an element would be negligible, and the processing of all the cases would then be uniform.

The complexity of deleting an element v_x from a binary search tree is thus not bounded by the level at which v_x appears in the tree, since it might involve the successor of v_x at a lower level. However, even in the worst case, the complexity is still bounded by the depth of the tree.

Exercises

4.1 Draw the 5 different forests as well as the 5 different binary trees with 3 nodes, and show how they correspond using the equivalence displayed in Figure 4.4.

4.2 Draw the binary tree whose in-order and post-order traversals are, respectively, B G L F I K A C N H J E M D and L F G K C N A I J D M E H B. What is the pre-order traversal of this tree? Is it possible to determine the tree on the basis of its pre-order and post-order traversals alone? Show how to do it, or give a counterexample.

4.3 A complete *ternary* tree is a tree in which each internal node has exactly 3 children. Show by induction on the structure of the tree that a complete ternary tree with n leaves has $(n-1)/2$ internal nodes.

4.4 Given is a sequence of n ordered integer sequences $A_1, \ldots, A_n$, of lengths $\ell_1, \ldots, \ell_n$, respectively. We wish to merge all the sequences into a single ordered sequence, allowing only pairs of adjacent already ordered sequences to be merged. The number of steps needed to merge a elements with b elements is $a + b$. If $n = 2$, there is only one possibility to merge A_1 with A_2, but for $n = 3$, one could merge $A_1(A_2A_3)$ or $(A_1A_2)A_3$. The corresponding times would be $(\ell_2 + \ell_3) + (\ell_1 + \ell_2 + \ell_3)$ or $(\ell_1 + \ell_2) + (\ell_1 + \ell_2 + \ell_3)$. For $n = 4$, there are 5 possibilities.

Find a connection between the different possibilities to merge n sequences under the given constraint and binary trees. How many possibilities are there to merge ten sequences?

4.5 Given are two binary search trees with k and ℓ nodes, respectively, such that $k + \ell = 2^n - 1$ for some $n > 2$. All the $2^n - 1$ elements are different. Describe an algorithm running in $O(k + \ell)$ time, that merges the two trees into one full binary search tree.

5

AVL Trees

5.1 Bounding the Depth of Trees

We saw earlier that binary search trees are a good compromise between sequentially allocated arrays, which allow direct access, but are not updated easily, and linked lists, that support inserts and deletes in constant time, but cannot be searched efficiently. There is, however, still a major challenge left to be dealt with: the shape of the tree, and in particular its depth, on which ultimately all update complexities depend, is a function of the order in which the elements are processed. The same set of elements, when given in different orders, may produce completely different trees (see Figure 5.1).

Yet, we have generally no influence on the order the elements are presented, so we might get the worst case scenario, in which the depth of the tree is $\Omega(n)$. This is unacceptable, as it would also imply search and update times of the same order. Nothing has then be gained by passing from a linear linked list to a tree structure. What we would like is a tree structure for n elements in which the update times are guaranteed to be as close as possible to the optimal, which is $\log_2 n$. Imposing, however, that the tree should be completely balanced, which yields the $\log_2 n$ bound on the depth, seems to be too restrictive: it would require reshaping the tree constantly.

An elegant tradeoff has been suggested by Georgy Adelson-Velsky and Evgenii Landis and is known by the acronym of its inventors as AVL trees. The idea is to define a condition that on one hand is easily enforceable, but on the other hand yields trees that are *almost* balanced. Let us recall some definitions.

Background Concept: Depth of a Tree
The *depth* of a tree, sometimes also called its *height*, is the number of edges one has to traverse on the path from the root to a most distant

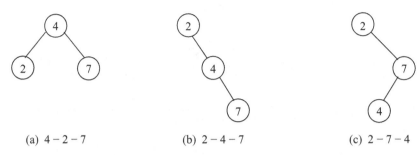

(a) $4 - 2 - 7$ (b) $2 - 4 - 7$ (c) $2 - 7 - 4$

Figure 5.1. Binary search trees for the set $\{2, 4, 7\}$. The different shapes correspond to different input orders.

leaf. The depths of the trees in Figure 5.1 are 1, 2 and 2, respectively. It is the number of levels minus 1, hence a tree consisting of a single node (the root is a leaf) has depth 0, and it is convenient to define the depth of an empty tree as -1. We shall denote the depth of a tree T by $d(T)$. For any node v of a tree T, denote by T_v the subtree of T rooted at v, and by $L(v)$ and $R(v)$ the left child, respectively right child, of v, if it exists.

Definition 5.1. A tree T is an AVL tree (also called *height-balanced tree*) if it is a binary search tree and for each node v of T, the difference of the depths of the subtrees of v is at most 1. Formally,

$$\forall v \in T \qquad |d(T_{L(v)}) - d(T_{R(v)})| \leq 1. \tag{5.1}$$

For example, the shape of the upper four trees of Figure 5.2 comply with the constraint of eq. (5.1), the tree in Figure 5.1(a) is also AVL, but the tree in Figure 5.2(e) is not, because of the black node: its left subtree is of depth 2 and its right one of depth 0.

What remains to be done is the following:

- show that the constraint of eq. (5.1) implies a logarithmic depth;
- show how, at low cost, the tree can be maintained complying with the condition after insertions and deletions.

5.2 Depth of AVL Trees

One can get a surprisingly exact lower bound on the depth of the tree in our special case.

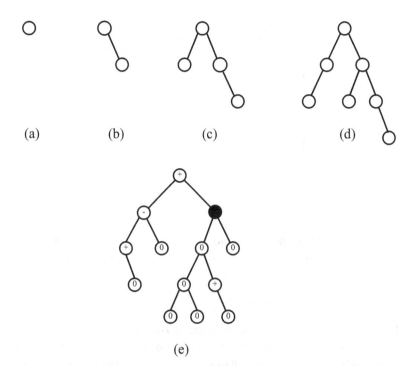

(a) (b) (c) (d)

(e)

Figure 5.2. (a)–(d) Minimal AVL trees of depths 0–3, respectively. (e) A non-AVL tree.

Theorem 5.1. The depth of an AVL tree T with n nodes is at most logarithmic in n, and more precisely

$$d(T) \leq 1.4404 \log_2(n+1) - 1.33. \tag{5.2}$$

How can one prove such a statement? A first thought might be to try induction on the number of nodes n, since this is the parameter of Theorem 5.1. But the depth of a tree must be an integer, and $\log_2 n$ is not, for most values of n. For example, for $n = 1000$ and $n = 1001$, the theorem yields the upper bounds 12.155 and 12.157, which have both to be rounded to the same integer 12. There seems thus to be a technical problem with the inductive step. To overcome the difficulty in this and similar cases, in particular when stating properties of trees, we shall formulate an alternative, equivalent, theorem, that is easier to prove, by changing our point of view.

Theorem 5.1′. The number of nodes n of an AVL tree with depth k is at least exponential in k, that is $n \geq a^k$ for some constant $a > 1$.

Background Concept: Proving Properties of Trees
One may wonder how the inequality suddenly changed direction. Theorem 5.1 asserts a relationship between two properties of a tree, as can

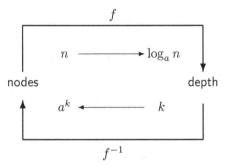

Figure 5.3. Schematic of the relation between the number of nodes of a tree and its depth.

be seen in the upper part of Figure 5.3. Given is a parameter n, the number of nodes in a tree, and the theorem reveals information about $f(n)$, the depth of the tree, stating that

$$f(n) \leq \log_a n, \text{ for some constant } a > 1. \tag{5.3}$$

One gets to the alternative formulation of Theorem 5.1′ by inverting the roles of the properties: assume now that the depth of the tree is given, denote it by k, and let the new theorem convey information about the corresponding number of nodes, as depicted in the lower part of Figure 5.3. If the function from the nodes to the depth is f, its inverse is usually denoted by f^{-1}. But f is not injective, that is, trees with different numbers of nodes may have the same depth, and therefore f^{-1} is not necessarily a function. This mathematical difficulty can be overcome if we restrict our attention to *minimal* AVL trees, defined as those AVL trees having a minimal number of nodes for their depth. For example, the trees in Figure 5.2(a)–(d) are minimal, but the tree in Figure 5.1(a) is not.

To get to the alternative theorem, we apply the function f^{-1} to both sides of the inequality in eq. (5.3), getting

$$f^{-1}\left(f(n)\right) \leq f^{-1}\left(\log_a n\right), \tag{5.4}$$

where the inequality did not change direction, because f, and thus also f^{-1}, are nondecreasing functions. Substituting k for $\log_a n$ and consequently a^k for n, we get

$$a^k \leq f^{-1}(k). \tag{5.5}$$

The inequality did not change, but the main function of the theorem now appears on the right-hand side. It is customary to rewrite such an inequality as $f^{-1}(k) \geq a^k$, which yields Theorem 5.1'. This is similar to interpreting $x < y$ both as "x is smaller than y" and as "y is larger than x", two quite different statements, but obviously equivalent. Nonetheless, there is a different nuance: reading left to right gives information about x, namely that it is smaller than y, where y is assumed to be known in this context; reading from right to left assumes that x is known and that the statement adds information about y.

Theorem 5.1' is easier to handle, because it calls for induction on the parameter k and all the values involved are integers. Note also that restricting the attention to minimal AVL trees did not do any harm, since if the theorem is true for minimal trees, it is *a fortiori* true for the nonminimal ones.

Proof by induction on the depth k. Define $N(k)$ as the number of nodes in a minimal AVL tree of depth k and let us try to evaluate it. For $k = 0$, there is only one tree with depth 0 (Figure 5.2(a)) and it contains a single node, thus $N(0) = 1$. To get a tree of depth 1, one needs at least one node in level 0 and in level 1, as in Figure 5.2(b). The tree in Figure 5.1(a) is also of depth 1, but it is not minimal. We conclude $N(1) = 2$. For $k = 2$, one could consider a tree as in Figure 5.1(b), but it is not AVL, because its root is unbalanced. Adding one more node yields a tree as in Figure 5.2(c), and we get $N(2) = 4$.

So far, the sequence is 1, 2, 4, which might suggest that the general term is of the form $N(k) = 2^k$, but this guess fails already at the next step. Indeed, Figure 5.2(d) shows that $N(3) = 7$, and not 8 as we could have expected.

For the general step, consider a minimal AVL tree T of depth $k > 2$. At least one of its subtrees has to be of depth $k - 1$, but must itself be an AVL tree, and minimal, thus with $N(k - 1)$ nodes. The depth of the other subtree cannot be larger than $k - 1$ (otherwise, T is of depth larger than k), nor smaller than $k - 2$ (otherwise the root wouldn't be balanced). It could also be of depth $k - 1$ from the AVL point of view, but then it would not be minimal. Therefore, it must have depth $k - 2$. Adding the root, we can conclude that

$$N(k) = N(k - 1) + N(k - 2) + 1. \tag{5.6}$$

As example, consider the tree in Figure 5.2(d); its subtrees appear in Figure 5.2(b) and (c).

The recurrence relation of eq. (5.6) should remind us the definition of the famous *Fibonacci* sequence.

Background Concept: Fibonacci Sequence

The Fibonacci sequence 0, 1, 1, 2, 3, 5, 8, 13, 21, ... is defined by

$$F(0) = 0, F(1) = 1 \quad F(i) = F(i-1) + F(i-2) \text{ for } i \geq 2, \quad (5.7)$$

and its properties have been investigated for centuries. The elements of the sequence can be represented as linear combinations with fixed coefficients of the powers of the roots of the polynomial $x^2 - x - 1$. These roots are

$$\phi = \frac{1 + \sqrt{5}}{2} = 1.618 \quad \text{and} \quad \hat{\phi} = \frac{1 - \sqrt{5}}{2} = -0.618, \quad (5.8)$$

the first of which is known as the *golden ratio*. The Fibonacci sequence is given by

$$F(i) = \frac{1}{\sqrt{5}} \left(\phi^i - \hat{\phi}^i \right) \qquad \text{for} \quad i \geq 0. \quad (5.9)$$

Note that the absolute value of $\hat{\phi}$ is smaller than 1, so $\hat{\phi}^i$ quickly becomes negligible with increasing i, and one gets a good approximation for $F(i)$ by taking just the first term of the right-hand side of eq. (5.9): $F(i) \simeq \frac{1}{\sqrt{5}} \phi^i$. Actually, $F(i)$ is $\frac{1}{\sqrt{5}} \phi^i$, rounded to the nearest integer, for all elements of the sequence.

Comparing the sequences $N(k)$ and $F(k)$, one gets

k	0	1	2	3	4	5	6	7	8	9	10
$N(k)$	1	2	4	7	12	20	33	54	88	143	232
$F(k)$	0	1	1	2	3	5	8	13	21	34	55

suggesting that $N(k) = F(k+3) - 1$. Indeed, this is true for $k \in \{0, 1\}$, and for larger k, by induction,

$$N(k) = N(k-1) + N(k-2) + 1$$
$$= (F(k+2) - 1) + (F(k+1) - 1) + 1 = F(k+3) - 1.$$

Putting it all together, it follows that n, the number of nodes in an AVL tree of depth k satisfies

$$n \geq N(k) = F(k+3) - 1 \simeq \frac{1}{\sqrt{5}} \phi^{k+3} - 1,$$

giving the required exponential bound for Theorem 5.1′, from which the bound on the depth k for Theorem 5.1 can be derived:

$$\log_\phi \left(\sqrt{5}(n+1) \right) \geq k + 3,$$

which is equivalent to eq. (5.2). ∎

We conclude that even in the worst possible case, the depth of an AVL tree is at most 44% larger than in the best possible scenario. The average depth can be shown to be only about $1.04 \log_2 n$, implying that accessing and searching AVL trees is very efficient.

5.3 Insertions into AVL Trees

Once it is known that the AVL constraints indeed imply logarithmic depth for the trees, we have to take care of how to maintain the validity of the constraints during possible tree updates. Recall that an AVL tree T is a search tree, so if we want to insert a new node with value x, the exact location of this new node is determined by T, and there is no freedom of choice. A new insert might thus well cause the tree to become unbalanced.

To avoid constantly recalculating the depths of subtrees, we add a new field to each node v, called its *Balance Factor*, defined by

$$BF(v) = d(T_{R(v)}) - d(T_{L(v)}). \tag{5.10}$$

By definition, each node v of an AVL tree satisfies $BF(v) \in \{-1, 0, 1\}$, which we shall indicate as $-$, 0, $+$ in the diagrams. Figure 5.4 depicts an example AVL

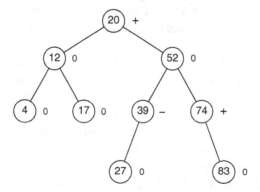

Figure 5.4. Example of AVL tree.

tree, with the *BF* fields appearing next to each node. *BF* can also be defined for non-AVL trees, as the one in Figure 5.2(e), where the nodes display their *BF*, except for the black node, which is unbalanced (its *BF* would be -2). A node with $BF = 0$ will be called *balanced*, otherwise unbalanced.

We shall assume that AVL trees are built incrementally from scratch, so there is no need to deal with how to turn an arbitrary tree into an AVL tree, and we may restrict our attention on how the balancing condition can be maintained during insertions and deletions.

To avoid a confusion between a node and the value it contains, we shall continue with the convention introduced earlier of denoting by v_x a node containing a value x.

To insert an element with value x into an existing AVL tree T, we proceed, in a first stage, according to the rules of binary search trees, ignoring for the moment the additional balancing constraints, and leaving the balance factors unchanged. After having inserted the new node (it forms a new leaf v_x), we check whether all the nodes of T still meet the conditions, take appropriate action if not, and finally update the *BF* fields.

Define the *insertion path* of x as the sequence of nodes, starting with the root of T, whose values are compared with x during the insertion. For example, if we were to insert the value 31 into the tree of Figure 5.4, the insertion path would consist of the elements with values 20, 52, 39, and 27. Consider a node w not belonging to the insertion path. The subtrees of w are not affected by the insertion of v_x, so their depths, and consequently also $BF(w)$, do not change. In other words, the only elements that have to be checked are those on the insertion path. Since these elements have to be processed bottom up, and there is usually no pointer from a node to its parent in a tree, it is convenient to store the elements of the insertion path in a stack S. In addition, we also store with each element a flag indicating whether the next element on the path is a left or right child of the current one. For our example of inserting the value 31, the stack would consist of: $S = [(v_{20}, R), (v_{52}, L), (v_{39}, L), (v_{27}, R)]$.

The inserted node v_x is always a leaf. If its parent node z has $BF(z) = 0$, it must have been a leaf prior to the insertion, but now $BF(z)$ has to be changed to $+$ if v_x is a right child of z, and to $-$ if it is a left child. This, however, changes the depth of T_z, the subtree rooted at z, one therefore has to continue to the next higher level. For example, when inserting the value 15 into the tree of Figure 5.4, $BF(v_{17})$ is changed to $-$, and $BF(v_{12})$ is changed to $+$. The update procedure thus climbs up the tree along the insertion path, by means of the elements stored in the stack S, as long as the *BF* of the current node is 0, and changes this value to $+$ or $-$.

This loop is terminated in one of the following three cases:

(i) When the root is reached. In this case, the depth of the entire tree T increases by 1, but the tree itself still complies with the AVL definition.

(ii) When an unbalanced node is reached from the side which corrects the imbalance. That is, the update algorithm reaches a node w with $BF(w) = -$ and we come from a right child (in other words, the element in the stack is (w, R)), or $BF(w) = +$ and we come from a left child (in other words, the element in the stack is (w, L)). In both cases, $BF(w)$ is changed to 0, and the iteration can stop, since the tree rooted at w did not change its depth, hence the BF fields of the ancestors of w are not affected. To continue the example of inserting the value 15, after changing $BF(v_{12})$ to $+$, one reaches the root, v_{20}. Its BF is $+$ and we come from the left, so we set $BF(v_{20}) = 0$.

(iii) When an unbalanced node is reached, but from the side which aggravates the imbalance. That is, the update algorithm reaches a node w with $BF(w) = -$ and we come from a left child, or $BF(w) = +$ and we come from a right child. The BF of w is thus temporarily ± 2, which violates the AVL rules. Returning to the example of inserting 31, $BF(v_{27}) = 0$ and is changed to $+$, but the next node is v_{39}, its BF is $-$ and we come from the left: there is thus a violation at v_{39}.

Figure 5.5(a) displays a generic view of this last case schematically. The node v_a is the first node with $BF \neq 0$ on the path from the newly inserted node v_x to the root of the tree. In this figure, $BF(v_a) = +$, and the case for $BF(v_a) = -$ is symmetrical. The left subtree of v_a is α, of depth h, and the right subtree of v_a is δ, of depth $h + 1$, with $h \geq -1$. The new element v_x is inserted as a leaf in δ, increasing its depth to $h + 2$. The challenge is now to rebalance the tree rooted at v_a.

It turns out that the actions to be taken for the rebalancing are different according to which of the subtrees of δ contains the new node v_x. We therefore have to take a closer look, given in Figure 5.5(b), which zooms in on δ: the root of δ is v_b and its subtrees are denoted β and γ. Note that both are of depth h, as we know that $BF(v_b) = 0$, because v_a is the *first* node we extract from the stack S for which $BF \neq 0$. The tree in Figure 5.5(b) gives enough information for the case that v_x is inserted into γ, the right subtree of v_b.

In the other case, when v_x is inserted into β, the left subtree of v_b, one needs to zoom in even further. Different actions are then required, and the update procedure separates the subtrees of β. This leads to the tree in Figure 5.5(c), where the tree β is given in more detail: if β is not empty, i.e., $h \geq 0$, then its root is v_c, and the subtrees are β_1 and β_2, both of the same depth $h - 1$, as

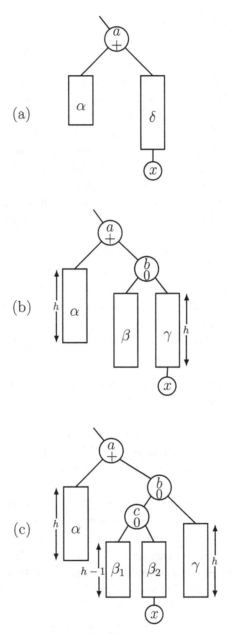

Figure 5.5. AVL insertion: the need for rebalancing.

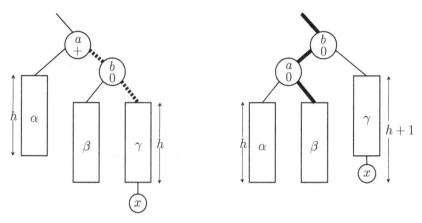

Figure 5.6. AVL insertion: single rotation.

explained earlier for β and γ. The inserted node v_x can now be either in β_2, as in the figure, or in β_1. This will not change the update commands, only the balance factors. If β is empty, the inserted node v_x is identified with the node v_c in Figure 5.5(c). The good news is that no further zooming in is required, and these are all the cases to be dealt with.

The rebalancing is achieved by performing what has become known as *rotations*. The subtree rooted at the node v_a, where the imbalance has occurred, is rearranged by changing some of the connections between its components. Figure 5.6(a) redraws the first case presented in Figure 5.5(b) (v_x inserted in γ), showing the structure before the rotation, whereas Figure 5.6(b) is the resulting subtree consisting of the same nodes, but after the rotation. The root of the subtree is now v_b, and v_a is its new left child. This does not violate the rules of search trees, since v_b was previously the right child of v_a, implying that $b > a$; the new connection means that $a < b$, and we mentioned already earlier that these are of course equivalent. The left subtree of v_a remained α and the right subtree of v_b remained γ, and only β changed its position from being previously the left subtree of v_b to become now the right subtree of v_a. Again, both layouts define the range of all the values y stored in β to be $a < y < b$. We conclude that also after the rotation, the tree remains a search tree.

The depth of the entire subtree after the rotation is $h + 2$, just as was the subtree prior to the insertion of v_x, and the *BF* fields are indicated in the figure. We have thus succeeded in adding a new node without changing the depth of this subtree, meaning that the insertion process can stop after the rotation.

Note that though the extent of the necessary update steps seems frightening at first sight, possibly encompassing a substantial part or even the entire tree, the actually needed programming commands are very simple: only the three pointers indicated as boldfaced edges in Figure 5.6(b) have to be changed. It

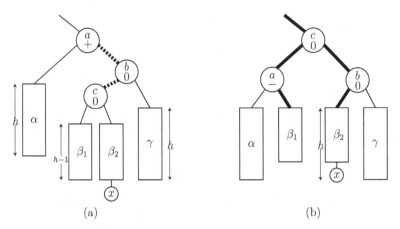

Figure 5.7. AVL insertion: double rotation.

is particularly noticeable that this small number of steps is independent of h, and might be performed quite far from the node v_x which triggered the whole update process. Nevertheless, after having located the exact position to perform the correcting steps, this can be done in $O(1)$.

A closer look also reveals why this is not a solution in the case v_x is inserted in β. In that case, the tree in Figure 5.6(b) would not be AVL, because the right and left subtrees of v_b would be of depths h and $h + 2$, respectively. This explains the need for a different rebalancing procedure.

If v_x is inserted in β, the corresponding rotations are shown in the two parts of Figure 5.7. The new root of the subtree is v_c and the three nodes v_a, v_b, and v_c are rearranged; they satisfy before and after the rotation $a < c < b$. The subtrees α and γ remain in place, but the subtrees β_1 and β_2 of v_c are separated and moved to become the left subtree of v_a and the right subtree of v_b, respectively. The defining conditions for the values y of the elements of β_1 are, before and after the update: $a < y < c$ and for β_2: $c < y < b$. If v_x would have been inserted into β_1, the rotation would be the same, but we would have $BF(v_a) = 0$ and $BF(v_b) = +$.

In both cases, the depth of the entire subtree after the rotation is $h + 2$, just as was the subtree prior to the insertion of v_x. The number of necessary pointer updates is now five, and they are indicated, as earlier, by boldfaced edges. Referring to the nodes v_a and v_b in Figure 5.6 and to the nodes v_a, v_b, and v_c in Figure 5.7, the first update is called a *single* and the second a *double* rotation.

One question still remains: how do we know which of the rotations to apply? The answer is to refer to the last two steps of the iteration using the stack to process the elements of the insertion path bottom up. Each node on this path has been stored together with a direction indicator, so the four possibilities for the directions of the last two steps are *LL*, *LR*, *RL*, and *RR*. If these steps are in the same direction, *LL* or *RR*, a single rotation is needed; if they are of opposite directions, *LR* or *RL*, we perform a double rotation. The edges corresponding to these last two steps appear in dashed boldface in Figures 5.6(a) and 5.7(a).

Summarizing the insertion, we ascend the tree, starting at the newly inserted leaf and passing from one node to its parent node, as long as we see $BF = 0$, changing it to + or − as appropriate. If a node w is reached with $BF(w) \neq 0$, then if we come from the "good" side, $BF(w)$ is set to 0 and the process stops; if we come from the "bad" side, the subtree rooted at w is rebalanced by means of a single or double rotation, and the process stops. In any case, there is only $O(1)$ of work per treated node, thus the entire insertion does not require more than $O(\log n)$.

5.4 Deletions from AVL Trees

As already mentioned in the previous chapter dealing with trees in general, insertions and deletions in search trees are not always symmetrical tasks. An insertion always adds the new element as a leaf, but we might want to delete any element, not necessarily a leaf.

When dealing with the deletion of a node v_x from an AVL tree, we may nevertheless restrict the attention to deleting a leaf. Indeed, if v_x has one child, this child must be a leaf, otherwise v_x would be unbalanced; and deleting a parent of a leaf can be considered as replacing its value with that of its child and then deleting the leaf. For example, in Figure 5.4, from the point of view of the layout of the nodes in the tree, deleting the node with value 74 results in exactly the same operations as if we were deleting the leaf with value 83. And if v_x has two children, we actually delete the successor of v_x, which is either a leaf or has only one child.

Assume then that we wish to delete a leaf v_x. Just as for the insertion, we start by storing in a stack the elements compared with x in its insertion path (which, formally, should rather be called now deletion path). Proceed then along this path from v_x toward the root, as long as the encountered nodes have $BF \neq 0$, and coming from the good side. More precisely, if the current node w has $BF(w) = +$ and we come from the right subtree, or if $BF(w) = -$ and we come from the left subtree, we set $BF(w) = 0$ and continue: the subtree rooted at w, T_w, was not balanced and now it is, but its depth is reduced by 1, hence one has to check also above w.

If a node w with $BF(w) = 0$ is encountered, this is changed to + (resp., −) if we come from the left (resp., right). This is the case in which T_w was balanced, and the deletion of v_x made it unbalanced, but without violating the AVL constraint. The depth of T_w, though, did not change, thus the update process stops.

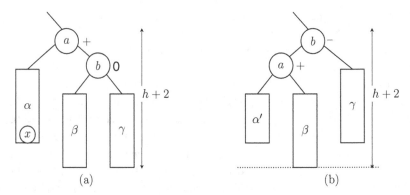

Figure 5.8. AVL deletion: $BF(b) = 0$.

If we get to an unbalanced node w, but from the bad side, that is, $BF(w) = +$ and we come from the left, or $BF(w) = -$ and we come from the right, the subtree T_w has to be rebalanced. Fortunately, the single and double rotations we saw earlier are all that is needed also in this case, just the conditions when to apply which kind of rotation differ. We shall treat, as before, only the case in which v_x is deleted from a left subtree α of a node v_a with $BF(v_a) = +$, see Figure 5.8(a), as the complementing case, with $BF(v_a) = -$, is symmetric.

The depth of the subtrees α, β, and γ is h, and the constraint on h is now $h \geq 0$, because α contains at least the node v_x and thus cannot be empty. Let v_b be the root of the right subtree of v_a. We need to know the balance factor of v_b to correctly draw its subtrees, but how can we know it? In the case of insertion, the node v_b was a part of the insertion path of x, so we knew from the algorithm that $BF(v_b)$ had to be 0. But for deletion, we assume that v_x is deleted from α, whereas v_b belongs to the *other* subtree of v_a. We thus have no information about $BF(v_b)$ and indeed, all three possibilities, +, – or 0, are plausible. These three possibilities give rise to the three cases to be treated for the deletion of an element from an AVL tree; the balance factor $BF(v_b)$ appears in boldface in the corresponding diagrams in Figures 5.8(a), 5.9(a), and 5.10(a).

Figure 5.8 assumes $BF(v_b) = 0$. The subtrees β and γ are then both of the same depth h as α, and when v_x is removed, the node v_a violates the AVL constraint. The solution, given in part (b) of the figure, is a single rotation. We denote by α', of depth $h - 1$, the tree obtained by deleting v_x from α. After the rotation, the new subtree T_{v_b} is of the same depth $h + 2$ as was T_{v_a} prior to the rotation; the update process may thus stop.

For the second case, given in Figure 5.9, assume $BF(v_b) = +$. The only difference with the previous case is that β is now shorter, but the solution seems at first sight to be the same: a single rotation. However, the tree in part (b) of

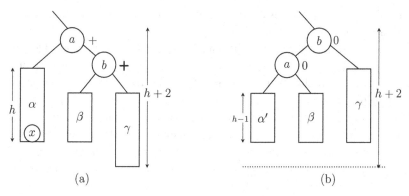

Figure 5.9. AVL deletion: $BF(b) = +$.

the figure has now depth only $h + 1$, which means that there might be more updates needed. This is the first example we see, in which the depth of the tree is changed during a rotation. It may thus happen that during our continuing ascent in the tree, more nodes are encountered that violate the AVL rules, triggering more rotations. Still, since only $O(1)$ operations are needed for rotating, the overall update time stays bounded by $O(\log n)$.

The third case is depicted in Figure 5.10, with $BF(v_b) = -$, implying that the left subtree of v_b is now deeper. The solution here is a double rotation, but as before, we ignore the balance factor of v_c. The figure assumes $BF(v_c) = 0$, with the subtrees β_1 and β_2 both of depth $h - 1$, but the same solution is also valid if $BF(v_c) = +$ and the depth of β_1 is only $h - 2$ (as indicated by the dotted line in β_1), or if $BF(v_c) = -$ and it is β_2 that has depth $h - 2$. As in the second

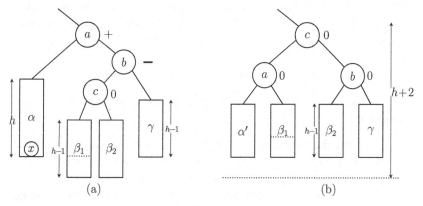

Figure 5.10. AVL deletion: $BF(b) = -$.

case, the double rotation results in a tree of depth $h + 1$, and one has to continue upward with the update process.

Summarizing the deletion, we ascend the tree, starting at the deleted leaf v_x and passing from one node to its parent node, as long as we see $BF = +$ or $-$ and we come from the good side, changing the BF to 0. If a node w is reached with $BF(w) = 0$, it is changed to $+$ or $-$ as appropriate and the process stops. If $BF(w) = +$ or $-$ and we come from the bad side, the subtree rooted at w is rebalanced by means of a single or double rotation, depending on the BF of the child u of w belonging to the *other* side, not that of v_x. Only in case $BF(u) = 0$ does the process stop, otherwise it continues to the next higher level. The entire deletion thus requires at most $O(\log n)$.

5.5 Alternatives

AVL trees are not the only possibility to enforce logarithmic update times. Many other balanced structures have been suggested, and we mention only trees that have become known as *red-black* trees, and *B-trees* that are treated in the next chapter, though the latter have different application areas.

The general mechanism, however, remains the same. One first defines a set of rules defining the trees. Then one has to show that these rules imply a bound on the depth. Finally, algorithms have to be devised that enable the constraints to be maintained, even when elements are adjoined or removed.

Exercises

5.1 Insert the elements of the following sequence, in order, into an initially empty AVL tree, taking care of rebalancing the tree after every insertion, if needed:

$$3, 14, 15, 9, 2, 6, 5, 35.$$

Now delete these elements, one by one, in the same order as they have been inserted.

5.2 We saw that the number of nodes $N(k)$ in an AVL tree of depth k is at least $N(k - 1) + N(k - 2) + 1$, which lead to a tight bound connected to the Fibonacci sequence. One can get a logarithmic bound for the depth more easily, by using the fact that $N(k - 1) > N(k - 2)$. What is the resulting bound on $N(k)$?

5.3 Define AVL2 trees as binary search trees, in which for each node v,

$$|d(T_{L(v)}) - d(T_{R(v)})| \leq 2.$$

(a) Derive a bound on the depth on AVL2 trees.
(b) What are the advantages and disadvantages of AVL2 trees relative to AVL trees?

5.4 We defined four kinds of *rotations* in the rebalancing of AVL trees: simple and double, to the left or right.

(a) Show that when given two binary search trees T_1 and T_2, not necessarily AVL, with the same set of values, one can transform the one into the other by a sequence of simple rotations. **Hint:** Show first how to deal with the root, then with the subtrees.
(b) Show that the number of rotations is $O(n^2)$.

5.5 Given is a connected, undirected, unweighed graph $G = (V, E)$ and a pair of vertices $u, v \in V$. Let $d(u, v)$ denote the length of a shortest path from u to v (in terms of number of edges). The *diameter* of the graph is defined as

$$D(G) = \max_{u,v \in V} d(u, v).$$

We wish to study the diameter of a binary tree, considering it as a special case of a graph rather than as a data structure.

(a) Show why the following claim is wrong for a binary tree T. **Claim:** *If the diameter of the tree is D, then there must be a path of length D passing through its root; therefore the diameter of a tree is simply the sum of the depths of its left and right subtrees, + 2.*
(b) Is the claim true for AVL trees?
(c) Write an algorithm getting an AVL tree as input and returning its diameter.

5.6 Denote the Fibonacci numbers by F_i for $i \geq 0$. Beside the direct way to compute F_i by eq. (5.9), one can obviously do it in time $O(n)$ using eq. (5.7). Let us show that one can do better. We assume that any multiplication, also of matrices 2×2, requires time $O(1)$.

(a) Define the matrix $A = \begin{pmatrix} 1 & 1 \\ 1 & 0 \end{pmatrix}$. We then have $\begin{pmatrix} F_i \\ F_{i-1} \end{pmatrix} = A \begin{pmatrix} F_{i-1} \\ F_{i-2} \end{pmatrix}$.
Derive from it a formula for $\begin{pmatrix} F_n \\ F_{n-1} \end{pmatrix}$, as a function of A and $\begin{pmatrix} F_1 \\ F_0 \end{pmatrix} = \begin{pmatrix} 1 \\ 0 \end{pmatrix}$.

(b) We thus would like to calculate A^k in time less than $O(k)$. Suppose A^8 is already known. Do we really need 8 more multiplications to calculate A^{16}? Show how to do it in a single operation.

(c) Using the same principle, how many operations are needed for the evaluation of A^8? Generalize to A^k when k is a power of 2.

(d) How do we calculate A^5 (note that 5 is not a power of 2)? And A^{12}? Generalize to any power A^k, where k is any integer.

(e) Summarizing: given any k, how many matrix multiplications are needed to calculate A^k? Deduce from it a bound for the evaluation of the nth Fibonacci number.

5.7 Build an example of an AVL tree with a minimal number of nodes, such that the deletion of one of the nodes requires two rotations. **Hint:** The number of nodes in such a tree is 12.

Generalize to find an AVL tree with a minimal number of nodes, for which the deletion of one of the nodes requires k rotations, for $k \geq 1$.

6

B-Trees

6.1 Higher-Order Search Trees

A simple way to generalize the binary search trees seen in previous chapters is to define m-ary search trees, for $m \geq 2$, in which any node may have up to m children and store up to $m - 1$ numbers. Binary search trees are the special case $m = 2$. Just as the only element x in a node v_x of a binary search tree partitions the elements stored in the subtrees of v_x into those that are smaller than x and stored in the left subtree, and those that are larger than x and stored in the right subtree, there are $k - 1$ elements $x_1, x_2, \ldots, x_{k-1}$ stored in a node $v_{x_1, x_2, \ldots, x_{k-1}}$ of an m-ary search tree, with $k \leq m$, and they partition the elements in the subtrees of this node into k disjoint sets of numbers, each corresponding to one of the subtrees.

The partition is done generalizing the ordering induced by binary search trees:

- The first (leftmost) subtree contains elements that are smaller than x_1.
- The ith subtree, for $2 \leq i < k$ contains elements that are larger than x_{i-1} but smaller than x_i.
- The kth (rightmost) subtree contains elements that are larger than x_{k-1}.

Figure 6.1 displays an example search tree for $m = 4$. The number of elements stored in each node is thus between 1 and 3. For instance, the root stores two elements, and partitions the rest of the elements into three subtrees, one for elements smaller than 23, one for elements between 23 and 56, and one for elements larger than 56. Arrows not leading to other nodes represent NIL-pointers.

One of the applications of these higher-order search trees is to files so large that they do not fit any more into the available memory. They have therefore to be split into *pages*, most of which are stored on some secondary storage device. The assumption is then that an access to such a page has to be done by a read

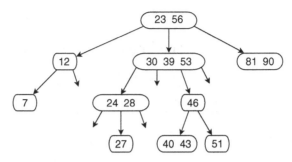

Figure 6.1. Example of a 4-ary search tree.

operation, which is much more time consuming than any processing within a given page, once it is loaded into the main memory. The idea is to choose the order m of the search tree so that a node, whose size depends on the given data, will roughly correspond to a page, whose size depends on the hardware used. Typical page sizes may be 4–8 KB, and typical values of m may be 200–400. To explain the algorithms and give manageable examples, we shall use small values of m, like $m = 4$, but one shall bear in mind that these structures are especially efficient for much larger values, like $m = 300$.

When coming to evaluate the processing time, one can thus restrict the attention to the number of nodes that have to be accessed; the work done within a node, be it by binary or by sequential search, will be deemed as negligible relative to the expensive read operations.

6.1.1 Searching in m-ary Search Trees

As in the binary case, the search for a number y always starts at the root $v_{x_1,x_2,\ldots,x_{k-1}}$ of the tree, only that several comparisons are needed to check whether y is stored there. If not, one continues recursively with the first pointer if $y < x_1$, with the ith pointer if $x_{i-1} < y < x_i$, for $2 \le i < k$, or with the last pointer if $y > x_{k-1}$. Reaching a NIL-pointer means that an element with value y is not in the tree. As for $m = 2$, the number of required steps is at most the depth of the tree.

Referring to Figure 6.1 and searching for $y = 29$, we see that y is not in the root, but that $23 < y < 56$, so we follow the second pointer; y is not in $v_{30,39,53}$ and $y < 30$, so the first pointer is chosen, leading to $v_{24,28}$; y is larger than 28, but the last pointer is NIL – we conclude that 29 is not in the tree.

To continue the similar treatment given here to higher-order search trees, we should now turn to how to insert or delete elements. We shall, however, skip over these details, because m-ary search trees without further constraints

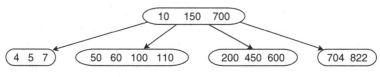

Figure 6.2. Example of a B-tree of order $m = 5$.

suffer from the same deficiencies as did their binary counterparts: in the worst case, the depth of the tree, on which the complexities of all required operations depend, may be $\Omega(n)$. We saw AVL trees in the previous chapter as a possible solution to this problem in the binary case. The alternative suggested in the next section presents a completely different approach.

6.2 Definition of B-Trees

As earlier, the solution will be some additional constraints, strong enough to imply a logarithmic depth of the tree, yet weak enough to be maintained efficiently when the tree is updated by insertions and deletions.

Definition 6.1. A *B-tree* of order m, with $m > 2$, is an m-ary search tree with the following additional constraints:

(i) Every node, except the root, stores at least $\lceil \frac{m}{2} \rceil - 1$ elements, and the root stores at least one element.

(ii) NIL-pointers emanate only from nodes on the lowest level.

The second condition implies that all the leaves of a B-tree are on the same level; this shows that the search tree in Figure 6.1 is not a B-tree. The first condition, together with the definition of m-ary search trees, bounds the number of children of an internal node, which is not the root, in a B-tree to be between $\lceil \frac{m}{2} \rceil$ and m, and accordingly, the number of stored elements to be between $\lceil \frac{m}{2} \rceil - 1$ and $m - 1$.

Because any newly allocated node would anyway reserve space for at least $m - 1$ elements and m pointers, imposing the lower bound of the first condition helps to avoid a waste of space. Requiring that any node should at least be about half full implies that the space utilized by the data structure is exploited at least to 50%.

Figure 6.2 shows a B-tree of order $m = 5$, so that any node may have between 3 and 5 children and contain between 2 and 4 elements. In this example, all the leaves are on level 1.

To evaluate the depth of a B-tree or order m, consider the lower bound on the number of elements stored at each level. At level 0, the root may contain a single element. At level 1, there are at least two nodes, each with roughly $\frac{m}{2}$ elements. At level 2, there are at least $2\frac{m}{2}$ nodes, with about $2\left(\frac{m}{2}\right)^2$ elements. For the general case, at level t, there are at least $2\left(\frac{m}{2}\right)^{t-1}$ nodes, with about $2\left(\frac{m}{2}\right)^t$ elements. If one considers a B-tree of order m storing N elements, N must be larger than the number of elements stored in the leaves, thus

$$N > 2\left(\frac{m}{2}\right)^t,$$

from which one can derive that

$$t < \log_{m/2}\frac{N}{2} = \frac{\log_2 N - 1}{\log_2 m - 1}.$$

To give a numerical example, suppose a huge file of half a billion items is to be handled. The depth of a completely balanced (full) binary tree would be 29 and that of an AVL tree at most 42, while a B-tree of order $m = 256$ would reach at most level $t = 4$. We conclude that typical B-trees are extremely flat structures with very little depth, even for very large files.

What has to be discussed next is how to perform the basic operations on B-trees. Search has already been discussed for general m-ary search trees, which leaves insertions and deletions. They are dealt with in the following sections.

6.3 Insertion into B-Trees

To insert a new value y into a B-tree, one first has to verify that y is not yet in the tree, which can be done by searching for y. An unsuccessful search is detected when a NIL-pointer is encountered, which in our case means that a leaf $v_{x_1,x_2,\dots,x_{k-1}}$ on the lowest level has been reached. If $k < m$, that is, the node has not yet reached its full capacity, the number y is just inserted at the proper place in the sequence $x_1, x_2, \dots, x_{k-1}$.

For example, to insert the value 9 into the tree of Figure 6.2, one reaches the leaf $v_{4,5,7}$; it contains only three values but could accommodate four, so the value 9 is added to form the sequence $4, 5, 7, 9$, and no further action needs to be taken.

Suppose we want now to insert the value 55. The corresponding leaf is $v_{50,60,100,110}$, but it is already filled to capacity. This is the case $k = m$, for which the content of the node cannot be further extended. The solution in this case is applied in several steps. In a first step, the new element is inserted into its proper

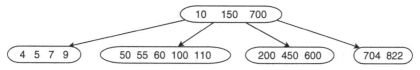

Figure 6.3. After inserting 9 and 55.

position in the node, disregarding the overflow it causes. Figure 6.3 shows the tree at this stage.

To rectify the situation, the violating node with m elements will be split into two nodes, each containing about half of the elements, that is, the list $S = r_1, \ldots, r_m$ of elements stored in this node is split into

$$\mathsf{SL} = r_1, \ldots, r_{\lceil m/2 \rceil -1} \qquad \text{and} \qquad \mathsf{SR} = r_{\lceil m/2 \rceil +1}, \ldots, r_m,$$

the node v_S is split into v_SL and v_SR, and the middle element $r_{\lceil m/2 \rceil}$, which has not been included in either SL or SR, will be inserted, recursively, into their parent node. To understand this operation, notice that when a node v is split into two, this is equivalent to inserting a new node w as an immediate brother of v, that is, as an additional child of $p(v)$, the parent node of v. But if $p(v)$ has an additional child, it needs an additional pointer to it, and thus, by the rules of search trees, an additional value to separate the corresponding subtrees. The most convenient choice for this value is one of the middle of the list of values originally stored in v.

To continue our running example, $\lceil \frac{m}{2} \rceil = 3$, the node $v_{50,55,60,100,110}$ is split into $v_{50,55}$ and $v_{100,110}$, and the middle element, 60, is inserted into the parent node, which is the root. There is enough space in the root for an additional element, so the insertion of 55 is thereby completed. The resulting tree is given in Figure 6.4.

The following is an example in which the insertion of a new element triggers a chain reaction. Let us insert the value 3, so the first step is to store it in $v_{4,5,7,9}$, and this leads to an overflow, as shown in Figure 6.5.

The second step of the insertion of 3 is therefore splitting the node $v_{3,4,5,7,9}$ into $v_{3,4}$ and $v_{7,9}$, and inserting the middle element 5 into the parent node, which is the root. This is shown in Figure 6.6.

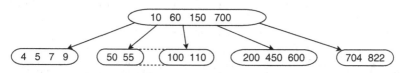

Figure 6.4. Example of splitting a node.

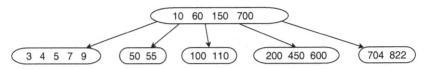

Figure 6.5. After inserting 3.

The problem is that the insertion of 5 into the root causes again an overflow, and the node $v_{5,10,60,150,700}$ has also to be split. Since this is not a leaf, the splitting process has also to take the corresponding pointers into account. In the general case, a node containing the m values $r_1, \ldots, r_m$ and the corresponding $m + 1$ pointers $p_0, p_1, \ldots, p_m$, will be split into

$$r_{\lceil m/2 \rceil}$$

$$\begin{array}{cc} r_1, \ldots, r_{\lceil m/2 \rceil - 1} & r_{\lceil m/2 \rceil + 1}, \ldots, r_m \\ p_0, p_1, \ldots, p_{\lceil m/2 \rceil - 1} & p_{\lceil m/2 \rceil}, \ldots, p_{m-1}, p_m \end{array} \quad ,$$

where the top line shows the middle element inserted into the parent node, and the left and right parts show the contents of the new nodes, namely the values and the corresponding pointers. Note that while the set of m values has been distributed over three nodes, the whole set of $m + 1$ pointers is accounted for in the two new nodes.

The insertion of $r_{\lceil m/2 \rceil}$ may in turn cause an overflow, and this chain reaction may continue for several steps. It may terminate either by reaching a node that can still absorb the element to be inserted without exceeding its limits, or when getting to the root, as in our example.

When the root has to be split, there exists no parent node into which $r_{\lceil m/2 \rceil}$ could be inserted, so a new node is created for this purpose, and this will be the new root. The only element stored in it will be $r_{\lceil m/2 \rceil}$, and its two pointers will lead to the two halves created from the root that has been split, as shown in Figure 6.7. This special case was the reason for formulating a different condition for the root than for the other nodes in the definition of a B-tree.

As a result of splitting the root, the B-tree has thus increased its depth by 1, and this is the only possibility for a B-tree to grow in height. Contrary to binary search trees, for which each inserted element creates a new leaf, the growth process of B-trees proceeds "backwards," and therefore, no special care

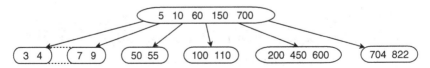

Figure 6.6. After splitting a node.

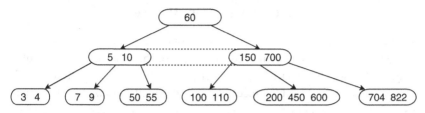

Figure 6.7. After a second split.

is needed during insertions to maintain the condition that all the leaves have to be on the same level.

Returning to our example, the new root contains only the value 60, and its two pointers are to the nodes $v_{5,10}$ and $v_{150,700}$. This ends the insertion process for 3, which involved two node splits and changed the shape and depth of the tree.

In the worst case, the number of node splits for a single insertion may thus be as the depth of the tree. Even though the depth is generally small, this might still seem a heavy price to pay. Fortunately, the picture is not as dark as it seems when considering the worst case. This is a good example for an application in which a more interesting evaluation can be given using *amortized analysis*: rather than concentrating on the pessimistically worst choice for an insertion operation, let us consider the total cost of inserting many elements into a B-tree.

Suppose N elements are inserted into an initially empty B-tree of order m. The total number of node splits caused by the N insertions is exactly equal to the number of nodes in the tree, since each split adds a single node. If we assume that roughly each node contains about $\frac{3}{4}m$ elements, then there are about $\frac{4N}{3m}$ nodes, and the amortized number of node splits per inserted element is $\frac{4}{3m}$. For example, if $m = 400$, the overwhelming majority of insertions will not result in any split at all; only about one of 300 insertions will cause a single split and a double split like in our second example will occur only for one of 90,000 insertions.

The readers might want to check their understanding by inserting, in order, the elements 25, 43, and 32 into the tree of the running example, given in Figure 6.7. This affects the left subtree, which should look like the one in Figure 6.8.

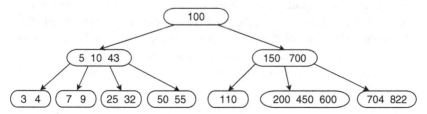

Figure 6.8. Replacing 60 by 100 and deleting 100 from its leaf.

6.4 Deletions from B-Trees

As in the previous chapters, we may restrict our discussion to the deletion of an element stored in one of the leaves. If one of the other elements should be deleted, it will be replaced by its *successor* so that the overall structure of the tree is maintained, and the successor will be erased. This has already been discussed for general binary trees and for AVL trees in particular. In the special case of a B-tree, the successor of an element x stored in an internal node is always in a leaf, and can be found as follows.

(i) Locate the node v that contains the value x, and follow the pointer immediately to its right.

(ii) While the current node is not a leaf, follow its leftmost pointer.

(iii) The successor of x is the leftmost element in the leaf that has been reached.

For example, in Figure 6.7, the successor of 700 is 704 and the successor of 60 is 100.

The simplest case of deleting an element x from a leaf is when it stores more than the minimum required $\lceil m/2 \rceil - 1$ numbers. In that case, x can simply be erased. This would be the case, for example, if we wanted to erase any of the elements of the leaf $v_{200,450,600}$ in the tree of Figure 6.7.

Suppose then that the element to be deleted is the one stored in the root, 60. It is replaced by its successor 100, which itself has now to be erased from its leaf $v_{100,110}$. This leads to an *underflow*, because the node now contains less than the minimum number of elements, which is 2. Figure 6.8 shows the tree of our running example at this stage.

If the remedy to an overflowing node was its splitting into two parts, one might have expected that the answer to an underflow is a merge. But it takes two to tango! While the possibility to split a node depends only on the node itself, a merge will only be possible if there is an appropriate partner node. The only possible candidates are therefore the immediate neighbors.

In our example, the underflowing leaf v_{110} has only one neighbor, $v_{200,450,600}$, but merging the two is not immediately possible. Recall that when a node was split for an insertion, a pointer, and therefore also a new value, had to be added to the parent node. Similarly, the fusion of two nodes reduces the number of children of their parent node, so the number of elements stored in it needs also to be decreased. We would thus like the merged node to contain the values 110, 150, 200, 450, and 600, but this is more than permitted.

The solution in this case is a step called *balancing*. In its general form, suppose a node gets below the limit, storing the elements $r_1, \ldots, r_{\lceil m/2 \rceil - 2}$, but its neighbor, say, the right one, stores the elements $s_1, \ldots, s_k$, with $k \geq \lceil m/2 \rceil$, that

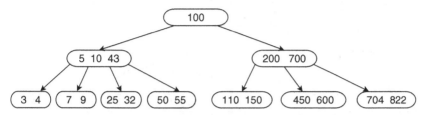

Figure 6.9. Example of a balancing step.

is, the neighbor has a surplus, above the minimum number of elements. Suppose that the separating value in their parent node is t, so that $r_{\lceil m/2 \rceil -2} < t < s_1$. All these elements will then be rearranged into two sequences of roughly equal length. Specifically, the total number of elements is $\ell = (\lceil m/2 \rceil - 2) + 1 + k$, and after renaming them $u_1, \ldots, u_\ell$, the left node will hold $u_1, \ldots, u_{\lceil \ell/2 \rceil -1}$, the right node will hold $u_{\lceil \ell/2 \rceil +1}, \ldots, u_\ell$, and the separating element in the parent node will be $u_{\lceil \ell/2 \rceil}$. Figure 6.9 shows how the nodes v_{110} and $v_{200,450,600}$, with separating element 150, have been rebalanced into $v_{110,150}$ and $v_{450,600}$, with separating element 200.

If we wish now to delete the element 600, then no balancing is possible, since both neighbors of $v_{450,600}$ are at their lowest permitted levels. In this case, when one of the nodes is at its lowest limit and the other is even one below it after the deletion of one of its elements, the two nodes may be merged, absorbing also the separating element.

Merging v_{450} with, say, its right neighbor gives $v_{450,700,704,822}$, as can be seen in Figure 6.10. The value 700 has to be erased, recursively, from the parent node, which again results in an underflow. Here again, balancing can be applied. Note that since this is not performed on the lowest level, one also has to take care of the pointers in a way that is symmetrical to the treatment for insertions.

As can be seen in Figure 6.11, the nodes $v_{5,10,43}$ and v_{200}, with separating element 100 are rebalanced into $v_{5,10}$ and $v_{100,200}$, with separating element 43; the leaf $v_{50,55}$ has not been touched, but it belongs now to another subtree.

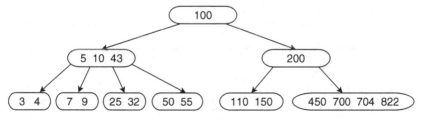

Figure 6.10. First step for the deletion of 600.

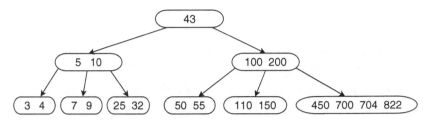

Figure 6.11. Balancing of internal nodes.

This concludes the deletion of 600, which involved a merging followed by a balancing step.

As a last example, let us delete the value 55. No balancing is possible, hence there will be a merging step at the leaf level, resulting in the tree of Figure 6.12.

As in Figure 6.10, the node v_{200} is below minimal capacity, but unlike the previous example, no balancing is possible. The two nodes $v_{5,10}$ and v_{200} should thus be fusioned, and the united node should also include the separating value 43, which has to be deleted, recursively, from the parent node. We are, however, in the special case for which 43 is the only element in its node, which is only possible if this node is the root. The old root will thus be erased and the newly merged node will be the new root, as shown in Figure 6.13.

This example shows the only possibility for a B-tree to shrink in height: when a chain of node mergers, triggered by the deletion of a single value, extends all the way up to the root, and the only value stored in the root has to be erased.

6.5 Variants

The basic definitions of B-trees have meanwhile been extended in many ways and we shall mention only a few of these variants. A first improvement may be obtained at almost no price, as in the following example.

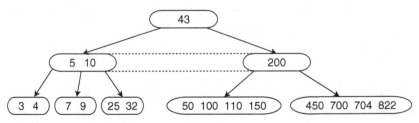

Figure 6.12. First step of the deletion of 55.

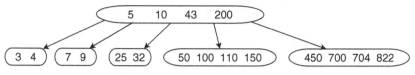

Figure 6.13. Erasing the root.

Suppose we wish to reinsert the element 55 into the tree of Figure 6.13. This would cause an overflow in the leaf $v_{50,55,100,110,150}$, which would be split into $v_{50,55}$ and $v_{110,150}$, with the middle element 100 being inserted into the parent node; this provokes a second split, this time of the root, and we get in fact back to the tree of Figure 6.11. The increase in height could however be avoided, by applying a *balancing* step with $v_{25,32}$, the left neighbor of the overflowing leaf $v_{50,55,100,110,150}$. The resulting tree is in Figure 6.14.

There is an essential difference for the use of balancing between insertions and deletions. For deletions, the balancing step prior to a merge is *mandatory*: if the neighboring node, with which the underflowing node should be merged, is not at its lowest permitted capacity, no merging is possible, so there is no other choice than balancing. On the other hand, for insertions, an overflowing node can be split without taking the status of its neighbors into consideration. A balancing step is therefore only *optional*. Since the balancing procedure needs to be written for deletion, and the same procedure can be used for insertion as well, it might be advantageous to try balancing also for insertion, as it might help reducing the height of the tree.

6.5.1 B⁺-Trees

A useful feature for some applications is the ability to scan the entire file sequentially in order in an efficient way. For larger values of m, like those used in practice, almost the whole file resides in the leaf nodes, and less than, say, 1%, in the other levels. Yet the values stored in these internal nodes disrupt the scanning order, so it could be preferable to have *all* the values in the leaves.

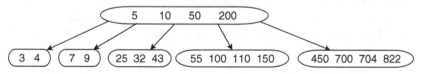

Figure 6.14. Using balancing for insertion.

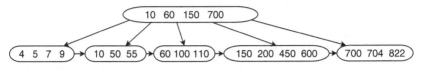

Figure 6.15. A B$^+$-tree.

This can be achieved with some small adaptations to the original B-trees. The resulting structure is known as a B$^+$-tree. The difference is that in a B$^+$-tree, all the data is stored in the leaves, hence they can be connected by means of pointers to form a linked list; the values in the internal nodes of the tree serve only as a guide to enable a faster access to the actual data.

Insertion

First, the leaf v into which the new element should be inserted is located. If it can accommodate another element, we are done. If the leaf overflows, it has to be split (unless balancing is applied, if possible), just that instead of moving the middle element r up to the parent node $p(v)$, it is *a copy* of r that will be inserted into $p(v)$. All the elements remain therefore at the leaf level, and the elements in the nodes above them are all copies of a part of these values.

A B$^+$-tree with the same elements as the B-tree of Figure 6.4 may look like the one in Figure 6.15. Pointers have been added to show how the leaves could form here a linked list.

When the insertion of the copy of the middle element into the parent node leads there too to an overflow, the insertion algorithm continues with further node splits, but like the algorithm for B-trees. That is, only on the lowest (leaf) level do we keep all of the elements and insert a copy of one of them into the parent node; when an internal node is split, we proceed as before, moving the middle element itself, and not just a copy of it. The reason for this asymmetric behavior is that one would need an additional pointer emanating from one of the newly created nodes. For the lowest level, there is no such problem, since all the pointers are NIL.

For example, insert the element 172 into the tree of Figure 6.15. The node $v_{150,\ldots,600}$ is split into $v_{150,172}$ and $v_{200,450,600}$ (including the element 200), and a copy of 200 is inserted into the root, yielding in a first stage $v_{10,60,150,200,700}$. Since this is again an overflow, the node is split, but in the regular B-tree way. The result can be seen in Figure 6.16. If the element 150 had been kept also in one of the nodes on level 1, as in, say, $v_{150,200,700}$, this would require four outgoing pointers from this node, and thus four corresponding leaves. But the

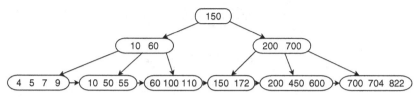

Figure 6.16. Insertion of 172.

total number of leaves in the tree is only six, not seven. The awkward distinction, applying a different split algorithm on the lowest (leaf) level than for the levels above, is therefore necessary.

Deletion

Since all the elements are in the leaves, one has only to deal with deletions at the leaf level. At first sight, it may seem that one has to check whether there is a copy of the element to be deleted in the upper part of the tree, so that the copy may also be removed. But in fact, such a check is not needed, for even if the value x is not any more in one of the leaves, it may still work perfectly well as a separator.

If the node from which an element has been removed underflows, the balancing procedure must be applied, taking care of replacing also the separating element. For example, if we remove the element 150 from the tree in Figure 6.16, the root containing a copy of 150 will not be touched, the nodes v_{172} and $v_{200,450,600}$ will be re-balanced into $v_{172,200}$ and $v_{450,600}$, and their parent node $v_{200,700}$ will be changed into $v_{450,700}$. If no balancing is possible, two nodes will be merged, and their separating element will simply be discarded. If deleting the separating element causes another underflow, we continue like for B-trees, similarly to what we have seen for the insertion.

Search

The only difference between the searches in B-trees or B$^+$-trees is that for the latter, the search has always to continue until the leaf level is reached. The reason is that even if the value is found in one of the internal nodes, this does not imply that the corresponding element is still in the tree; it might have been deleted.

Summarizing, the processing of B$^+$-trees is only slightly more involved, the time complexity is about the same and the space is only marginally increased. In many situations, this will seem as a reasonable tradeoff for getting the improved sequential scan.

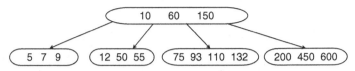

Figure 6.17. Example of a B*-tree with $m = 6$.

6.5.2 B*-Trees

Another extension of the basic B-tree concentrates on reducing the wasted space within the nodes, which can reach about 50%. This is improved in the variant called B*-trees to about $\frac{1}{3}$. The exact definition is as follows:

Definition 6.2. A *B*-tree* of order m, with $m > 2$ and m being a multiple of 3, is an m-ary search tree with the following additional constraints:

  (i) Every node, except the root, stores at least $\frac{2m}{3} - 1$ elements.
 (ii) The root stores at least one and at most $\frac{4m}{3} - 2$ elements.
(iii) NIL-pointers emanate only from nodes on the lowest level.

The restriction to orders that are divisible by 3 is for convenience only, as it simplifies the presentation. For the large values of m used in practice, it has no importance. Figure 6.17 is an example of a B*-tree, with $m = 6$. All the nodes store at least three elements.

Since more data than for B-trees is stored in each node, the number of nodes will tend to be smaller, and hence also the depth of the tree may be reduced. The search algorithm for B*-trees, which is the same as for B-tree, may be expected to work faster. The question is, of course, how to maintain the stricter bounds on the number of elements per node during updates.

Insertion

Unlike B-trees, for which a balancing step in case of an overflow was optional, an overfull node v in a B*-tree *requires* a balancing attempt, to assure that one of the neighbors w of v has reached full capacity. The reason is that the splitting process is applied to two neighboring nodes simultaneously, of which one should be with a maximum number of elements $m - 1$, and the other even beyond, storing, temporarily, m elements. If one adds the element separating v and w, this gives $2m$ elements, that should be redistributed into three nodes.

It will be easier to work through an example and infer from it the general case. Assume $m = 99$, so that any node has between 66 and 99 outgoing pointers and thus stores between 65 and 98 values. Suppose a new value is added to a node v, causing an overflow, that the right neighbor w of v is full, and that the separating value between v and w is a, $r_{99} < a < r_{100}$. The situation can be described schematically like earlier as

$$a$$

$$r_1, \ldots, r_{99} \qquad\qquad r_{100}, \ldots, r_{197}$$
$$p_0, p_1, \ldots, p_{99} \qquad\qquad q_{99}, q_{100}, \ldots, q_{197}$$

Splitting the two nodes into three yields

$$r_{66} \qquad\qquad\qquad\qquad\qquad\qquad r_{132}$$

$$r_1, \ldots, r_{65} \qquad r_{67}, \ldots, r_{99}, a, r_{100}, \ldots, r_{131} \qquad r_{133}, \ldots, r_{197}$$
$$p_0, p_1, \ldots, p_{65} \qquad p_{66}, p_{67}, \ldots, p_{99}, q_{99}, q_{100}, \ldots, q_{131} \qquad q_{132}, \ldots, q_{197}.$$

Note that the middle node contains one more element than the minimal allowed.

The insertion of r_{66} and r_{132} instead of a into the parent node may again cause an overflow, which is handled recursively, like for B-trees.

If v does not have any neighbor, it must be the root, which has to be split on its own. But if the upper bound on the number of elements in the root had been $m - 1$ like for the other nodes, the result of the split would be two nodes that contain only about $m/2$ elements, violating the lower bound. This is circumvented by defining, only for the root, which anyway already gets a special treatment, an upper bound of about $\frac{4}{3}m$, by $\frac{1}{3}$ larger than for the other nodes. More precisely, on our example, the root may hold up to 130 values. Suppose then that it overflows and denote the values by $r_1, \ldots, r_{131}$ and the pointers by $p_0, \ldots, p_{131}$. This gives, after the split,

$$r_{66}$$

$$r_1, \ldots, r_{65} \qquad\qquad r_{67}, \ldots, r_{131}$$
$$p_0, p_1, \ldots, p_{65} \qquad\qquad p_{66}, p_{67}, \ldots, p_{131}.$$

Deletion

As for B$^+$-trees, we deal only with the deletion of an element in a leaf node v. If this induces an underflow, balancing should be attempted, but this time with *both* left and right neighbors of v, if they exist at all. If no balancing is possible, this is the situation where v has one element short of the minimum, and its two neighbors are exactly at minimum capacity, as in

$$a \qquad\qquad\qquad\qquad b$$

$$r_1, \ldots, r_{65} \qquad s_1, \ldots, s_{64} \qquad t_1, \ldots, t_{65}$$
$$p_0, p_1, \ldots, p_{65} \qquad q_0, q_1, \ldots, q_{64} \qquad y_0, y_1, \ldots, y_{65}.$$

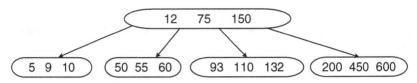

Figure 6.18. Example of extended balancing.

The three nodes will then be merged into two as shown:

$$s_{33}$$

$$r_1, \ldots, r_{65}, a, s_1, \ldots, s_{32} \qquad\qquad s_{34}, \ldots, s_{64}, b, t_1, \ldots, t_{65}$$

$$p_0, p_1, \ldots, p_{65}, q_0, q_1, \ldots, q_{32} \qquad\qquad q_{33}, q_{34}, \ldots, q_{64}, y_0, y_1, \ldots, y_{65}.$$

Note that the right node contains one less element than the maximum allowed.

There is a slight complication in this case, relating to nodes that are leftmost or rightmost children of their parent nodes: they do not have two immediate neighbors, like, e.g., the node $v_{5,7,9}$ in Figure 6.17. But for the merging to work properly, three nodes have to be handled together. The solution for this particular case is to allow *extended balancing*, not just with the immediate neighbor, but even with the neighbor's neighbor. Returning to Figure 6.17, if the element 7 is deleted, extended balancing would involve the three leftmost leaves and transform the tree into the one shown in Figure 6.18.

If even extended balancing cannot be performed, the three nodes that will be merged into two will be v, its neighbor and the neighbor's neighbor.

And what if there is no further neighbor to the neighbor? This can only happen if there is only a single value in the parent node of v; this parent must therefore be the root. The starting situation is thus

$$a$$

$$r_1, \ldots, r_{65} \qquad\qquad s_1, \ldots, s_{64}$$

$$p_0, p_1, \ldots, p_{65} \qquad\qquad q_0, q_1, \ldots, q_{64}.$$

and the nodes will be merged to form a new root with maximum load

$$r_1, \ldots, r_{65}, a, s_1, \ldots, s_{64}$$

$$p_0, p_1, \ldots, p_{65}, q_0, q_1, \ldots, q_{64}.$$

6.5.3 2-3-Trees

A special case of a B-tree that deserves being mentioned is for $m = 3$. Any node then contains one or two elements, and may have two or three children if it is not a leaf. Actually, 2-3-trees have been invented earlier than the more general B-trees. The application area is also different, since B-trees are often used with large values of m, as mentioned previously. Therefore 2-3-trees can be seen as an alternative to AVL-trees for controlling the depth of a search tree with n elements, which will be bounded by $O(\log n)$.

Exercises

6.1 Given is a B-tree of order 5 with four levels.

    (a) A new element x is inserted, and immediately afterward, x is deleted. Is the B-tree after these two operations necessarily identical to that before the operations?

    (b) What if the order of the operations is inverted: first, an element x is deleted, and then it is re-inserted?

6.2 Consider two B-trees A and B, both of order m. Denote the number of their elements by a and b, respectively, and assume $a \geq b$. Assume also that all the elements in A are smaller than any element in B. Show how to merge A and B in time $O(h)$ into a single B-tree of order m, where h is the height of A.

6.3 Given is the B-tree of order 5 in the following figure. Draw the tree after having removed the element 40 in the following cases:

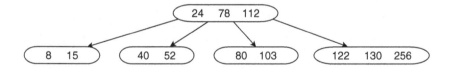

    (a) merging with the left neighbor;
    (b) merging with the right neighbor;
    (c) merging three elements into two;
    (d) using extended balancing;
    (e) assuming the order of the tree is 4.

6.4 Show how the B-tree of Exercise 6.3 changes if you insert, in order, the elements 104, 105, 106, 107, 108, using balancing, if necessary. Then insert 109, splitting the two rightmost leaves into three. Finally, insert 140, 150, and 158.

6.5 To increase the space exploitation of the nodes even further, one may define a B-tree variant in which every node, except the root, stores between $\frac{3m}{4} - 1$ and $m - 1$ elements.

(a) How should the number of elements in the root be defined?

(b) Show how to adapt the insertion and deletion procedures to comply with the new constraints.

7

Heaps

7.1 Priority Queues

One of the first data structures we encountered in Chapter 2 was a queue. The idea of dealing with some records on a FIFO – first in, first out – basis seems to be a reasonable choice and enjoys widespread acceptance. Nonetheless, there are situations in which the order should be different. A case in point would be the emergency room of any hospital: there is a constant influx of new potential patients, all waiting to being taken care of. However, they will be treated by order of medical urgency (which some professional has to assess) rather than by arrival time. Similarly, we all have many items on our to-do lists, but some of these items may be given a higher priority than others.

Translating the problem into mathematical terms, we are looking for a data structure we shall call a *priority queue*, storing a collection of records, each of which has been assigned a value considered as its *priority*. We wish to be able to perform updates, as inserting new elements, deleting others, or changing the priority of some. In addition, there should be fast access to the element with highest priority.

A simple solution could be a list that has been sorted by nonincreasing priority. The element with highest priority would then be the first, but updates might require $\Omega(n)$ time for a list of n records. Another option would be to use a search tree, which takes $\Omega(n \log n)$ time to be built, as we shall see in Chapter 10, but then updating and extracting the maximum element can be done in time $O(\log n)$.

This chapter presents a better alternative. It uses a special form of a binary tree, called a *heap* and achieves $O(\log n)$ time updates and access to the maximum element in $O(1)$. The time to build a heap of n elements is only $O(n)$.

The name comes possibly from the fact that beside the rules given in the definition, there is little order between the elements of a heap, which conveys

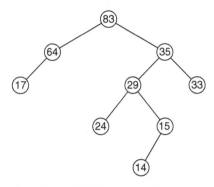

Figure 7.1. Example of a heap.

the impression of a disordered pile or elements that have been thrown one on another. It might remind many card games, in which the players throw cards in turn onto some pile, and only the top card is considered as being accessible.

7.2 Definition and Updates

Definition 7.1. A *heap* is a binary tree for which the value stored in any node is larger or equal to the values stored in its children, if they exist.

An immediate consequence of this definition is that the largest element of a heap is always stored in the root, as can also be seen in the sample heap shown in Figure 7.1.

The elements along any path from the root to a leaf appear in non-increasing order, but there is no specific order if one scans the elements by layers.

To remove the maximal element, or in fact any other node, one proceeds similarly to what we saw for binary search trees: only the value of the node is erased, and it has to be replaced. In the case of a heap, the value of a node v to be deleted should be replaced by the larger of the values of the children of v, if they exist. This process continues top-down until a leaf is reached, which can be removed without causing problems. For example, removing the root v_{83} of the heap in Figure 7.1 is done by replacing it with v_{64}, which in turn is replaced by v_{17}; the latter is then simply removed from the tree.

For the insertion of a new element, there is a certain degree of freedom: the new node should first be inserted in time $O(1)$ as a leaf, but there is no restriction on which of the potential leaves to choose. Obviously, this might violate the heap property, so a series of comparisons is performed, this time bottom-up, until the modified tree is a heap again. For example, one could choose to insert

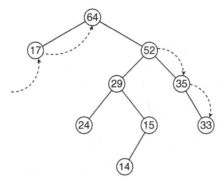

Figure 7.2. Inserting into and deleting from a heap.

first the node v_{52} as the right child of the leaf v_{33} in Figure 7.1. Since $52 > 33$, the values of the leaf v_{52} and its parent node v_{33} are swapped; but 52 is also larger than 35, so there is another exchange between v_{52} and v_{35}. Now $52 < 64$ and the update is done. Figure 7.2 shows the heap of Figure 7.1 after the deletion of the root and insertion of the value 52.

The number of operations for such updates is thus again dependent on the depth of the tree, and similarly to what we saw for binary search trees, this depth may be as large as $\Omega(n)$. The way to overcome such worst case behavior is by imposing some additional constraints, as done previously for AVL-trees and B-trees.

The best possible performance of updates in binary trees like heaps or search trees is attained by full binary trees with $n = 2^d - 1$ nodes, which have all their leaves on the same level of depth $d - 1$. For search trees, such a constraint was too restrictive and led to a more relaxed one, that of AVL-trees. For heaps, on the other hand, requiring the shape of a full tree may be efficiently supported, and we shall henceforth assume that a heap is a full binary tree. The definition of a full binary tree has to be extended for any number of nodes n, not just those of form $2^d - 1$ for some d:

Definition 7.2. A full binary tree with n nodes is a binary tree in which all the leaves are on the same level $d - 1$, if $n = 2^d - 1$, or, when $2^d \le n < 2^{d+1}$, the leaves are on adjacent levels, with $n - 2^d + 1$ leaves left justified on level d, for some $d \ge 1$.

For example, the structure of the tree in Figure 7.3 is that of a full binary tree, with $n = 12$ nodes. Accordingly, there is one leaf on level $d - 1 = 2$, and there are $n - 2^d + 1 = 5$ leaves that are left justified on the lowest level $d = 3$. The values in the nodes show that the tree is a heap.

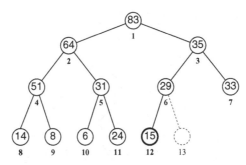

Figure 7.3. A heap as a full binary tree.

We saw earlier that to insert a new element, one has to create a new leaf, but that there is much freedom of where this leaf should be in the tree. Now the choice is more restricted. In fact, to maintain the shape of a full binary tree, a new element is first inserted as a leaf at the only location not violating the constraint: continuing the sequence of left justified leaves on the lowest level, or, if this level is already filled, as the leftmost leaf of the next level. For our example tree, this location is indicated in broken lines in Figure 7.3. In a second stage, the inserted element is then propagated bottom up if necessary, to its proper place in the order imposed by the heap.

Similarly, the only leaf that can be removed without losing the shape of a full binary tree is the rightmost one on the lowest level, which, in the example of Figure 7.3, is emphasized and contains the value 15. Denote this extreme element by v_e. Therefore, the procedure given earlier for the removal of the maximum element, or any other node w, has to be modified. We cannot simply erase the value of a node and move repeatedly the larger of its children's values to the higher level, because that could create a gap on the lowest level. So we start the deletion process by *replacing* the value of the node w to be removed by the value of v_e, and by removing the leaf v_e from the heap. Then the new value of w is percolated top down, if necessary, swapping its value with the larger of its children's values, until the heap property is restored. All the update operations can thus be performed in time $O(\log n)$.

The upper tree in Figure 7.4 is the result of deleting the largest value 83 from the heap of Figure 7.3. The root v_{83} is replaced by the leaf v_{15}, which is swapped twice with its left child. The lower tree in Figure 7.4 is obtained by inserting the value 42 into the heap of Figure 7.3. The new leaf v_{42} is inserted as the 13th node of the heap, and is then swapped twice with its parent node.

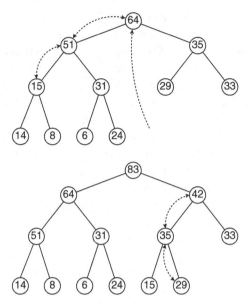

Figure 7.4. Deleting 83 from and inserting 42 into the tree of Figure 7.3.

7.3 Array Implementation of Heaps

There remains a small technical problem. In the trees we have seen so far, there were only pointers from a node to its children, not to its parent, but here we need the ability to navigate both downward and upward in the tree. This was true also for the updates in the AVL trees of Chapter 5, but there no upward pointers were needed, because one could save all the necessary nodes, those on the path from the root to a leaf, in a stack.

Fortunately, the fact that heaps are restricted to have the form of a full binary tree enables a much simpler implementation, without any pointers at all. Any full binary tree with n nodes can be implemented as an array of size n, indexed by the numbers 1 to n. To build the correspondence between nodes of the tree and array cells, just number the nodes sequentially top down, and in each level from left to right. For example, this numbering appears in the heap of Figure 7.3, just underneath the nodes. The heap can therefore be represented in an array as

1	2	3	4	5	6	7	8	9	10	11	12
83	64	35	51	31	29	33	14	8	6	24	15

Denote by $v(i)$ the node indexed by i in the heap. The simple rules are that the left child of the node $v(i)$ is $v(2i)$ and the right child of $v(i)$ is $v(2i + 1)$, for

$1 \leq i \leq \lfloor n/2 \rfloor$, and hence the parent node of $v(j)$ is $v(\lfloor j/2 \rfloor)$, for $2 \leq j \leq n$. This explains why it is important to start the indexing with 1, and not with 0, as would be set by default in the C/C++ languages. There is thus no need for any pointers, and one can pass from one node to the next or previous level just by multiplying or dividing the index by 2. These operations are, moreover, easily implemented, since all one has to consider is the standard binary representation of the index. If i is represented by $b_k \cdots b_2 b_1 b_0$, with $b_j \in \{0, 1\}$, that is $i = \sum_{j=0}^{k} b_j 2^j$, then the parent of $v(i)$ is indexed by $b_k \cdots b_2 b_1$, the grand-parent by $b_k \cdots b_3 b_2$, and so on. The left child of $v(i)$ will be indexed by $b_k \cdots b_2 b_1 b_0 0$, and its right child by $b_k \cdots b_2 b_1 b_0 1$.

For example, the following is a list of indices of nodes, given in both decimal and binary, starting with the node $v(25)$, and passing from one node to its parent, up to the root $v(1)$:

25	11001
12	1100
6	110
3	11
1	1

Going from $v(25)$ to its two children yields

25	11001
50	110010
51	110011

Any element to be deleted will first be replaced by the one in the last entry of the array, indexed n, and any new element is first inserted in the next available spot, which should be indexed $n + 1$. The time complexity of all the updates clearly remains $O(\log n)$.

7.4 Construction of Heaps

A heap can obviously be constructed by inserting its elements in any order into an initially empty tree or array. This could take about $\sum_{i=1}^{n} \log i = \Omega(n \log n)$ time. The question is whether it can be done faster when the whole set of records is given at once. One could sort the array by non-increasing values, since a sorted array is a particular form of a heap, but sorting will also require at least $\Omega(n \log n)$ time, as we shall see in Chapter 10. The order imposed by a heap is less restrictive than strictly sorted order, so there is hope for the complexity of the construction of a heap to be less than the lower bound for sorting.

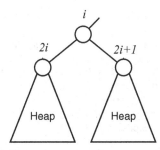

Figure 7.5. Schematic of the input of Heapify.

As a first step, consider a function called Heapify(i, j), working on the sub-array between and including the indices i and j. More precisely, Heapify(i, j) works on the subtree $T_{v(i)}$ rooted at the node $v(i)$, but excluding all nodes with indices larger than j. The usefulness of the second argument j will become clear later. One has to remember that the array is only a convenient way to represent the heap, which is still defined as a tree. Therefore, the subarray $[i, j]$ processed by Heapify(i, j) does not really refer to all the elements in the range, but only to those belonging to the subtree rooted at $v(i)$. For example, Heapify(2, 10) deals only with the grayed entries in

1	2	3	4	5	6	7	8	9	10	11	12

which is most easily understood when comparing the array with the corresponding tree form in Figure 7.3: the elements 3, 6, 7, and 12 remain white because they are not in the subtree rooted by 2, and element 11 is excluded because it is not in the given range [2, 10].

The purpose is to transform the subrange of the array given as parameter, or rather the corresponding subtree $T_{v(i)}$, into a heap. The definition of Heapify will be simplified by the additional assumption that the two subtrees of $T_{v(i)}$, which are $T_{v(2i)}$ and $T_{v(2i+1)}$ are already heaps, as given schematically in Figure 7.5.

Therefore, denoting the given array by A, if the value at the root $v(i)$ is not smaller than the values of its children, that is, if

$$A[i] \geq A[2i] \qquad \text{and} \qquad A[i] \geq A[2i + 1],$$

then the entire subtree is already a heap, and no further action is needed. Otherwise, let us swap the values of $v(i)$ and the larger of its children, for example $v(2i)$. But then we are again in a situation in which a subtree is given that is *almost* a heap: its own subtrees, $T_{v(4i)}$ and $T_{v(4i+1)}$ are heaps, and only the root

Heapify(i, j)
> $maxind \longleftarrow i$
> if $2i \leq j$ and $A[2i] > A[maxind]$ then
> > $maxind \longleftarrow 2i$
>
> if $2i + 1 \leq j$ and $A[2i + 1] > A[maxind]$ then
> > $maxind \longleftarrow 2i + 1$
>
> if $maxind \neq i$ then
> > $A[i] \longleftrightarrow A[maxind]$
> > Heapify$(maxind, j)$

Figure 7.6. Heapify transforms a tree into a heap, assuming its subtrees are heaps.

$v(2i)$ may violate the heap condition. This may therefore be treated recursively. Figure 7.6 shows the formal definition of Heapify(i, j).

After the first two if statements, the variable $maxind$ will be the index of the largest element among $\{A[i], A[2i], A[2i + 1]\}$, which are the root and its two children. The fact that they are in the given range at all is checked by the conditions $2i \leq j$ and $2i + 1 \leq j$. If at this stage $maxind = i$, the tree is a heap and we are done; otherwise the value of the larger of the two children is swapped with the value of the root (this action is symbolized by the two-sided arrow $\longleftrightarrow$), and Heapify is invoked recursively for the subtree.

Background Concept: Swapping Two Elements
The swap of two elements used here is a frequent action that appears in many algorithms and therefore deserves some comments. The simplest and possibly also the best way to swap the values of two variables x and y is by means of a third, auxiliary, variable T:

swap1(x, y)
> $T \longleftarrow x$
> $x \longleftarrow y$
> $y \longleftarrow T$

An alternative, using also only three assignment, but no extra space for a temporary variable, exploits the properties of the Boolean bit-wise XOR operation, denoted by $x \oplus y$:

swap2(x, y)
> $x \longleftarrow x \oplus y$
> $y \longleftarrow x \oplus y$
> $x \longleftarrow x \oplus y$

This elegant procedure, consisting of three copies of almost the same command, uses the fact that XOR is both associative and commutative. At the end of the execution of the second line, one gets

$$y = x \oplus y = (x \oplus y) \oplus y = x \oplus (y \oplus y) = x \oplus 0 = x.$$

And after the third line, one gets:

$$x = x \oplus y = (x \oplus y) \oplus x = (y \oplus x) \oplus x = y \oplus (x \oplus x) = y \oplus 0 = y.$$

To evaluate the time complexity of the procedure, note that invoking Heapify(i, j) generates a sequence of recursive calls to Heapify, and that the number of commands between consecutive calls is bounded by a constant. On the other hand, since $i \geq 1$ and $j \leq n$, the number of calls is bounded by the number of times i can be doubled until it exceeds j, which is at most $\log_2 n$.

The question is now how to employ the Heapify procedure to build a heap from scratch. The answer lies in the simple idea of processing a given input array *backward*, or in terms of the corresponding binary tree, building the heap *bottom-up*. A full binary tree with n nodes has $\lceil \frac{n}{2} \rceil$ leaves, each of them being a heap, as the heap condition is trivially fulfilled for nodes without children. The trees rooted by the parent nodes of these leaves, in our example of Figure 7.3, the nodes indexed 6, 5, 4 and 3, satisfy then the condition that their own subtrees are heaps, so Heapify can be applied on them. This paves the way to apply subsequently Heapify to the trees rooted by the grand-parents (2 and 1 in the example), etc. This yields the simple construction routine:

Buildheap(n)

    for $i \longleftarrow \lfloor \frac{n}{2} \rfloor$ by step -1 to 1

        Heapify(i, n)

An immediate upper bound on the complexity, given that Heapify takes $O(\log n)$ time and that there are about $n/2$ iterations, is $O(n \log n)$. This turns out to be overly pessimistic. A tighter bound can be achieved if one realizes that only the entire tree has depth $\log_2 n - 1$, and that the subtrees on which the recursive calls of Heapify act are shallower.

To simplify the notation, assume that $n = 2^{k+1} - 1$, that is, we consider a full tree of depth k having all its $\frac{n+1}{2}$ leaves on the same level k. In Buildheap, there is a single call to Heapify with a tree of depth k, there are two such calls with trees of depth $k - 1$, and more generally, there are 2^i calls to Heapify with trees of depth $k - i$, for $0 \le i < k$. The total number N of calls is therefore

$$N = 1 \cdot k + 2(k-1) + 2^2(k-2) + \cdots + 2^{k-1} \cdot 1 = \sum_{i=0}^{k-1} 2^i(k-i).$$

Such a summation can be dealt with by writing it out explicitly line by line, starting with the last index $k - 1$ and going backward, and then summing by columns:

$$
\begin{aligned}
N = \quad & 2^{k-1} \\
& + 2^{k-2} + 2^{k-2} \\
& + 2^{k-3} + 2^{k-3} + 2^{k-3} \\
& + \quad \cdots \\
& + 2^{k-k} + 2^{k-k} + 2^{k-k} + \cdots + 2^{k-k}.
\end{aligned}
$$

The first column is the geometric series $\sum_{i=0}^{k-1} 2^i$, well known to sum up to $2^k - 1$. The second column is similar, but the last index is $k - 2$, so the sum is $2^{k-1} - 1$, and in general, we get that the jth column is $\sum_{i=0}^{k-j} 2^i$ summing up to $S(j) = 2^{k-j+1} - 1$, for $1 \le j \le k$. Summing the summations, we finally get

$$N = \sum_{j=1}^{k} S(j) = \sum_{j=1}^{k} (2^{k-j+1} - 1) = \sum_{i=1}^{k} 2^i - k = 2^{k+1} - 2 - k < n.$$

The overall complexity of building a heap of n elements is thus only $O(n)$.

7.5 Heapsort

We conclude this chapter on heaps by preponing the description of a sorting method that should in fact be dealt with only in Chapter 10. It is, however, strongly connected to the current subject and a good example of an important application of heaps.

Suppose that an array of n numbers is given and that it has already been transformed into a heap. The array can then be sorted by repeatedly extracting the largest number. Since on one hand the extracted numbers have to be stored somewhere, and on the other hand, the shrinking heap should form a contiguous block in the array including the first element, it is natural to store the extracted elements at the end of the array. The sorted sequence is thus constructed backward using the cells that are vacated, so that no additional space is needed for the sort.

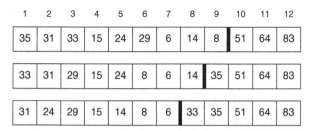

Figure 7.7. Partially sorted array during Heapsort.

More precisely, at the end of iteration j, $1 \le j \le n$, the elements $A[1] \cdots A[n - j]$ form a heap and the rest of the elements, those in $A[n - j + 1] \cdots A[n]$, store the j largest numbers of the original array in increasing order. The initial stage is considered here as the end of iteration 0. Figure 7.7 shows the array corresponding to the heap of Figure 7.3 at the end of iterations 3, 4, and 5. The heap is to the left of the black bar, the partially sorted array to its right.

In iteration j, the largest element of the heap, the one stored in position 1, is swapped with the last one in the current heap. This places the extracted element into its final position in the sorted array. Then the heap has to be updated, but we are in the special case in which all the elements satisfy the heap property, except possibly the root. The heap can thus be repaired, in time $O(\log j)$, by a single application of Heapify, in which the second argument is used to limit the scope of the current heap. Overall, the updates will take

$$\sum_{j=1}^{n} \log j < \sum_{j=1}^{n} \log n = O(n \log n),$$

and the formal algorithm is given by

Heapsort(n)
    Buildheap(n)
    for $j \longleftarrow n$ by step -1 to 2
        $A[1] \longleftrightarrow A[j]$
        Heapify($1, j - 1$)

In fact, Heapsort consists of two quite similar loops. The first builds the heap and the second retrieves repeatedly the largest element remaining in the heap. An easy way to remember the varying parameters of Heapify is the rhombus shaped diagram in Figure 7.8. It shows in its upper part, corresponding to

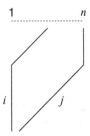

Figure 7.8. Schematic of the parameters of Heapsort.

Buildheap, that i passes from $n/2$ to 1 while j stays fixed at n; in the lower part, i remains equal to 1, but j decreases from n to 2.

As a final note it should be mentioned that though the definition of a heap given herein places the largest element at the root, one could clearly also define a *min-heap* with the smallest element on top and with the obvious adaptations to the earlier procedures. What we have defined as a heap is therefore often referred to in the literature as a *max-heap*.

Exercises

7.1 Given are two heaps A of size m and B of size n. The heaps are given explicitly as binary trees, not as arrays. Assume that all $m + n$ elements are different, that $m = 2^k - 1$ for some integer k and that $m/2 < n \le m$. The task is to build a heap C consisting of the elements of $A \cup B$.

   (a) What is the depth of the tree A, and what is the depth of the tree B?
   (b) What will be the depth of the tree C?
   (c) Suggest an efficient algorithm for the construction of C. What is its complexity?

7.2 What happens to the correctness and efficiency of the Buildheap procedure, if one changes the control of the main loop from

   for $j \longleftarrow \lfloor \frac{n}{2} \rfloor$ by step -1 to 1   to

   (a) for $j \longleftarrow n$ by step -1 to 1   ?
   (b) for $j \longleftarrow 1$ to n ?

   If the procedure does not work, show a counterexample with smallest possible n.

7.3 A possible generalization of a heap is a *ternary heap*, which is a full ternary tree (each internal node has 3 children). The procedure **Heapify** is generalized accordingly to **Heapify3**.

(a) A full ternary tree can also be represented as an array. How does one pass from a node to its three children? How from a node to its parent?

(b) To remove the maximum element and then restore the heap, how many calls to **Heapify3** and how many comparisons on each level of the tree are needed?

(c) What may be concluded in comparison with binary heaps?

7.4 Let T be a binary tree in which each node is annotated by a pair of integers (s, h). T is a *search-heap* if it is a search tree according to s and a heap according to h.

(a) Given is the following set of (s, h) pairs: $\{(26, 16), (17, 8), (5, 1), (24, 34), (12, 5), (41, 12), (49, 3), (52, 9), (54, 29), (34, 2), (38, 14), (10, 6)\}$. Build the search-min-heap and the search-max-heap for this set.

(b) Assuming that all s-values are different, and all h-values are different, show that there is exactly one search-heap (more precisely, one for *min*, one for *max*) for any set of pairs.

(c) For a given such set of (s, h) pairs, write an algorithm for the construction of the corresponding search-heap.

7.5 Suggest a data structure supporting the following operations in the given time complexities:

(a) **Build** in time $O(n)$ for a set of n elements.

(b) **Insert**(x), inserting a new element x into the structure in time $O(\log n)$.

(c) **min** and **max**, finding minimum and maximum elements in time $O(1)$.

(d) **delete-min** and **delete-max**. removing the minimum and maximum elements in time $O(\log n)$.

7.6 Apply **Heapsort** with a max-heap to sort an array of length n into increasing order. How many comparisons and swaps are executed if the array

(a) is already given in increasing order?

(b) is given in decreasing order?

8

Sets

8.1 Representing a Set by a Bitmap

The topic of this chapter is different from that of the previous ones, in that a *set* is not a data structure, but rather a mathematical entity that appears frequently enough in our programs to raise the question of how to implement it efficiently. Generally, a set $S = \{a_1, a_2, \ldots, a_n\}$ of n elements is defined, and one is interested in certain subsets of S and their interactions.

A straightforward representation of a subset is by means of a *bitmap*, also referred to as a bit-vector, which we have encountered already in the example of Section 3.4.1. A subset $C \subseteq S$ will be represented by the bitmap $\mathcal{B}(C) = b_1 b_2 \cdots b_n$ of length n, in which $b_i = 1$ if and only if $a_i \in C$. For example, if $n = 10$ and $C = \{a_2, a_6, a_7\}$, then the corresponding bitmap is

$$\mathcal{B}(C) = 0100011000.$$

For the entire set, one gets $\mathcal{B}(S) = 1111111111$ and for the empty set $\mathcal{B}(\emptyset) = 0000000000$. Intersection, union, and complementation are handled with the corresponding Boolean operators:

$$\mathcal{B}(X \cap Y) = \mathcal{B}(X) \wedge \mathcal{B}(Y),$$

$$\mathcal{B}(X \cup Y) = \mathcal{B}(X) \vee \mathcal{B}(Y),$$

$$\mathcal{B}(\overline{X}) = \overline{\mathcal{B}(X)},$$

where $\overline{X}$ denotes the complementing set $S \setminus X$, $\overline{b} = 1 - b$ is the complementing bit of b, and the complement of a bit-vector is the vector of the bit-complements.

If the size of the set n is relatively small, it may fit into a computer word (32 bits) and all the operations can then be performed in a single step, but even for larger n, the necessary operations are simple loops and easily parallelized.

It will be convenient to prepare a set of *masks* $I_1, \ldots, I_n$, which are bitmaps representing the singletons $\{a_1\}, \ldots, \{a_n\}$, respectively, that is, $I_1 = 1000 \cdots$, $I_2 = 0100 \cdots$, $I_3 = 0010 \cdots$, etc. Some of the basic operations can then be translated as follows:

add element a_r to the set X	$\mathcal{B}(X) \longleftarrow \mathcal{B}(X) \vee I_r$
delete a_r from X	$\mathcal{B}(X) \longleftarrow \mathcal{B}(X) \wedge \overline{I_r}$
check whether $a_r \in X$	if $(\mathcal{B}(X) \wedge I_r) = I_r$
check whether $Y \subseteq X$	if $(\mathcal{B}(X) \wedge \mathcal{B}(Y)) = \mathcal{B}(Y)$

This set representation is familiar to all users of the Unix operating system, in which the *access rights* to a given file are represented by a string of the form -rwxrw-r-, for example. This would mean that the owner may read, write and execute the file, other members of the group the owner belongs to may only read or write, and the rest of the users has only read access. In fact, the access rights may be written as a bitmap of length 10, since the interpretation of each bit position is fixed. For example, the third bit from the left indicates whether the owner has write permission. The preceding string would thus be 0111110100. Indeed, it is customary to set the access rights by the chmod command, using the octal representation of the 9 rightmost bits. For example the command setting the given string would be

chmod   764   filename.

Another instance of representing a set by a bitmap has been encountered in Section 3.2: the rows of the adjacency matrix of a graph give the sets of outgoing edges, whereas the columns correspond to the incoming edges for all the vertices.

8.1.1 Application: Full-Text Information Retrieval

Computers were initially just large machines performing calculations, and it took some time to realize that they can also be used to manipulate large texts. This might seem obvious for somebody growing up with internet access, but in the 1960s when large Information Retrieval Systems were built, this was a small revolution. The basic algorithms in these systems process various sets, which is why they are a good example for the topic of this chapter.

The general problem can be described as follows. In the background, a large corpus of natural language texts T is given and may be pre-processed. The system is then accessed by means of some *query* Q, and the task is to retrieve all the passages that satisfy the query. For example, the query could be

$$Q = \text{information} \textsc{ and } (\text{processing} \textsc{ or } \text{retrieval}), \qquad (8.1)$$

and it could retrieve all the documents of T containing the first term and at least one of the other two. As extension, if the number of text passages satisfying Q is too large, one could be interested only in the most relevant results. To continue the example, one might restrict the retrieval to documents containing one of the *phrases* information processing or information retrieval, and not just happen to include the terms without any connection between them.

The algorithms to be used actually depend on the size of the underlying textual database. For small enough texts (and the definition of what *small* means clearly changes with time), a brute-force approach may be feasible, using a fast *string matching* algorithm, like the one of Boyer and Moore presented in the first chapter. For larger corpora, even a fast scan may take too long. The solution, called *inverted files,* is then to build the following auxiliary files.

- A *dictionary D*, containing the lexicographically sorted list of all the different terms in T; and
- A *concordance C*, containing, for each term $x \in D$, the sorted list $L(x)$ of the exact references of all occurrences of x in T. These references may be given as *coordinates*, which can be just document numbers, or when more fine grained queries are to be supported, the coordinates can be tuples, as (*document, paragraph, sentence, word*), or in any other hierarchical form.

The algorithm processing a query Q would then access the dictionary D with all the terms of Q and get there pointers to their coordinate lists in C. These lists have then to be merged or intersected, according to the Boolean structure induced by the query. For the example query, the sought list would be

$$L(\text{information}) \cap \big(L(\text{processing}) \cup L(\text{retrieval})\big).$$

In the case more precise metrical constraints are supported, the intersection is more involved. Suppose the query is $\mathsf{X}\ [\ell]\ \mathsf{X}'$, meaning that we are looking for occurrences of X and X' within the same sentence, but at most ℓ words apart, with $\ell = 1$ standing for adjacent terms. Then if $(d, p, s, w) \in L(\mathsf{X})$ and $(d', p', s', w') \in L(\mathsf{X}')$, this pair of coordinates should be retrieved if it satisfies

$$d = d' \ \wedge \ p = p' \ \wedge \ s = s' \ \wedge \ |w - w'| \leq \ell.$$

For queries caring only about the document level, bitmaps acting as occurrence maps can be used, as explained in Section 3.4.1: the length of each bitmap will be the total number of documents in the system, and the bit in position i of the bitmap $B(A)$ of term A will be set to 1, if and only if the term A appears in document i. The query (8.1) would then be processed by evaluating

$$B(\text{information}) \wedge \big(B(\text{processing}) \vee B(\text{retrieval})\big),$$

and the list of document indices to be retrieved would just be the list of the indices of the 1-bits of the resulting bitmap.

8.2 Union-Find

In many applications involving sets, the scenario is the following. Given is a set $S = \{x_1, \ldots, x_n\}$ of n elements and its partition into k disjoint subsets $S_1, \ldots, S_k$, that is,

$$S = \bigcup_{i=1}^{k} S_i \quad \text{and} \quad S_i \cap S_j = \emptyset \quad \text{for} \quad i \neq j.$$

Two operations are to be supported:

(i) Find(x): given an element $x \in S$, find the index of the (unique) subset $S_i \subseteq S$ to which x belongs, i.e., $x \in S_i$;

(ii) Union(S_i, S_j): merge the subsets S_i and S_j into a single subset and return a pointer to the merged set.

If the partition is given and static throughout the process, one could use a simple array R of integers to implement the Find operation, by defining

$$R[i] = j \quad \text{if and only if} \quad x_i \in S_j \quad \text{for } 1 \leq i \leq n, \ 1 \leq j \leq k.$$

This would enable a constant time evaluation of Find(x). A Union(i, j) request, however, would force a linear scan of the array, to change all i entries to j or vice versa, and would thus cost $\Omega(n)$.

To improve the time complexity of the Union command, one could think of representing each set S_i in the partition as a circular linked list with a sentinel element containing the index i of the subset. The lists can then be concatenated in time $O(1)$ as already mentioned in Section 2.4.1, but given an element x, one needs to follow pointers until getting to the sentinel element to retrieve the name of the set in a Find command, so the number of steps may be the length of the subset, which could be $\Omega(n)$.

This dilemma should remind a similar one of the beginning of Section 4.1, concerning the efficient implementation of a data structure supporting both efficient searches and updates. The compromise there was to pass to a tree structure, and a similar idea will be useful also for the present case.

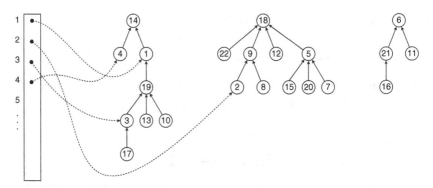

Figure 8.1. Representing disjoint sets by rooted trees.

8.2.1 Representing a Set by a Forest of Rooted Trees

Each element of the set S will be associated with a node in some tree. A set in the partition will be represented by a *rooted tree*, which is a tree in which every node has only one outgoing pointer, to its parent. Figure 8.1 displays three such rooted trees. Using again the notation v_x to design a node containing the value x, the root of the leftmost of the trees in Figure 8.1 is v_{14}, and it has two children, the leaf v_4 and v_1, which has a single child v_{19}. Note that the pointers, symbolized by the solid arrows, are pointing upward, so it is easy the reach the root from any node in the tree, but there is in fact no way of passing from a root to any of its offsprings.

We shall use the convention to name a set according to its root. The three trees in Figure 8.1 therefore represent the sets S_{14}, S_{18} and S_6. To implement the Find operation, an array of pointers is used, allowing direct access to each of the nodes. This array is shown on the left-hand side of the figure. For example, to process Find(x_3), the array is accessed at entry 3 that contains a pointer to the node v_3. From v_3, one follows then a series of parent pointers, passing through v_{19} and v_1, until reaching v_{14}, which is recognized as the root, because its outgoing pointer is NIL. The conclusion is that $x_3 \in S_{14}$. Similarly, one would get that $x_{20} \in S_{18}$ and that $x_6 \in S_6$, so there is no danger of confusing an element and the set it belongs to. The number of steps needed for Find(x) is thus related to the depth of x in its tree.

The merging of two sets for the Union(S_i, S_j) command is achieved in $O(1)$ time by letting one of the roots point to the other root. For example, for Union(S_{14}, S_{18}), one could set either

$$parent(v_{14}) \longleftarrow v_{18} \quad \text{or} \quad parent(v_{18}) \longleftarrow v_{14}. \qquad (8.2)$$

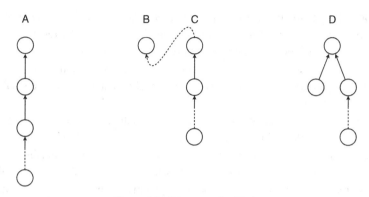

Figure 8.2. Worst case for Find.

Suppose the first possibility is chosen and that a Find(x_3) command is issued again. This time the pointer chain would not stop at v_{14}, but continue to the new root v_{18} of the merged set, resulting in the new conclusion that $x_3 \in S_{18}$.

It should be noted that we restrict our attention here only to the Union and Find commands, and shall not deal with other operations like inserting or deleting nodes into one of the trees. We may therefore assume that the given form of a tree has been achieved by a series of Union operations, where initially the partition of the set S was into n singletons $\{x_1\}, \ldots, \{x_n\}$. A second observation is that our discussion in terms of trees is for convenience only, and that the forest may well be represented simply by an array P of parent indices. For example, the array for the forest of Figure 8.1 would be

1	2	3	4	5	6	7	8	9	$\cdots$	17	18	19	20	21	22
14	9	19	14	18	0	5	9	18	$\cdots$	3	0	1	5	6	18

with the NIL pointer represented by the value 0, for example for $P[6]$.

So far, the solution suggested by these rooted trees does not seem satisfactory. While Union can be performed in $O(1)$, Find might require $\Omega(n)$, so this does not improve on our previous attempts. There is, however, still a degree of freedom that has not been exploited: there are two possible choices in (8.2) for merging two sets, and we might take advantage of that.

To see how the two ways of merging two trees can influence the depth of the merged tree, consider the tree labeled A in Figure 8.2, representing a tree of depth $m - 1$ with m nodes, which is the worst possible form in this context. There is only one way of getting such a tree by Union operations: the last step must have been the merging of a single node, like the tree labeled B, with a tree of depth $m - 2$, like the tree labeled C. Moreover, the Union must have been performed by letting the root of C point to that of B, as indicated by the broken line arrow in the figure. Had we chosen to let B point to C, the resulting tree would be like the one labeled D, and not A.

This leads to the intuition that to avoid degenerated trees and thereby restrict the depth of the trees, one should prefer, in the Union steps, to let the smaller tree point to the larger one.

The question is then, how should one define which of two trees is the smaller one? Two plausible definitions come to mind: referring to the depth or to the number of nodes. That these are not equivalent can be seen by inspecting again the trees of Figure 8.1. The left tree S_{14} has 8 nodes and depth 4, whereas the middle tree S_{18} has 10, thus more nodes, but is only of depth 2. So how should we decide to perform the merge? Since the purpose is to restrict the depth of the trees, it seems natural to take the depth as criterion for smallness. We shall, however, do exactly the opposite.

The total number of steps to be performed depends obviously on which elements will be searched for. Lacking any reasonable model for these elements, we shall assume that all the nodes will appear once in a Find command, and use the total number of steps in these n Find operations as comparative measure.

Let us compare the two possibilities for merging the leftmost trees of Figure 8.1. If v_{18} will point to v_{14}, the depth of the merged tree will remain 4 as for S_{14}, a Find on any of the 8 nodes of S_{14} will take the same number of steps as it did before the merge, but a Find for any of the 10 nodes of S_{18} will require one more step than before, as the search will have to traverse the additional pointer from v_{18} to v_{14}. The increase caused by the merge is thus of 10 steps. On the other hand, if v_{14} will point to v_{18}, the depth of the merged tree will become 5, a Find on any of the 10 nodes of S_{18} will take the same number of steps as it did before, but a Find for any of the 8 nodes of S_{14} will require an additional step, giving together a total increase of just 8.

The simple explanation for this fact is that the depth of a tree may be determined by a single leaf on the lowest level, while the complexity of applying Find should depend on the levels of all the nodes, according to our model. The conclusion is that when applying Union, the smaller tree in terms of number of nodes should point to the larger one.

8.2.2 Depth of Trees in Union-Find Forests

Even though the criterion for deciding how to merge the trees is based on the number of their nodes, we are still interested in a bound on the depths of the resulting trees, since this is also a bound on the complexity of the Find operation. Fortunately, a precise bound can be derived.

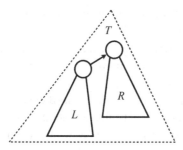

Figure 8.3. Schematic of inductive step.

Theorem 8.1. If the Union operations are implemented by letting the tree with the smaller number of nodes point to the tree with the larger number of nodes, then the depth of a tree with m nodes is at most $\lfloor \log_2 m \rfloor$.

To get a logarithmic depth might have been expected, but why should the base of the logarithm be 2? The $\log_2 n$ depth we encountered earlier was due to the fact that the trees were binary; m-ary trees, like the B-trees of Chapter 6, had a depth of $O(\log_m n)$. Our rooted trees are not binary, and in fact, there is no limit on the number of children a node can have, since no explicit pointer to the children is kept. So what is the explanation of the base 2 of the logarithm? We shall return to this question after the proof.

We saw already in Section 5.2 that a theorem with such a formulation might be hard to prove, which is why it will be convenient to formulate another, equivalent, theorem, by changing our point of view. Instead of assuming the number of nodes is given and deriving an upper bound on the depth, we assume that the depth is given and derive a lower bound on the number of nodes.

Theorem 8.1′. If the Union operations are implemented as described earlier, then the number of nodes in a tree of depth h is at least 2^h.

Proof By induction on the depth h. For each depth, let us consider the *minimal* tree, defined as a tree with smallest number of nodes among all trees attaining this depth. This is no real restriction, because if one shows a lower bound on the number of nodes for a minimal tree, this bound holds even more so for nonminimal trees of the same depth.

For $h = 0$, the only possible tree consists of the root alone, like the tree labeled B in Figure 8.2. Indeed, it has $2^0 = 1$ node. This is enough to prove the basis of the induction. Just for the exercise, let us also check the case $h = 1$. A tree of depth 1 must have at least one node on level 1, and one (the root) on level 0, like the leftmost tree in Figure 4.3. The number of its nodes is $2^1 = 2$.

Assume now the truth of the statement up to depth $h - 1$ and let us show it for h. Let T be a minimal tree of depth h. Since any tree is the result of a Union of two other trees, let us call L and R the two trees merged to yield T. More precisely, we assume that as a result of the Union, the root of L points to that of R. as depicted in Figure 8.3.

The depth of T being h, this can be obtained either if R itself is already of depth h, or if L has depth $h - 1$. The first possibility has to be ruled out: R being a subtree of T, it has obviously less nodes, contradicting the assumption that T is minimal. It follows that the depth of L must be $h - 1$, so the inductive assumption can be applied to yield $|L| \geq 2^{h-1}$, where $|X|$ denotes the number of nodes in a tree X.

What is the depth of R? If it were $h - 1$, we could reach the desired conclusion, but R can be much more shallow. Nevertheless, we can bound its size, not by the inductive hypothesis, but by the rules of the Union algorithm. Since L points to R, the latter must have at least as many nodes as the former.

Summarizing, given any tree G of depth h, we get

$$|G| \geq |T| = |L| + |R| \geq |L| + |L| \geq 2^{h-1} + 2^{h-1} = 2^h, \qquad (8.3)$$

where the first inequality is due to the minimality of T, the second to the rules of Union, and the third to the inductive assumption. ∎

The proof also solves the riddle posed earlier about the base 2 of the logarithm. Although the unified trees are not necessarily binary, the Union operation itself is a binary operation in the sense that it is always applied on a pair of trees. This implied the doubling of the number of nodes with each new level, as shown in eq. (8.3).

Note that a consequence of the theorem is that not all the shapes of trees are possible. In particular, the leftmost tree of Figure 8.1 cannot be obtained by the given Union commands, because with depth 4, it would need at least 16 nodes. The smallest tree of depth 2 cannot consist just of a chain of 3 nodes, as tree A of Figure 8.2, but needs at least 4 nodes, as the rightmost tree in Figure 8.1.

There is still an open question: how do we know the size of each tree? A tree is identified by its root, but there are no outgoing pointers from there. Even if there were, it would not be reasonable to evaluate the size on the fly. The solution is to keep track of the sizes of the trees from the beginning. A field $size(x)$ will be added to each node, indicating the number of nodes (including itself) in the (sub)tree rooted by x. Initially, all the sets are singletons and all sizes are 1. In a Union, when x will be set to point to y, the only node for which the size field needs an update is the root y of the unified tree, for which

$$size(y) = size(y) + size(x).$$

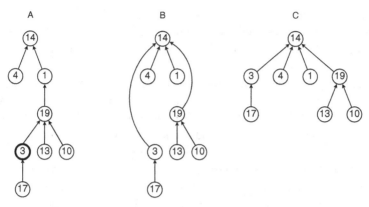

Figure 8.4. Path compression.

8.2.3 Path Compression

The performance of the Find can be improved at almost no cost with the following simple amendment, known as *path compression*. Consider the tree labeled A of Figure 8.4 and suppose the command to be executed is Find(x_3) as before, which leads us to the emphasized node in the tree. The algorithm inspects then all the nodes on the path from v_3 to the root v_{14}. If there is subsequently another Find(x_3) command, does it make sense to traverse the same path again, including v_{19} and v_1?

In binary search trees we would like to have as many nodes as possible close to the root, but the space there is limited; hence, most of the nodes have to be at logarithmic depth, which implies a logarithmic search time. However for the special trees of this chapter, the shape of the tree is not useful in itself, but rather a byproduct of the way a Union is performed. From the point of view of optimizing the Find, it would be preferable if all the elements in a tree would directly point to the root, which is possible since there are no limitations on incoming edges.

The idea is thus to take advantage of the fact that the Find command visits a chain of nodes, by letting all these nodes ultimately point to the root of the tree. The tree labeled B of Figure 8.4 shows the modified tree, in which v_3 and v_{19} point directly to the root v_{14} (v_1 is also on the path, but its parent pointer was already to the root). The tree labeled C is the same tree, but redrawn in the more standard way to emphasize how path compression will result in a tendency of the trees to get flatter.

For any Find(v) command, there is hardly any loss caused by the additional pointer updates, but there is a large potential gain, not only for the nodes on the path from v to the root, but also for all the nodes in the subtrees rooted at any of the nodes on this path. For the preceding example, if one searches for v_{17} after the search for v_3, the root will be reached by 2 parent-pointers, instead of 4 without path compression.

Evaluating the depth of the trees for this case is not a simple task. It clearly depends on which elements have participated in a Find command, so the worst case did not change. On the other hand, in the long run, all the trees might end up with depth 1, if there are enough Find queries. We give here the complexity of the procedure without proof or details: using an appropriate model, the *average* cost of a Find on a set of n elements will be $O(\log^* n)$. The function $\log^*$ (also called iterative logarithm or log star) is the number of times the function $\log_2$ can be applied iteratively until the result is ≤ 1. For example, reading right to left,

$$0.54 = \log_2(1.45 = \log_2(2.73 = \log_2(6.64 = \log_2(100))))$$

thus $\log^*(100) = 4$. This function grows extremely slowly: the lowest argument for which $\log^*$ will be 5 is $2^{16} = 65536$, and it will stay at value 5 for all reasonable numbers (up to 2^{65536}). For any practical use, we can thus consider $\log^* n$ as being a constant, even though theoretically, it tends to ∞.

The following table summarizes the complexities of applying a single Union-Find operation on a set of n elements. The values correspond to worst cases, except the Find in the last line:

	Union	Find	
Simple array	$O(n)$	$O(1)$	
Linear linked list	$O(1)$	$O(n)$	
Rooted trees	$O(1)$	$O(n)$	
Smaller tree pointing to larger	$O(1)$	$O(\log n)$	
With path compression	$O(1)$	$O(\log^* n)$	average

8.2.4 Formal Algorithms

The formal Union-Find algorithms, including all the variants mentioned earlier, are given in Figure 8.5.

It uses the array implementation of the trees, so the parameters are indices in $\{1, \ldots, n\}$ rather than nodes or sets. The field $size(x)$ of a node v_x is implemented here as an additional array $size[]$. The first while loop in Find reaches the root of the tree. At the end of this loop, the index of the root is stored in y. The second loop implements path compression and traverses again the path from v_x to v_y, letting each node now point directly to the root.

Union(v, w)   Find(x)
    if *size*[*v*] < *size*[*w*] then   *y* ⟵ *x*
        P[*v*] ⟵ *w*   while *P*[*y*] ≠ 0 do
        size[*w*] ⟵ *size*[*w*] + *size*[*v*]   *y* ⟵ *P*[*y*]
        return *w*   while *P*[*x*] ≠ *y* do
    else   *z* ⟵ *x*
        P[*w*] ⟵ *v*   *x* ⟵ *P*[*x*]
        size[*v*] ⟵ *size*[*v*] + *size*[*w*]   *P*[*z*] ⟵ *y*
        return *v*   return *y*

Figure 8.5. Formal Union-Find algorithms.

Exercises

8.1 The game of *Hex* is played on a honeycomb like board, representing a
2-dimensional matrix of $n \times n$ hexagonal cells. Two cells are considered
adjacent if the hexagons share a common side. The players B and W alter-
nate to pick at each turn one of the free (gray) cells, which is then colored
black, respectively white. The winner is the first to build a sequence of adjacent cells of the same color that connects opposing edges of the matrix, for
example NW to SE for B, or NE to SW for W. A possible situation after 9
turns for each of B and W is shown in Figure 8.6.

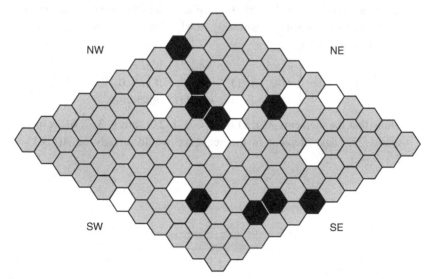

Figure 8.6. The game of Hex, with $n = 11$.

Show how to implement a program that checks after each turn whether
the last move was a winning one.

8.2 The Union algorithm sets the smaller tree as a subtree of the larger one, where *small* and *large* are defined in terms of the number of nodes. If instead *small* and *large* are defined in terms of the depths of the trees, how will this affect the bound on the depths of all the trees in the forest?

8.3 The Minimum Spanning Tree problem for a graph $G = (V, E)$ with weights $w(x, y)$ on its edges $(x, y) \in E$ has been presented in Section 3.1.1. One of the algorithms solving it is due to J. B. Kruskal. The edges are first sorted into nonincreasing order according to their weights, and the tree T is initially empty. The edges are then considered in the given order, and an edge is adjoined to T unless it closes a cycle. The algorithm stops when there are $|V| - 1$ edges in T.

(a) What is the complexity of Kruskal's algorithm when BFS or DFS is used to check whether an edge closes a cycle?

(b) What is the complexity when Union-Find is used instead?

(c) What is the connection between the trees in the Union-Find forest and those forming the connected components of T at each stage of Kruskal's algorithm?

8.4 The expected depth of the trees when path compression is used has been stated previously to be bounded by $\log^* n$. Another analysis shows that the bound is $\alpha(n) = A^{-1}(n, n)$, which is known as the *Inverse-Ackermann* function, which also grows extremely slowly. One of the definitions of Ackermann's function is

$$A(m, n) = \begin{cases} n + 1 & \text{if } m = 0, \\ A(m - 1, 1) & \text{if } m > 0 \land n = 0, \\ A(m - 1, A(m, n - 1)) & \text{otherwise.} \end{cases}$$

Show that the elements $A(n, n)$ for $n = 0, 1, 2, 3$, are 1, 3, 7, 61, respectively. The next element in the sequence would already be $A(4, 4) = 2^{2^{65636}} - 3$.

9

Hash Tables

9.1 Calculating instead of Comparing

In what we saw so far, the search time for an element could be reduced from $O(n)$ to $O(\log n)$, which is a significant improvement. However, even logarithmic time might be, for certain applications, too high a price to pay. Consider, for instance, a very large computer program, with thousands of variables. We sometimes write quite complicated arithmetic expressions, involving many of these variables, and having to search for the values of each of them may impair the execution time.

We can get faster access by changing the approach altogether. In previous chapters, an element x was sought for by comparing its value to that of some elements stored in a list or a tree, until x was found or could be declared as missing. The new approach is to access the data structure at an address which is not the result of a comparison, but which can be calculated by means of x alone.

The basic idea is not new and is familiar to everybody. Many institutions, like schools, stores, hospitals, or clubs, used to assign *membership numbers* to their students, clients, patients, or members. If a group had n adherents, these numbers were 1 to n, and information about member i was stored in a table T at entry $T[i]$. With the growing number of such organizations, it became unpractical to manage different indices for a single person, and it was preferred to use some official, unique, identification number, which is provided in many countries to each of their inhabitants as ID or Social Security number. These numbers need to be larger and consist generally of 8 to 10 digits.

It is obviously not reasonable to allocate a table with a number of entries of the order of 1 billion, only to get direct access to some n elements by using their ID numbers as index, when n may be a few hundred. The 8- to 10-digit ID number should thus be shortened. This has been realized by bank tellers long

ago, when they had to compile, by hand, a list of the check numbers for a batch
of checks: they do not use the full check numbers, but rather only their, say,
three rightmost digits, hoping that there are no clashes.

This simple idea has then been generalized as follows. We assume that the
identifiers of the elements, large numbers or character strings, are drawn from
some very large, or even infinite universe $\mathcal{U}$; we further consider a table T with
M entries, into which the information about the elements has to be stored. The
problem is to find an appropriate function

$$h : \mathcal{U} \longrightarrow \{0, 1, \ldots, M - 1\}$$

so that the element identified by X should be stored in T at $h(X)$. Additional
constraints on the function h are as follows:

(i) It should be easy to evaluate $h(X)$ for any X.
(ii) The values $h(X)$ should be evenly distributed over the possible table
entries.

If the first condition is not met, the evaluation of $h(X)$ might take longer than
the sequence of comparisons it was designed to replace. The second condition
is needed to assure that there are not too many collisions. Hoping that there will
be no collisions at all is not realistic: the universe $\mathcal{U}$ is often much larger than
the set $\{0, 1, \ldots, M - 1\}$, so the function h cannot be injective, and since we
have generally no control of which subset of $\mathcal{U}$ will be chosen, we shall have
to cope with pairs of different identifiers X and Y, such that $h(X) = h(Y)$.

The challenge is therefore to come up with a good compromise between
the two demands. If the choice of the function h is too simplistic, like in the
example of the bank teller, for which $h(X) = X \bmod 1000$, the distribution of
the $h(X)$ values can be strongly biased for certain applications. The problem
with considering only the last few digits is that all the other digits of X have
no influence on $h(X)$. This could give biased results for subsets of $\mathcal{U}$ in which
mostly these other digits vary. We would prefer a function for which every bit
in X is significant, and the resulting value should be obtained by reshuffling
all the input bits in some sophisticated way, that is nevertheless fast to implement. Such functions are therefore known under the name of *hashing* or *hash*
functions, and the tables storing elements at indices obtained by applying hash
functions are called *hash tables*.

Our study of hashing will first concentrate on possible functions, and then
deal with various strategies to handle the unavoidable collisions. We also
assume for the moment that elements may be added or searched for, but not
deleted from the table. Deletion is problematic for hashing, and we shall deal
with it later.

9.2 Hash Functions

The following is an example of a simple hash function, known as *Middle square method* and attributed to John von Neumann. Starting with a natural number $n > 0$, its hash value should fit into a table of size 2^m, for some given integer m, so that the index should consist of m bits. One can, of course, represent n in its standard binary form in $k = 1 + \lfloor \log_2 n \rfloor$ bits, and take a subset of m of these bits. Taking the rightmost $m = 3$ bits was the check number example, and any other proper subset would have the same flaw of not letting all the input bits influence the hash value. To overcome this, take first the square of n. If the binary form of n is $n = b_{k-1} \cdots b_2 b_1 b_0$, then the rightmost bit of n^2 is b_0^2. The next to rightmost bit is $b_1 b_0 \oplus b_0 b_1$, where $\oplus$ stands for addition modulo 2, and will always be 0. The closer the bit position i is getting to the middle of the $2k$ bits representing n^2, the more bits of the representation of n are involved in the determination of the bit at position i. The hash function will therefore be defined as the middle m bits of the $2k$ bits of n^2. Formally, let $\ell = k - \frac{m}{2}$ be the number of bits to be ignored at the right end of n^2, then

$$h(n) = \left(\lfloor n^2 / 2^\ell \rfloor \right) \bmod 2^m.$$

For example, consider $n = 1234567$ and $m = 16$ bits. The number of necessary bits to represent n is $k = 21$. Squaring n, one gets $n^2 = 1524155677489$, which is

0101100010110**1111011000001111**1101100110001

in binary. The decimal value of the emphasized middle 16 bits is 62991, so we conclude that $h(1234567) = 62991$. The middle square method has been suggested as a pseudo random number generator, but it fails many randomness tests and is not recommended. It is brought here only as example for the construction of hash functions.

The next example, taken from the data compression component of some operating system, will illustrate the choices in the design of a hashing function. The universe $\mathcal{U}$ consists of all the possible character pairs, and they are to be hashed into a table T with 2048 entries. An index into T is accordingly of length 11 bits, but, using the standard 8-bit ASCII representation for a character, the input consists of 16 bits. Figure 9.1 shows the evaluation of the hash function for the pair (Y, V).

The characters are first converted into their binary ASCII equivalents and then moved together, so that the overlapping part is of length 5 bits. Then some Boolean operation should be applied: an OR operation would produce too many 1-bits, and an AND operation would favor 0-bits, so a better choice seems to be

Y	0 1 0 1 1 0 0 1
V	0 1 0 1 0 1 1 0
h(YV)	0 1 0 1 0 0 1 1 1 1 0

Figure 9.1. Example of hashing two characters to 11 bits.

to apply XOR. The mathematical definition is thus

$$h(x, y) = (8 \times x) \text{ XOR } y,$$

where the multiplication by 8 simulates a left shift of 3 bits.

While at first sight this function seems to fulfill all the constraints, applying it to an input file consisting mainly of textual data gives disastrous results: practically all the items are then squeezed into just one quarter of the table, between indices 512 and 1023. The reason for this strange behavior is that the ASCII representations of most printable characters, including all lower and upper case letters, start with 01 in their two leftmost bits. Since the overlapping part of the two bit-strings in the definition of the hash function h covers only the five rightmost bits of the first parameter, most of the resulting 11-bit values will remain with this 01 bit-pattern in their two leftmost bits, as seen in the example of Figure 9.1.

To rectify this deficiency, the bit-strings are cyclically shifted so as to move the leading 01 bits to the overlapping part; they then get a chance to be modified by the XOR operation. Figure 9.2 shows the result of this amended function, in which the first parameter is cyclically shifted left by 4 bits, and the second parameter by 5 bits. The previously leading 01 bits are emphasized to show their new positions.

The mathematical definition of the modified function is

$$h(x, y) = \Big(\big((x \bmod 16) + \lfloor x/16 \rfloor \big) \times 8 \Big) \text{ XOR } \big((y \bmod 32) + \lfloor y/32 \rfloor \big).$$

The resulting function takes only slightly more time to be evaluated, as a cyclic shift is a basic operation in assembly languages, but the distribution of the values over the possible table entries will be much more uniform, even for purely textual input.

The simplest way of adapting the range of a hash function to fit a given table size M is to use the remainder function $h(X) = X \bmod M$, returning

Y	1 0 0 1 0 **1** 0 1
V	1 1 0 **0** 1 0 1 0
h(YV)	1 0 0 0 1 1 0 0 0 1 0

Figure 9.2. Example of improved hashing of two characters to 11 bits.

values in the range $[0, 1, \ldots, M - 1]$. We saw already that the usefulness of
such a function may depend on the value of M. For instance, as explained
earlier, $M = 1000$ is not a good choice. For similar reasons, $M = 1024$ is not
much better: even if there is no obvious connection between the digits of X
and $h(X) = X \bmod 1024$, notice that $1024 = 2^{10}$ is a power of 2, so if X is
given in binary, $h(X)$ is again just the extraction of the 10 rightmost bits.
Returning to the previous example, the binary representation of $X = 1234567$
is 100101101011010000111, and that of $X \bmod 1024 = 647$ is 010000111.

Actually, M does not need to be a power of any number to yield a skewed
distribution for certain input sequences. If M is even, then every even input
value X would imply that $X \bmod M$ is even. So if all the elements to be hashed
happen to be even, half of the hash table, the entries with odd indices, would
be empty! If M is a multiple of 3, a similar bias can be observed, and in fact, M
should not be chosen as a multiple of 2, or 3, or 5, or any other smaller constant.
This restricts the potential choices for M only to numbers that are not multiples
of any others – that is, M should be a prime number.

Background Concept: Prime Numbers

A *prime number* is an integer larger than 1 that is divisible only by 1 and
by itself. Many properties of prime numbers were known already to the
Ancient Greek, but only in the last 100 years or so has their usefulness
been discovered for many applications, in particular in cryptography. A
natural number that is not prime is called *composite*.

There are infinitely many prime numbers, and the number of prime
numbers up to n is approximately $\frac{n}{\ln n}$. The difference between consecutive prime numbers can become arbitrarily large, but can be as small as
2, for example, for 99989 and 99991. Such pairs are called *twin primes*,
and it is not known whether there are infinitely many of them.

The simplest way to check if a number p is prime is by trying to divide
it by smaller primes 2, 3, 5, up to $\sqrt{p}$. If no divisor has been found, then
p must be prime. This procedure is, however, not feasible for the large
primes, spanning hundreds of bits, used in cryptographic applications. To
check whether $n = 2^{400} - 3$ is prime (it is not!), one would need about 2^{200}
divisions, which requires billions of CPU-years even on the most powerful
computers. Fortunately, there are *probabilistic algorithms* allowing to test
the primality of a number in logarithmic time.

The suggested algorithm is therefore to choose a prime number M which
is close to the size we intended to allocate to the hash table, and to use as

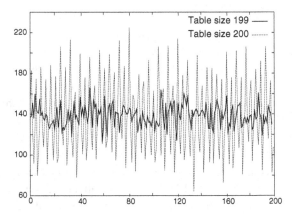

Figure 9.3. Distribution of hash values for King James Bible.

hash function

$$h(X) = X \bmod M.$$

This is an interesting case of a data structure for which it might be worth not to exploit all the available memory to get a better performance. For example, if there is enough space for 1000 entries, it may be better to prefer $M = 997$.

The following test shows the superiority of a prime sized hash table. The King James Version of the English Bible is used as input, viewing it as a sequence of blocks of length 4 characters each. There are 813352 such blocks B, of which 27590 are different ones, and using the ASCII representation of each character, each block is considered representing a 4-byte = 32 bit integer. The hash functions are $B \bmod 200$ and $B \bmod 199$. Figure 9.3 plots the number of hashes to entry i, for $0 \le i < 200$, for both functions.

The solid line corresponds to the prime value $M = 199$, and can be seen fluctuating around the expected value $27590/199 = 139$. The lighter, broken, line corresponds to the nonprime size $M = 200$: the fluctuations are much more accentuated, and there are peaks at regular intervals of size 8, both above and below the average middle line. Such regular patterns are contradicting the expected uniformity.

And what if the element to be hashed is not a number, but a character string? This may happen, as in the example of variable names in a large computer program. There is an obvious way to convert a character string into an integer, using a standard encoding of the characters, like ASCII. The C Programming language even identifies characters with small integers from 0 to 255. To get the number N corresponding to a character string S, just concatenate the ASCII encodings of the individual characters of S and consider the resulting bit-string as the binary representation of N. For example, for $S = \text{AB}$, we have $\text{ASCII}(\text{A}) = 65 = 01000001$ and $\text{ASCII}(\text{B}) = 66 = 01000010$; the binary representation of N is thus 0100000101000010, so $N = 16706$.

This works for input strings of any length, just that the numbers to be manipulated may get out of control. Taking, for instance, the string A-LONG-EXAMPLE-STRING as input, the corresponding integer N would be 168 bits long and correspond, in decimal notation, to

$$95\,256\,212\,776\,338\,074\,265\,619\,361\,588\,642\,035\,558\,695\,416\,974\,919.$$

Most programming languages are not able to process such numbers with their standard tools. What comes to our rescue are the handy properties of modular arithmetic.

Background Concept: Modular Arithmetic
Let p be a fixed integer larger than 1 we shall call the *modulus*. For any natural number n, $n \bmod p$ is defined as the remainder of the division of n by p, that is $n \bmod p = r$ if $0 \le r < n$ and n can be written as $n = kp + r$ for some integer k. As the modulus is assumed to be fixed, we may abbreviate the notation by setting $\bar{n} = n \bmod p$, and call it the *modulo* function. The following properties follow directly from this definition,

First note that $\bar{n} = \bar{\bar{n}}$, implying that the modulo function can be applied once or more times without changing the result. It follows that for all integers n and m,

$$\overline{n + m} = \overline{\bar{n} + \bar{m}} \quad \text{and} \quad \overline{n \times m} = \overline{\bar{n} \times \bar{m}},$$

which enables the decomposition of one operation on large arguments into several operations on smaller ones. For example, for $p = 13$, let us calculate $\overline{29 \times 72} = \overline{2088}$. Most of us will find it difficult to multiply these number in their heads, and even more so to divide the result by 13 to find the remainder. Applying the modulo repeatedly simplifies this task to

$$\overline{29 \times 72} = \overline{3 \times 7} = \overline{21} = 8,$$

for the evaluation of which we need no paper or pencil.

For the evaluation of a large integer, originating from a character string, modulo p, suppose the string is $S = c_t c_{t-1} \cdots c_2 c_1 c_0$, where the c_i are characters we shall identify with numbers between 0 and 255, like in C. The numerical value N of S can be written as

$$N = c_t 256^t + c_{t-1} 256^{t-1} + \cdots + c_2 256^2 + c_1 256 + c_0.$$

By *Horner's rule*, this can be rewritten as

$$N = \big(\cdots ((c_t 256 + c_{t-1})256 + c_{t-2})256 + \cdots \big)256 + c_0.$$

When evaluating $\overline{N}$, we may apply the modulo function on each of the nested parentheses, yielding

$$\overline{N} = \big(\cdots \overline{(\overline{(c_t 256 + c_{t-1})}256 + c_{t-2})256} + \cdots \big)256 + c_0,$$

so that at no stage of the calculation does the current value exceed p^2. Returning to the string A-LONG-EXAMPLE-STRING and choosing the modulus as the prime number $p = 2^{16} - 39 = 65497$, we get that

$$\overline{N} = \big(\cdots \overline{((65 \cdot 256 + 45)256 + 76)256} + \cdots \big)256 + 71 = 20450,$$

where all the operations could be performed with 32-bit integers. The general algorithm is given by

$$
\begin{array}{l}
\underline{N \text{ modulo } p} \\
\quad a \longleftarrow 0 \\
\quad \text{for } i \leftarrow t \text{ to } 0 \text{ step } -1 \\
\quad\quad a \longleftarrow (a \times 256 + c_i) \bmod p \\
\quad \text{return } a
\end{array}
$$

9.3 Handling Collisions

For a small enough set of arguments, it may be possible to model a custom tailored hash function that is injective and thus avoids any collision. Refer, for example, to the first 80 digits of π following the decimal point, and consider them as a sequence of 20 four-digit numbers that we wish to hash into a table of size 33, filling the table only up to about 60%, so there is ample space. The numbers are

$$1415, 9265, 3589, 7932, 3846, 2643, 3832, 7950, 2884, 1971,$$

$$6939, 9375, 1058, 2097, 4944, 5923, 0781, 6406, 2862, 0899.$$

It may take a while and require several trial and error iterations, but an appropriate injective function can certainly be found. Here is a possible one: denote the four digits of a given number by m, c, x and i, from left to right, then

$$h(mcxi) = \left(3m + \left\lfloor \frac{c}{3} \right\rfloor + \left\lfloor \frac{7xi}{4} \right\rfloor + \left(x + i = c\right)\right) \bmod 33.$$

The sequence of the hash values for the preceding numbers is then

$$12, \quad 13, \quad 4, \quad 1, \quad 20, \quad 29, \quad 21, \quad 24, \quad 31, \quad 18,$$

$$2, \quad 23, \quad 7, \quad 17, \quad 10, \quad 28, \quad 16, \quad 19, \quad 30, \quad 11.$$

Suppose, however, that we would like to extend the sequence to include also the following four-digit number of the digits of π, which is 8628. Applying h gives $h(8628) = 21$, which collides with $h(3832)$. To repair this, the whole work of the hash function design has to be restarted from scratch. Just choosing the function at random will most probably not help: the number of functions from a set of size 21 to a set of size 33 is 33^{21}, and the number of one-to-one functions for such sets is $\frac{33!}{12!}$. The probability of choosing an injective function, by selecting arbitrarily one of the possible functions, is the ratio of these numbers, which is 0.0002.

We have generally no a priori knowledge about the distribution of the elements to be stored in a hash table, but even if they are chosen at random from a much larger set, there are high chances that some of the numbers may cause a conflict, as illustrated by the following famous fact.

Background Concept: The Birthday Paradox

What is the probability that in a random group of 23 people, there are at least two which share the same birthday? Most of us would estimate it to be very low, yet it can be shown to be larger than $\frac{1}{2}$, that is, it is more likely to occur than not. This seems to be so surprising that many are reluctant to accept it, even after having seen the mathematical proof, which explains it being named a paradox.

Consider the complementing event of all the people in a group having different birthdays. More generally, a set of n elements is given, from which an element should be drawn at random k times, and we ask what the probability would be that all k elements will be different.

The probability for the second element not to be equal to the first is $\frac{n-1}{n}$. The probability for the third element to be different from both the first and the second is $\frac{n-2}{n}$, and in general, the probability of the event E_i, defined as the ith element being different from the preceding ones, is $\frac{n-i+1}{n}$. All the events $E_2, \ldots, E_k$ should occur simultaneously, and since they are mutually independent, the probability of all k elements being different is

$$\left(\frac{n-1}{n}\right)\left(\frac{n-2}{n}\right)\cdots\left(\frac{n-k+1}{n}\right)=\prod_{i=1}^{k-1}\left(1-\frac{i}{n}\right). \qquad (9.1)$$

This is a product of factors that all seem close to 1, and if there are just a few factors, the product would still be close to 1. But in fact, the factors are slowly decreasing, while their number grows. There will thus be an index for which the product will not be so close to 1 any more. More formally, let us just take the last $\frac{k}{2}$ factors. Each of the left out factors being smaller than 1, the product will increase:

$$\prod_{i=1}^{k-1}\left(1-\frac{i}{n}\right)<\prod_{i=k/2}^{k-1}\left(1-\frac{i}{n}\right)<\prod_{i=k/2}^{k-1}\left(1-\frac{k/2}{n}\right)=\left(1-\frac{k/2}{n}\right)^{k/2}.$$

Substituting $k=2\sqrt{n}$, we get

$$\left(1-\frac{1}{\sqrt{n}}\right)^{\sqrt{n}}\xrightarrow[n\to\infty]{}\frac{1}{e}=0.368.$$

This shows that it suffices to choose randomly just of the order of $\sqrt{n}$ elements out on n, for large enough n, to get already collisions with probability larger than $\frac{1}{2}$. In particular, for $n=365$ and $k=23$, the exact value of the product in (9.1) is 0.493, so the probability of two people in a group of 23 having the same birthday is 0.507. For a group of 40 people, it would already be 0.891.

As example, consider the 25 first Nobel laureates, all those who got the price in the years 1901–1904. Among them, Élie Ducommun (Peace) and Svante Arrhenius (Chemistry) were both born on February 19. Moreover, Henri Becquerel (Physics) and Niels Ryberg Finsen (Medicine) shared a birthday on December 15.

The conclusion is that some strategy is needed resolving the case $h(X)=h(Y)$ for $X\neq Y$. One of the possibilities is to use the hash table as an array of size M for header elements, each pointing to a linked list. An element Y with $h(Y)=k$ will be appended at the end of the list headed by the kth element, as shown in Figure 9.4. To search for an element X, we first evaluate $\ell=h(X)$ and then search in the list headed by ℓ. In the worst case, all the elements might hash to the same location, but if the assumption of the even spread of the hash values holds, the average search time will just be $\frac{n}{M}$, where n is the number

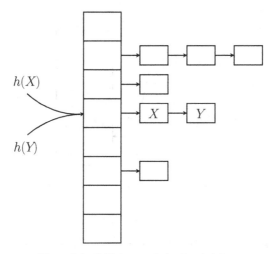

Figure 9.4. Collision resolution by chaining.

of elements to be inserted. If n and M are of the same order of magnitude, the average search time will be $O(1)$.

This approach is called *chaining* and has the advantage that the number of treated elements n might even exceed the size M of the table, so there is no need to have an exact estimate of n prior to the initialization of the hash table. However, for certain applications, one may wish to save the wasted space of the pointers, and prefer to store all the elements directly in the table itself. This can be achieved by the following methods, called *open addressing*.

The function $h(X)$ returns a value between 0 and $M - 1$ that can be used as an index into the hash table T. If the spot is empty, X will be stored in T at index $h(X)$. Refer to Figure 9.5 to see what to do in case another element Z hashes to the same value $h(Z) = h(X)$, and should therefore be stored in the same place. A similar situation arises when we arrive to our assigned seat in the cinema, but find it occupied. Our reaction then probably depends on the size of the occupant; if he seems considerably stronger than us, we rather find an alternative place to sit. Here, too, Z will just move, for example, forward, to the closest free table entry, leaping over a block of occupied ones, shown in gray in the figure. In the example of Figure 9.5, the next spot is also occupied, by Y, so Z can only be stored in the following one. If the bottom of the table is reached, consider the table as cyclic and continue from the top. This is easily implemented by indexing the table entries from 0 to $M - 1$ as shown, and incrementing the index by 1 modulo M during the search for an empty spot.

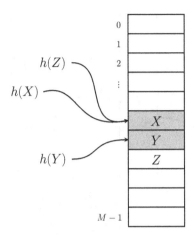

Figure 9.5. Open addressing using following empty location.

This works fine as long as only a small part of the table entries is used. When the table starts to fill up, the occupied cells will tend to form clusters. The problem is that the larger the cluster, the higher the probability of a new element being hashed into one of its locations, so the higher the probability of this specific cluster getting even larger – this contradicts the requested uniform spread of the values.

A better idea thus seems to be looking for an empty cell in jumps of size k, for some fixed number $k > 1$ of table entries. If k is chosen prime to M, that is, if the greatest common divisor of k and M, GCD(k, M), is 1, then this jump policy will get us back to the starting point only after having visited all the entries in the table. This is yet another incentive to choose M as a prime number, since then any jump size k is prime to M, so every k is appropriate. In the example of Figure 9.6, $M = 13$ and $k = 5$. Since $h(Z) = 5$ is occupied by X, the current index is repeatedly increased by k. The sequence of the checked indices, called the *probe sequence*, is 5, 10, 15 mod $M = 2$, and finally 7. This is the first empty location in the order imposed by the probe sequence, so Z will be stored there.

The truth is, that this last change is only a cosmetic one: there will still be clusters just as before, they might only be harder to detect. To see this, consider a probe sequence visiting the entire table. For the example with $M - 13$ and $k = 5$, one such sequence could be 5, 10, 2, 7, 12, 4, 9, 1, 6, 11, 3, 8, 0. This is in fact a permutation of the table indices 0 to $M - 1$, and if we would rearrange the table entries in the order given by this permutation, the same clustering effect we observed earlier would also be evident here.

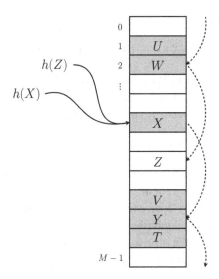

Figure 9.6. Open addressing using a probe sequence in jumps of size k.

To avoid these clusters, one can replace the fixed jump size k used in the case of a collision, by one which also depends on the element to be inserted. In fact, this suggests using two independent hash functions $h_1(X)$ and $h_2(X)$, which is why the method is called *double hashing*. The first attempt is to store X at the address

$$\ell \longleftarrow h_1(X).$$

If this entry is occupied, a jump size is defined by

$$k \longleftarrow h_2(X),$$

such that $1 \leq k < M$. The following attempts to store X are then, in order, at addresses

$$(\ell + k) \bmod M, \quad (\ell + 2k) \bmod M, \quad (\ell + 3k) \bmod M, \dots,$$

until an empty location $(\ell + rk) \bmod M$ is found at the $(r + 1)$st index of the probe sequence. The search for an element X is done accordingly. One first checks whether X is stored at $h_1(X)$, and if not, one defines k as $h_2(X)$ and checks at addresses $h_1(X) + ik$, for $i = 1, 2, , \dots$, until X is found or an empty location is encountered. In the latter case, the conclusion is that X is not in the table.

What would be a good choice for a second hash function $h_2(X)$? The requested range of values is between 1 and $M - 1$ (a jump size of 0 or M would results in a probe sequence of identical indices), so

$$h_2(X) \longleftarrow 1 + X \bmod (M - 1)$$

seems to be appropriate. But M has been chosen to be prime, thus $M - 1$ will be even, and we saw already that the function $h(X) = X \bmod Q$, for a composite number Q, is not recommended. This leads to the suggestion of using

$$h_2(X) \longleftarrow 1 + X \bmod M',$$

where M' is the largest prime smaller than M. The largest possible range for $h_2(X)$ will then be obtained for $M' = M - 2$. Indeed, such pairs of *twin* prime numbers, differing only by 2, do exist, as mentioned earlier.

Summarizing, to apply double hashing, we first choose a pair of twin primes M and $M - 2$, close to the size we wish to allocate for the hash table. The functions can then be defined as

$$h_1(X) \longleftarrow X \bmod M$$
$$h_2(X) \longleftarrow 1 + X \bmod (M - 2).$$

9.4 Analysis of Uniform Hashing

The idea of double hashing can be extended to the use of three, four, or more hashing functions. Ultimately, this leads to a theoretical method, called *uniform hashing*, in which the number of independent different functions used, $f_1, f_2, f_3, \ldots$, is not bounded. In practice, the two functions used in double hashing give already satisfying results, and the additional overhead of using more hash functions is not worth their marginal expected improvement. Nevertheless, we shall use uniform hashing as a theoretical model to evaluate the performance of double hashing, which has been shown to give very similar results, though using a more involved analysis.

Consider then an infinite sequence of hash functions $f_i(X)$, for $i \geq 1$. We assume that they all behave well, that is,

$$\forall i \geq 1 \quad \forall j \in \{0, \ldots, M - 1\} \qquad \mathsf{Prob}\big(f_i(X) = j\big) = \frac{1}{M},$$

and that they are mutually independent. Deviating from the notation used earlier, for which $h_1(X)$ was an address in a table of size M, and $h_2(X)$ was a leap size, we shall now adopt a more symmetric definition, in which all the $f_i(X)$ are possible addresses in the table, so that in fact $f_1(X), f_2(X), f_3(X), \ldots$ is the probe sequence for X. The insertion algorithm is accordingly to try the locations $f_i(X)$ in order, until the first empty space is found. This also explains why infinitely many functions are needed, and not just M: there is a (low) probability that $f_1(X) = f_2(X) = \cdots$, so one cannot assure that all the table entries have been checked, for any finite sequence of tests.

The quantities to be evaluated are the numbers of trials needed to insert a new element or to search for an element in the table. The analysis will be based on the following observations.

(i) A first observation is that the number of trials needed to insert some element X is equal to the number of trials to find X in subsequent searches. Moreover, even the sequences of comparisons will be identical, and they are a prefix of the probe sequence of X.

(ii) The number of collisions during an insertion depends on the number of elements already stored in the table. When the table is almost empty, there are good chances to find an empty spot already at the first trial. However, when the table is almost full, many more comparisons might be needed to get to an entry that is not yet occupied. If there are already n elements stored in the hash table, define

$$\alpha = \frac{n}{M}$$

as the *load factor* of the table. We expect the number of trials for insertion to be a function of α, where $0 \leq \alpha < 1$.

(iii) There is a difference between a successful and an unsuccessful search. An unsuccessful search is equivalent to the insertion of a new element. The number of trials is thus equal to the number of trials for insertion at the current load factor α. For a successful search, however, the number depends on when the given element has been inserted, and does *not* depend on the number of elements stored in the table at the time of the search. This is quite different from what we saw for search trees in Chapters 4, 5, and 6!

9.4.1 Insertion

Define C_n, for $0 \leq n \leq M$, as a random variable representing the number of comparisons needed to insert an element into the hash table in which n elements are already stored. Theoretically, C_n can be 1, or 2, or in fact any number, since the number of collisions is not necessarily bounded. We are interested in the mean value, or *expectation*, of C_n, usually denoted by $E(C_n)$. By definition, this expected value is the weighted sum of the possible values the random variable

C_n can assume, where the weights are the probabilities, i.e.,

$$E(C_n) = \sum_{i=1}^{\infty} i \, \text{Prob}(C_n = i).$$

Abbreviating $\text{Prob}(C_n = i)$ by p_i, and repeating the summation technique, used in the analysis of Heapify in Chapter 7, of writing a summation in rows and summing then by columns, we get

$$E(C_n) = \sum_{i=1}^{\infty} i \, p_i = \quad p_1$$
$$+ \, p_2 + p_2$$
$$+ \, p_3 + p_3 + p_3$$
$$+ \quad \cdots .$$

The first column of this infinite triangle is just $\sum_{i=1}^{\infty} p_i = 1$, the second column is $\sum_{i=2}^{\infty} p_i = \text{Prob}(C_n \geq 2)$, etc., yielding

$$E(C_n) = \sum_{i=1}^{\infty} \text{Prob}(C_n \geq i).$$

But the event $C_n \geq 2$ means that there has been a collision in the first trial, and this event occurs with probability α. The event $C_n \geq 3$ means that there were collisions both in the first and the second locations, so the probability of the event is α^2, where we have used the assumption that f_1 and f_2 are independent. In general, we get that the ith term will be α^i, so that

$$E(C_n) = 1 + \alpha + \alpha^2 + \alpha^3 + \cdots .$$

Background Concept: Infinite and Finite Summations

In the analysis of algorithms, one often encounters summations that are not given explicitly, but rather using an ellipsis ($\cdots$) from which a general term is supposed to be inferred. The following technique might be useful for getting a closed form of such summations. The example we shall follow here is a finite *geometric progression*,

$$A_n = 1 + \alpha + \alpha^2 + \cdots + \alpha^n. \tag{9.2}$$

We try to create another Identity that should be similar to, but different from, (9.2). If we have similar equations, it might be possible to subtract them side by side and get thereby some useful information, as because of the similarity, many of the terms may cancel out. This leaves us with the problem of how to generate the other equation.

The use of ellipses is generally restricted to cases in which the reader may derive some regularity from the context. This is not unlike the number sequences given often in IQ tests, in which you have to guess the next element. So the next term in $6 + 7 + 8 + \cdots$ should apparently be 9, and $3 + 6 + 9 + \ldots$ is probably followed by 12. In our case, it seems that each term is obtained from the preceding one by multiplying by α. This suggests to try to multiply the whole identity by α, to get

$$\alpha A_n = \alpha + \alpha^2 + \alpha^3 + \cdots + \alpha^{n+1}. \tag{9.3}$$

Subtracting (9.3) from (9.2), each side of the equation separately, yields

$$A_n - \alpha A_n = 1 - \alpha^{n+1},$$

in which there are no more ellipses. The left-hand side is $(1 - \alpha)A_n$, so two cases have to be considered. If $\alpha = 1$, then $A_n = 1 + 1 + \cdots + 1 = n + 1$. Otherwise, we can divide by $(1 - \alpha)$ to get

$$A_n = \frac{1 - \alpha^{n+1}}{1 - \alpha}.$$

Returning to the expectation of C_n, the number of comparisons to insert the $(n + 1)$st element into a hash table,

$$E(C_n) = \lim_{n \to \infty} A_n = \frac{1}{1 - \alpha} = \frac{M}{M - n},$$

as $\alpha < 1$ because we assume that the table is not full. For example, if the table is filled to about half, that is $\alpha = \frac{1}{2}$, then we expect about 2 comparisons only. Note in particular, that this number does not depend on M, the size of the table! Even if both the table size and the number of inserted elements grow linearly, but keeping a constant ratio, the insertion time will be $O(1)$.

9.4.2 Search

As mentioned, the number of comparisons for an unsuccessful search is also given by C_n. For a successful search, we have to decide which of the stored elements will be sought. As measure for the search performance, we shall use C'_n, for $1 \leq n \leq M$, defined as the average of the number of searches, assuming that each of the n elements currently stored in the table is equally likely to be the target,

$$C'_n = \frac{C_0 + C_1 + \cdots + C_{n-1}}{n}.$$

Using the fact that the expectation is a linear function, this implies

$$E(C'_n) = \frac{1}{n} \sum_{j=0}^{n-1} E(C_j) = \frac{1}{n} \left(1 + \frac{M}{M-1} + \frac{M}{M-2} + \cdots + \frac{M}{M-n+1} \right)$$

$$= \frac{M}{n} \sum_{j=0}^{n-1} \frac{1}{M-j} = \frac{M}{n} \sum_{i=M-n+1}^{M} \frac{1}{i},$$

where the last equality follows from a change of parameters $i = M - j$ and from reversing the order of summation. This is a part of the *harmonic series* $\sum_{i=1}^{\infty} \frac{1}{i}$ which is known to be divergent. The question is, at what rate it goes to infinity. This is a good opportunity to recall a useful tool for the approximation of similar discrete sums.

Background Concept: Approximating a Sum by an Integral

Let f be a monotonic function defined on the integers, and let a and b be two given integers, with $a \leq b$. A sum of the form

$$S = f(a) + f(a+1) + \cdots + f(b) = \sum_{i=a}^{b} f(i)$$

does frequently occur in the evaluation of the complexity of an algorithm. To approximate S, we assume that f can be extended to be defined on all the reals in the range $(a - 1, b + 1)$, not just on the integers, which is often the case for functions typically appearing in complexity expressions. We also assume that the function f is integrable on the given range.

A graphical interpretation of the sum S can be seen in Figure 9.7. The function is monotonically decreasing in our example, and the quantities $f(a), f(a+1), \ldots, f(b)$ are shown as bars connecting the x-axis with a point of the graph of the function. The problem is that we have not been taught to evaluate sums of lengths. But we know how to evaluate areas. This leads to the following idea, suggested in Figure 9.8.

Extend the bar of length $f(i)$ to its left, forming a rectangle of width 1 and height $f(i)$. The area of this rectangle is thus $f(i) \times 1 = f(i)$, so it is equal to the length of the bar. Of course, the purist will object that lengths and areas cannot be compared, since they use different units, neverthe-less, the number measuring the length is equal to the number quantifying the area. Repeating for all i from a to b, we get that the sum $S = \sum_{i=a}^{b} f(i)$ we wish to estimate is equal to the area in form of a staircase, delimited

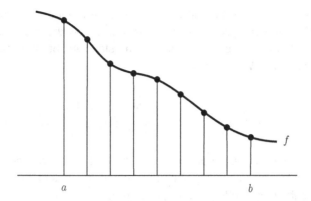

Figure 9.7. Graphical interpretation of $S = \sum_{i=a}^{b} f(i) = $ sum of the lengths of the bars.

by the broken line in Figure 9.8. But this staircase is completely below the graph of the function f, so the area of the staircase is smaller than the area below f, with appropriate limits, which is given by a definite integral:

$$S = \begin{array}{c} \text{area of broken line} \\ \text{staircase} \end{array} \leq \int_{a-1}^{b} f(x)dx. \tag{9.4}$$

This gives an upper limit for the sum S. To get a double sided approximation, apply the same procedure again, extending this time the bars to the right, yielding the dotted line staircase of Figure 9.8. Note that the areas of both staircases are the same: just imagine the dotted line

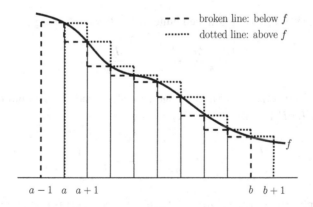

- - - broken line: below f
······· dotted line: above f

Figure 9.8. Replacing a sum of lengths by sums of areas.

staircase to be pushed to the left by one unit – it will then overlap with the broken line staircase. Now it is the area below the function that is bounded by the area below the dotted line staircase, but the limits have slightly changed. We get that

$$\int_a^{b+1} f(x)dx \leq S = \frac{\text{area of dotted line}}{\text{staircase}}. \tag{9.5}$$

A nice feature of this approximation is that it uses the integral of the same function twice, so only one primitive function has to be calculated. If $F(x)$ is the primitive function of $f(x)$, we get

$$F(b+1) - F(a) \leq S \leq F(b) - F(a-1).$$

If $f(x)$ is increasing instead of decreasing, the inequalities in (9.4) and (9.5) are reversed. If the function is not monotonic, we may try to approximate it separately on subranges on which it is monotonic, but care has to be taken to add the correct quantities when collecting the terms.

For the part of the harmonic series, we use the fact that the primitive function of $f(x) = \frac{1}{x}$ is $F(x) = \ln x$, the natural logarithm, and we get

$$\ln(M+1) - \ln(M-n+1) \leq \sum_{i=M-n+1}^{M} \frac{1}{i} \leq \ln(M) - \ln(M-n).$$

The sum is therefore approximated quite precisely as belonging to

$$\left[\ln \frac{M+1}{M-n+1}, \ln \frac{M}{M-n} \right],$$

which is a very small interval for large enough M and n. Substituting in the expression for $E(C_n')$, we conclude that

$$E(C_n') = \frac{M}{n} \sum_{i=M-n+1}^{M} \frac{1}{i} \simeq \frac{M}{n} \ln\left(\frac{M}{M-n}\right) = \frac{1}{\alpha} \ln\left(\frac{1}{1-\alpha}\right).$$

For example, if the load factor is 0.9, the expected number of comparisons is only 2.56. Even for a table filled up to 99% of its capacity, the average

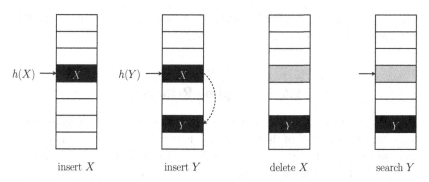

Figure 9.9. The problem with deletion in open addressing.

successful search does not take more than 4.65 trials, whereas a new insertion
would be expected to require about 100 attempts.

9.5 Deletions from Hash Tables

So far, we have considered only insertions and searches. If an element should
be removed, and the hash table is managed by means of chaining, the deletion
of an element is done just like for the linked lists studied in Chapter 2. For open
addressing. deletion is more problematic.

Figure 9.9 shows what might happen if an element to be deleted is just
erased from the table. Proceeding from left to right, suppose an element X is
inserted at $h(X)$, and that later, a second element Y is added, hashing to the same
address, so that it will be stored elsewhere, say at the second address in its probe
sequence. Suppose now that we remove X. A subsequent search for Y will fail,
because it will try to locate Y at its first potential location $h(Y) = h(X)$, and
since the spot is empty, it will erroneously conclude that Y is not in the table.

The problem can be overcome, if we define each entry of the table to be in
one of three possible *states*: it may be either **free** (white), or **occupied** (black)
or **erased** (gray). An **erased** cell will act like a **free** one for insertions, but like
an **occupied** one for searches. That is, a new element may be inserted in the first
free or **erased** entry encountered when scanning the element's probe sequence,
but a search for X has to continue as long as the inspected entries are **occupied**
or **erased**, until either X is found, or a **free** cell is reached for an unsuccessful
search.

If the number of deletion is not large, this is actually a good solution. However, in a highly dynamic application, with many insertions and deletions, there

will be no free cells left in the long run, only occupied or erased ones, and the average search time may significantly increase.

9.6 Concluding Remarks

Summarizing this chapter, hash tables may be very efficient in many applications, though not in all of them. Their use is widespread, not only as a stand alone technique, but also as a standard building block in many others. If they are managed with care, they allow the reduction of insertion and access times from logarithmic to constant time. Here are just a few of the interesting applications of hashing.

(i) Deduplication: Consider a large backup system, in which the entire available electronic storage of some corporation has to be saved at regular time intervals to prevent the loss of data. The special feature of such backup data is that only a small fraction of it differs from the previously stored backup. This calls for a special special form of data compression, known as *deduplication*: trying to store duplicates only once. The challenge is, of course, to locate as much of the duplicated data as possible.

A standard deduplication system achieves its goal in the following way. Partition the input database into blocks, apply a hash function on each of them, and store the different hash values, along with the address of the corresponding block, in a hash table. For an update, we assume that a new copy of the data is given, which is also partitioned into similar blocks. The hash value of each of these new blocks is searched for in the table, and if it is found, there is a good chance that the new block is an exact copy of a previous one, so all one needs to store is a pointer to the earlier occurrence.

(ii) String matching: The basic problem of finding a string S of length m in a text T of length n has been treated in Chapter 1. The following *probabilistic* algorithm is due to R. M. Karp and M. O. Rabin. Let T_i denote the substring of T of length m starting at the ith character of T, that is,

$$T_i = T[i]T[i+1] \cdots T[i+m-1] \qquad \text{for } 1 \leq i \leq m-n+1.$$

Instead of comparing S to T_i for all possible values of i, which would require $O(m)$ comparisons for each i, apply a hash function h and compare $h(S)$ with $h(T_i)$, which can be done in $O(1)$ if the hash values are small enough, say up to $k \leq 64$ bits. The overall complexity is then only $O(n)$, because $h(S)$ is evaluated only once, and, for a good choice of h, $h(T_i)$ can be derived from $h(T_{i-1})$ in constant time. A good hash function could be $h(X) = X \bmod P$, where P is a randomly chosen prime number with k bits. For large enough k, it can be shown that the probability of an error is negligible.

(iii) **Bloom filters:** Another efficient way to check the membership of an element in a set, a problem we dealt with in Chapter 8. It uses a bit-vector A of size n bits and k independent hash functions $h_1, \ldots, h_k$, each returning integers between 1 and n. For each element x added to the set, the bits in positions $h_1(x), \ldots, h_k(x)$ of A are set to 1. Membership tests are then executed similarly: given an item y, one checks whether all the bits in positions $h_1(y), \ldots, h_k(y)$ are set. If not, then y cannot be in the set; if yes, then y might be in the set, but there is no evidence, as the bits may have been set by a combination of other items. If m items are to be stored, one can adapt the parameters n and k to the required efficiency and error probability.

(iv) **Signature files:** Two approaches for the processing of information retrieval systems have been mentioned in Section 8.1.1: the one, for smaller texts, based on pattern matching, as in Chapter 1, the other, for larger corpora, by means of inverted files. Actually, there is a third alternative, adapted to intermediate text sizes, known as *signature files,* and they are an extension of Bloom filters.

The text is partitioned into logical blocks A_i, like, say, one or more paragraphs. Each block is assigned a bit-vector $B(A_i)$ of length n bits and Bloom filters are used for each different significant word in A_i to set a part of the bits in $B(A_i)$ to 1. The parameters n and k are chosen as a function of the average number of terms in the blocks, so that the number of 1-bits in each vector is about $\frac{n}{2}$. Typical values could be $n = 128$ and $k = 2$ or 3. To process a query, each of its terms is hashed with the same functions, yielding a query-vector Q of length n. This helps to filter out a (hopefully large) part of the potential blocks to be retrieved. For each i, if

$$Q \text{ AND } B(A_i) \neq Q, \qquad (9.6)$$

that is, if the 1-bits of Q are not a subset of those of $B(A_i)$, then the block A_i cannot contain all the terms of the query. If there is equality in (9.6), this does not assure that the block A_i does contain all the terms, but if the number of such blocks is low, each of them can be individually checked for the occurrence of the terms of Q.

On the other hand, the following situations are not handled well by hashing techniques, so if one of them occurs, it might be a better idea to choose some alternative.

(i) The worst case for hashing occurs when all the items hash to the same location. If this is not unreasonable, hashing should be avoided, as the corresponding insertion and search times may be linear in the number of stored items.

(ii) Open addressing requires that the number of elements to be inserted in the table does not exceed its size M. If it does, the table cannot be extended, a new table has to be allocated and all the elements need to be rehashed. This problem does not apply to chaining.

(iii) The only information gained from an unsuccessful search is that the item is not in the table. Consider the case of a list L of numbers and the problem of finding the element in L which is closest to some given number x. This is easily solved with an ordered list or a search tree, but a hash table may only locate the element itself, if it is in L. Thus hashing is not suitable for *approximate* searches.

(iv) In a *range query*, we want to retrieve all the elements in a list L between some constants a and b. When using a sorted list, we may locate the limits and return all the elements between them. For a search tree, the procedure is more involved, but two searches in the tree suffice to delimit the sought elements. In a hash table, locating a and b alone does not help.

Exercises

9.1 Every French child learns the following test, which helps detecting multiplication errors, in school. The test is based on a hashing function h. Given are two numbers X and Y we wish to multiply. To verify whether the calculated product $Z = X \times Y$ is correct, we apply h to the three numbers, and check if

$$h\big(h(X) \times h(Y)\big) = h(Z).$$

If the numbers differ, we must have made a mistake. If there is equality, the result is (most probably) correct. The function h is simply defined as taking repeatedly the sum of the digits, until only one digit is left, where 9 counts as 0.

For example, if $X = 123456$ and $Y = 98765432$, then $Z = 12193185172992$, and

$$h(X) = h(21) = 3, \qquad h(Y) = h(44) = 8, \qquad h(Z) = h(60) = 6,$$

and indeed, $h(3 \times 8) = h(24) = 6 = h(Z)$. To understand why the test is working, note that the digit 9 has no influence on the calculated result of the function h, for example $h(49) = h(13) = 4$. The test is accordingly known under the name *la règle par neuf*, the rule by nine.

Give a simple mathematical expression for $h(X)$ and deduce from it the correctness of the test.

9.2 Consider the $n = 21$ numbers extracted from the expansion of π and listed at the beginning of Section 9.3: $1415, 9265, \ldots, 0899, 8628$. Store them in a hash table of size 31 by means of double hashing using the functions

$$h_1(X) = X \bmod 31 \qquad h_2(X) = 1 + X \bmod 29.$$

Evaluate the actual value of C'_n and compare it to the theoretical expected value for this number of items if uniform hashing had been used. **Hint:** To check your results, the ratio of the two numbers should be 1.131.

9.3 Give an estimate for the following sums:

$$\sum_{i=2}^{n} i \log i, \qquad \sum_{i=1}^{n} i^3 \sqrt{i}, \qquad \sum_{i=1}^{n} \arctan i.$$

9.4 The following hash function h has been suggested to store a set of real numbers x such that $0 \le x \le 1$ in a table of size N: $h(x) = \lfloor Nx^2 \rfloor$. If the input values are uniformly distributed on the interval $[0, 1]$, is it also true that the hash values $h(X)$ are uniformly distributed on the range $[0, N]$? What is the conclusion?

9.5 Using uniform hashing, you would like to store 1000 elements in a hash table of size M.

(a) What should be the size M of the table if you wish to get an average of 2.5 comparisons for the last inserted element?

(b) If you choose $M = 1500$, what is the average number of trials to find one of the stored elements, if they all have equal chance to be the element to be searched for?

10

Sorting

10.1 A Sequence of Sorting Algorithms

Arranging the elements of a data set according to some specific order is one of the most basic tasks a program might perform, and there are even claims that most of the CPU time of many computers is spent on sorting. Although the relevant algorithms cannot be identified with some specific data structure, the topics connected to sorting are important enough to deserve being treated here in their own chapter. There is no intention to compile an exhaustive inventory of sorting techniques, but rather to study some noteworthy ones and related matters.

There is no need for the existence of a computer to understand the importance and advantage of keeping some items we wish to process in order, and the action of sorting is probably as old as mankind. Here is a several thousand years old written evidence:

> He searched, beginning with the oldest and ending with the youngest, . . .
>
> Genesis *44:12, New American Standard Bible*

To facilitate the discussion, we shall use numerical data in our examples, to be arranged into ascending sequences, but the order could of course also be reversed, the data can be alphabetic, and moreover, the same set of items may be arranged differently according to varying criteria. For example, the orders of months

January, February, March, April, May, June;

April, February, January, June, March, May;

February, April, June, January, March, May;

May, June, March, April, January, February

are, respectively, chronological, alphabetical, sorted by the lengths of the months or by the lengths of their names.

Some sorting methods have already been mentioned earlier: **Mergesort** in Chapter 2 and **Heapsort** in Section 7.5. Both have a worst case time complexity of $O(n \log n)$ for an input of n elements, which, as we shall see, is the best one can expect. The simpler methods, however, those used in real life applications rather than in programs, are generally less efficient and require up to $\Omega(n^2)$ comparisons. Examples are the way a card player incrementally updates her or his hand by adding new cards into their proper place (**Insertion sort**), or arranging a team of game players by their increasing heights, allowing only neighbors to swap places (**Bubble sort**).

The following technique generates a sequence of sorting methods with gradually improving performances. For all of them, the input sequence is supposed to be given in an array A_1 of size n. We start with a method of repeatedly removing the largest element from the remaining set, using $i - 1$ comparisons to find the maximum in the ith iteration, and storing the removed items in the order of their processing in another array B. This is called **Selection sort** and requires $(n - 1) + (n - 2) + \cdots = \sum_{i=1}^{n-1} i = O(n^2)$ comparisons.

A better performance can be achieved by partitioning the set A_1 into $\sqrt{n}$ subsets of $\sqrt{n}$ elements each (rounding, if necessary). The maximal element m can then be retrieved in two stages. We first find the maximum in each subset, using $\sqrt{n} - 1$ comparisons for each of them, and define the set A_2 of these maxima. The maximum element of A_1 is then the maximum of A_2, which again can be found in time $\sqrt{n} - 1$. So the total time to find m is

$$\sqrt{n} \times (\sqrt{n} - 1) + \sqrt{n} - 1 = n - 1,$$

just as before. However, for the second element of A_1, we need only to locate the subset from which the maximum originated, repeat the search in this subset, as well as again in A_2. This takes only $2(\sqrt{n} - 1)$ comparisons.

As example, refer again to the expansion of π and take the 25 first pairs of digits after the decimal point, yielding the set A_1 of Figure 10.1. The number of comparisons to get $m = 93$ is 24, but for the second largest element, we retrieve again the maximum of the last subset $\{69, 39, 75, 10\}$, after having removed 93, and then from the updated set A_2, $\{92, 89, 79, 84, 75\}$.

All the subsequent elements can be found similarly in $2(\sqrt{n} - 1)$ comparisons, so the total time for sorting the set is

$$(n - 1) + (n - 1) \times 2(\sqrt{n} - 1) \simeq 2n\sqrt{n}.$$

To further improve the complexity, we can try a similar solution in three instead of only two stages. The set A_1 is partitioned into subsets of size $\sqrt[3]{n}$, so the number of subsets will be $\sqrt[3]{n^2}$. The maximum elements of these subsets are stored in A_2, which in turn is partitioned itself into $\sqrt[3]{n}$ subsets of size $\sqrt[3]{n}$, and their maxima will form the set A_3, as can be seen in Figure 10.2. The largest element is now found by

$$\sqrt[3]{n^2}(\sqrt[3]{n} - 1) + \sqrt[3]{n}(\sqrt[3]{n} - 1) + \sqrt[3]{n} - 1 = n - 1$$

comparisons, as in the 2-stage algorithm. To find the second largest element, one only needs to re-evaluate the maximum of one subset of size $\sqrt[3]{n}$ for each level, thus using $3(\sqrt[3]{n} - 1)$ comparisons. The same is true also for the subsequent elements. For the example in Figure 10.2, after removing the global maximum 93, the three processed subsets to find the second element are $\{39, 75\}$ in A_1, $\{71, 75, 10\}$ in A_2 and $A_3 = \{92, 84, 75\}$. The complexity of this 3-stage approach is therefore

$$(n - 1) + (n - 1) \times 3(\sqrt[3]{n} - 1) \simeq 3n\sqrt[3]{n}.$$

In fact, since increasing the number of stages seems to reduce the number of requested comparisons, there is no reason to stop here. In the general case, k layers representing the sets $A_1, A_2, \ldots, A_k$ are constructed, and the set A_i, for $1 \leq i < k$ is partitioned into $n^{(k-i)/k}$ subsets of size $n^{1/k}$. The maximal element of each of the subsets of A_i is taken to form the set A_{i+1} of the next layer. The number of comparisons to find the global maximum is then $n - 1$, and for the subsequent elements it is $kn^{1/k}$, yielding a total complexity of about $kn^{1+1/k}$ for the k-layer sort. This is a decreasing function of k, which suggests to let k grow as large as possible. There is, however, an upper limit for k, because the size of the subsets in the partitions is $n^{1/k}$, which is also a decreasing function of k. To have any comparisons at all, this size has to be at least 2, and from $n^{1/k} = 2$ one can derive that the largest possible value of k is $\log_2 n$.

For our example of 25 elements, the number of layers will be $\lceil \log_2 25 \rceil = 5$, and each subset will be of size 2, as depicted in Figure 10.3. In fact, if the maximum element 93 is added as a single element in an additional layer A_6, this structure can be seen as a binary tree in which each node is the maximum of its two children – this is the definition of a *heap*. Finding the maximum element is equivalent to building the heap, and can be done in time $O(n)$, but then repeatedly removing the maximal element requires only one comparison for each of the $\log_2 n$ layers, for a total of $O(n \log n)$ comparisons. Building a heap and then maintaining the heap property while removing the elements in order is the basic idea of **Heapsort** we have seen in Section 7.5.

There are some technical differences between the heaps we studied in Chapter 7 and the heap resulting from the preceding derivation process, as given in

A_2	92	89	79	84	93
A_1	14 15 92 65 35	89 79 32 38 46	26 43 38 32 79	50 28 84 19 71	69 39 93 75 10

Figure 10.1. Partition into $\sqrt{n}$ subsets of $\sqrt{n}$ elements.

A_3	92			84			93		
A_2	92	89	79	46	79	84	71	93	10
A_1	14 15 92	65 35 89	79 32 38	46 26 43	38 32 79	50 28 84	19 71 69	39 93 75	10

Figure 10.2. Partition into $\sqrt[3]{n}^2$ subsets of $\sqrt[3]{n}$ elements.

A_5	92								93				
A_4	92				79				93				10
A_3	92		89		46		79		84		93		10
A_2	15	92	89	79	46	43	38	79	84	71	69	93	10
A_1	14 15	92 65	35 89	79 32	38 46	26 43	38 32	79 50	28 84	19 71	69 39	93 75	10

Figure 10.3. Partition into subsets of two elements – Heapsort.

Figure 10.3. All the elements of the original set A_1 appear here in the lowest layer, and the other sets contain just copies of some of the elements, whereas the heaps of Chapter 7 had no duplicates. The difference has thus some similarity with the difference between B-trees and B$^+$-trees of Chapter 6. Moreover, the update process here proceeds bottom-up in each iteration. By contrast, the definition in Chapter 7 insisted on representing a heap as a full binary tree, so to remove the root, it was swapped with a leaf and the comparisons were performed top-down. Nevertheless, the algorithm and its complexity are essentially the same.

Summarizing, we have seen a family of connected sorting procedures, starting with the trivial **Selection sort** which requires quadratic time, and leading naturally to **Heapsort** with its optimal worst case complexity of $O(n \log n)$.

10.2 Lower Bound on the Worst Case

An obvious question arises, and not only for sorting algorithms: how can we know that an algorithm we found for a given problem is reasonable in terms of its time complexity? Sorting by **Bubblesort** in time $O(n^2)$, for instance, might have looked as a good solution before a better one, like **Mergesort**, has been discovered, with time $O(n \log n)$. So maybe somebody will come up with an even faster sorting procedure?

This is not just a theoretical question. If I found some solution to a problem, but my boss is not satisfied with its performance, I might invest a major effort to design an improved algorithm, which may not always be justified. If one can prove mathematically that the suggested solution is already *optimal*, the waste of time could be avoided. However, it is often not possible to show such optimality, and then we might settle for finding a so-called lower bound for a given problem.

A *lower bound* for a problem P with input size n is a function $B(n)$ such that it can be shown that no algorithm solving P in time less than $B(n)$ can possibly exist. Note that this does not imply the existence of an algorithm that does solve P in time $B(n)$. For example, it might be possible to show that a lower bound for P is n^2, but that the best known algorithms for its solution require $\Omega(n^3)$. Much of the research in Computer Science strives to reduce, and possibly, close, this gap between a lower bound and the complexity of the best known algorithm. Sorting is one of the problems for which this goal has been achieved.

In what follows, we show how to derive a lower bound for the time complexity of sorting, but the technique is general enough to be applied also to other computational problems. We also restrict the discussion to sorting techniques based on comparisons between the elements, and all the sort algorithms mentioned so far belong to this class. There are, however, sorting methods like **Radix sort** or **Counting sort**, that place an element according to its own value rather than comparing it with another element, and the lower bound that we shall derive does not apply to them. For example, for comparison based methods, the input $\{4, 9, 7\}$ is equivalent to $\{40, 90, 70\}$ and even to $\{40, 90, 54\}$, as they all exhibit the same order: the smallest element first, then the largest, finally the middle one. The sequence of comparisons will thus be the same. For **Radix sort**. on the other hand, 4 is treated differently from 40.

Suppose then that a sequence of n different elements $a_1, a_2, \ldots, a_n$ is given that should be arranged into increasing order. It will be convenient to reformulate this sorting task as finding the permutation $\{\pi(1), \pi(2), \ldots, \pi(n)\}$ of the indices $\{1, 2, \ldots, n\}$ for which

$$a_{\pi(1)} < a_{\pi(2)} < \cdots < a_{\pi(n)}.$$

Obviously, if the permutation is known, the actual sorting is just a matter of re-arranging the items in a linear scan.

To abbreviate the notation, we shall identify a given permutation of the elements $a_1, a_2, \ldots, a_n$ by the ordered string of the indices of the terms. For example, if $n = 4$ and the order of a given permutation is $a_2 < a_4 < a_1 < a_3$, it will be represented by the string **2413**.

A common pitfall for showing lower bounds is to claim that the task can "obviously" only be done is some specific manner, which requires a complexity of at least $\Omega(f)$ for some function f. This is generally wrong, as there might be infinitely many options to tackle the problem. The difficulty of showing a lower bound is thus that the proof has to encompass all the possible algorithms, even those that have not yet been invented! The proof must therefore refer generically to all these algorithms and cannot restrict the discussion just to some specific ones.

We shall therefore describe a sorting algorithm by the only information we have about it: that it consists of a sequence of comparisons. Indeed, most of the methods mentioned earlier can be specified by some comparison pattern. Writing $i:j$ as a shorthand for the comparison between $A[i]$ and $A[j]$, some of these sequences are as follows:

for **Bubblesort** $- 1:2, 2:3, 3:4, \ldots, (n-1):n, 1:2, \ldots,$

for **Mergesort** $- 1:2, 3:4, 1:3, 5:6, 7:8, 5:7, 1:5, 9:10. \ldots,$

for **Quicksort** (to be seen later) $- 1:2, 1:3, 1:4, \ldots.$

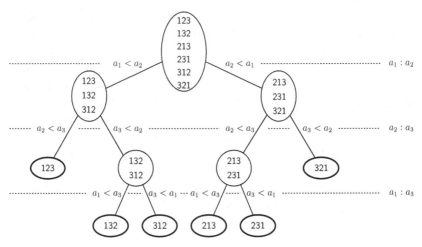

Figure 10.4. Example of a decision tree for sorting three elements.

However, not all sorting methods follow such well defined and regular comparison patterns, and most of the procedures do not even have names. In particular, the best methods for sorting a small set of items might be custom tailored to the size n of the set and not a particular case of any of the known general algorithms.

The tool by means of which the lower bound will be derived is called a *decision tree*. This is a binary tree corresponding to a specific sorting algorithm, that is, to a specific sequence of comparisons. Figure 10.4 is an example for a small decision tree, corresponding to the algorithm of sorting three elements a_1, a_2, a_3 using the sequence of comparisons 1:2, 2:3, 1:3. Each level of the tree corresponds to one of the comparisons, in order, and the nodes on level i of the tree contain the state of our knowledge after the first i comparisons. In particular, the root, on level 0, reflects the fact that there has not been any comparison yet, so we have not gained any information so far.

The knowledge is described as a set of permutations. The root contains all the $n!$ permutations of the numbers $\{1, \ldots, n\}$, $3! = 6$ in our example. If it is not a singleton, the set of permutations P_v in a node v on level $i - 1$ is split pursuant to the ith comparison into two nodes that will be the children of v on level i: if the comparison is $k : \ell$, one of these nodes will contain the permutations in P_v for which $a_k < a_\ell$, and the other node will contain the complementing set, those permutations of P_v for which $a_k > a_\ell$; the edges leading to these children nodes will be labeled accordingly. For example, let v be the left node on level 1 of the tree in Figure 10.4 that contains the permutations $P_v = \{123, 132, 312\}$; the second comparison is 2:3, hence P_v is split into $\{123\}$ for which $a_2 < a_3$, and {132, 312} for which $a_2 > a_3$, and these sets are stored in the left and right children of v on level 2, respectively.

The state of knowledge at a given node w on level i is a consequence of the *decisions* written as labels on the path from the root to w, which is why this is called a decision tree. For example, let w be the node on level 2 with $P_w = \{213, 231\}$. The decisions leading to w are $a_2 < a_1$ and $a_2 < a_3$, which are not enough to completely sort the three elements, because there are two permutations, 213 and 231 that are compatible with these outcomes of the first two comparisons. If the decisions had been $a_2 < a_1$ and $a_3 < a_2$, that would lead us to the node storing just one permutation 321, so in this case, the two first comparisons are sufficient to determine the order.

The aim of a sorting algorithm is to perform sufficiently many comparisons such that each leaf of the corresponding decision tree will contain just a single permutation. In other words, whatever the outcomes of these comparisons, we must be able to determine the exact order of the n elements. Note that the number of necessary comparisons is therefore the depth of the deepest leaf, which is the depth of the tree. As can be seen, for the example in Figure 10.4, three comparisons are sufficient: the tree has six leaves, which are emphasized, each containing a different single one of the six possible permutations. We also see that the first two comparisons alone are not enough: although there are some leaves on level 2, there are also nodes containing more than one permutation, so the sorting job is not completed.

How can this be generalized to a generic sorting algorithm? We obviously do not know which comparisons are used, and in which order. The answer is that we rely on certain properties of binary trees, of which decision trees are a special case. The number of different sorting orders of the given n elements is $n!$, and each of the corresponding permutations is stored as a singleton in one of the leaves of the decision tree, thus the number of leaves of this tree is $n!$.

As to the depth of the decision tree, let us again change our point of view, as we did, e.g., in the proof of Theorem 5.1 about AVL trees in Chapter 5. There is only one leaf in a tree of depth 0, which is a single node. There are at most two leaves in a binary tree of depth 1, and, by induction, there are at most 2^h leaves in a binary tree of depth h. The number of leaves of a binary tree will thus reach $n!$ only if h is large enough so that

$$2^h \geq n!,$$

from which we derive a lower bound on the depth:

$$h \geq \log_2 n!. \tag{10.1}$$

In particular, returning to our example, after 2 comparisons, the tree has at most 4 leaves. Since there are 6 permutations, there must be at least one leaf that contains more than a single permutation. This shows that not only this specific comparison order fails to sort the input of three elements in two steps, but that *any* sequence of two comparisons will equally be unsuccessful. To give a larger example, the number of permutations of 5 elements is $5! = 120$; after *any* 6 comparisons, the decision tree will only have $2^6 = 64$ leaves, so there is no way to sort 5 elements in 6 comparisons. Are 7 comparisons enough? It could be, since $2^7 = 128 > 120 = 5!$, but the technique of using the decision tree gives no clue about if it is indeed feasible and if so, about how to do it. Actually, it *is* possible to sort 5 elements in 7 steps, see the exercises.

Rewriting eq. (10.1) into a more convenient form, we get

$$\log(n!) = \log(2 \cdot 3 \cdot 4 \cdots (n-1) \cdot n) < \log(n \cdot n \cdots n)$$
$$= \log(n^n) = n \log n, \tag{10.2}$$

which sets an upper bound. To derive also a lower bound, the symmetric technique does not succeed. In (10.2), we have replaced each factor by the maximum value, but if we replace it now by the minimum, we get that $n! > 2^n$, which is true but not useful. A better bound is achieved by proceeding in two steps:

$$\log(n!) = \log(2 \cdot 3 \cdot 4 \cdots (n-1) \cdot n)$$
$$> \log\left(\left(\frac{n}{2}+1\right) \cdot \left(\frac{n}{2}+2\right) \cdots (n-1) \cdot n\right)$$
$$> \log\left(\left(\frac{n}{2}\right) \cdot \left(\frac{n}{2}\right) \cdots \left(\frac{n}{2}\right)\right) = \log\left(\left(\frac{n}{2}\right)^{\frac{n}{2}}\right) = \frac{n}{2} \log \frac{n}{2},$$

where the first inequality is obtained by dropping the first $\frac{n}{2}$ factors, and the second by replacing each factor by a lower bound on each of the remaining factors.

The conclusion is that the lower bound on the number of comparisons needed to sort n elements is in $\theta(n \log n)$. Since we have already seen algorithms that achieve this goal in $O(n \log n)$, these algorithms are *optimal*.

10.3 Lower Bound on the Average

The worst case behavior of an algorithm is surely an important criterion, since it provides a bound for all the cases, but for many problems, the worst case scenario is unrealistic. If so, it does not seem reasonable to compare competing methods considering only extreme situations that might hardly appear in practice, if at all. A better measure in such a context would then be the *average* performance of the algorithm, which depends on all its possible instances.

Background Concept: Average Complexity of an Algorithm

The *average* complexity of an algorithm will be defined as an extension of the notion of average or expectation of a random variable X. Let $\mathcal{V}$ be the (finite or infinite) set of possible values X can assume. The average or expectation of X is defined by

$$E(X) = \sum_{v \in \mathcal{V}} v \ \text{Prob}(X = v).$$

By analogy, given an algorithm $\mathcal{A}$, let $\mathcal{V}$ denote the set of all possible inputs of $\mathcal{A}$. The average complexity of $\mathcal{A}$ is defined by

$$E(\mathcal{A}) = \sum_{v \in \mathcal{V}} \left(\begin{array}{c} \text{number of steps executed} \\ \text{by } \mathcal{A} \text{ on input } v \end{array} \right) \text{Prob} \left(\begin{array}{c} \text{the input} \\ \text{of } \mathcal{A} \text{ is } v \end{array} \right). \quad (10.3)$$

For the evaluation of such an average, it is thus mandatory that the probability of occurrence of each of the possible inputs be given. The evaluation also requires the calculation of the number of steps in the execution of the algorithm on each of these inputs. Refer, for example, to the sorting problem, and consider again the decision tree of Figure 10.4. Each possible input corresponds to one of the permutations, which in turn are identified with the leaves of the tree. If $\mathcal{L}$ denotes the set of leaves of the decision tree, eq. (10.3) can be rewritten as

$$E(\mathcal{A}) = \sum_{\ell \in \mathcal{L}} \text{depth}(\ell) \ \text{Prob} \left(\begin{array}{c} \text{the input of } \mathcal{A} \text{ is ordered} \\ \text{by the permutation in } \ell \end{array} \right). \quad (10.4)$$

For example, if the probabilities of the permutations in the leaves of Figure 10.4 are, from left to right, $0.1, 0.4, 0.2, 0.1, 0.05$, and 0.15, the corresponding average is

$$0.1 \times 2 + 0.4 \times 3 + 0.2 \times 3 + 0.1 \times 3 + 0.05 \times 3 + 0.15 \times 2 = 2.85.$$

Lacking any other information, one often assumes that all the possible inputs are equally likely. This is not a part of the definition of an average, and it has to be stated explicitly if such uniform distribution is assumed. For the sorting problem, it would mean that each permutation appears with probability $\frac{1}{n!}$. For the example of Figure 10.4, assuming equal probabilities would yield an average of

$$\frac{1}{6}(2+3+3+3+3+2) = \frac{16}{6} = 2.67.$$

To derive a lower bound on the average complexity of any sorting algorithm, we again refer to the decision tree as a model for comparison based sorting methods. We also assume that all the $n!$ possible input permutations appear with equal probability $\frac{1}{n!}$. Let $\mathcal{A}$ be such a sorting algorithm, let T be the corresponding decision tree, and denote by $\mathcal{L}$ the set of the leaves of T. We then get from eq. (10.4) that according to our assumptions

$$E(\mathcal{A}) = \frac{1}{n!} \sum_{\ell \in \mathcal{L}} \text{depth}(\ell). \tag{10.5}$$

We are confronted with the same problem as in the worst case analysis of the previous section: the right-hand side of eq. (10.5) includes the sum of the depths of all the leaves of the decision tree, but the shape of this tree varies with the different sequences of comparisons. The solution, as before, is to consider properties that are common to all binary trees, and thus in particular to decision trees.

Let T be a complete binary tree with m leaves, that is, all internal nodes of T have two children. Define

$$D(T) = \sum_{\ell \in \{\text{leaves of } T\}} \text{depth}(\ell)$$

as the sum of the depths of all the leaves of T, which is a function depending on the shape of the given tree. To get a function which is independent of the shape, and only relies on the number of leaves, we further define

$$d(m) = \min\{D(T) \mid T \text{ has } m \text{ leaves}\}.$$

For example, the tree T in Figure 10.5(d) has $D(T) = 1 + 2 + 3 + 3 = 9$, and that in Figure 10.5(e) $2 + 2 + 2 + 2 = 8$. Since these are the only possible shapes for complete binary trees with 4 leaves (there are symmetric shapes, with the same depths), we get that $d(4) = \min\{8, 9\} = 8$.

To study the general behavior of the function d, we start with the first values. The trees in Figure 10.5 appear with the number m of their leaves above them, and with the depths written in the leaves. For $m = 1, 2, 3$, there is only one option for a complete binary tree (again, up to symmetry) and the trees appear in Figures 10.5(a), (b), and (c), respectively. The corresponding values of D, and

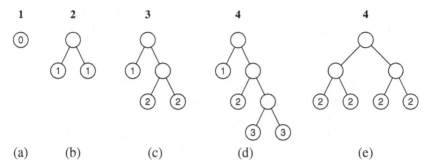

Figure 10.5. Complete binary trees with one to four leaves.

thus also of d, are 0, 2, and 5. We saw already that $d(4) = 8$, but for larger m, there are clearly many options of tree shapes (see the discussion in Section 4.2 on the number of trees).

Let us derive a recursive formula for D. Consider the tree T_m in Figure 10.6, where the subscript refers now to the number of leaves in the tree. Suppose the left subtree of T_m has i leaves, for some $1 \le i < m$, and let us therefore denote the tree by T_i; the right subtree has then $m - i$ leaves and will be denoted T_{m-i} accordingly. To express $D(T_m)$ as a function of $D(T_i)$ and $D(T_{m-i})$, note that for each leaf, its depth in the subtree is one less than its depth in the tree itself. For example, in Figure 10.6, the depth in T_i of the leaf appearing as a small white circle is the number of edges in the broken line showing the path from the root of T_i, indicated by a black dot, to this leaf; if the path starts at the root of T_m, just one edge is added, so the depth of the leaf is increased by 1. Since this is true for each of the m leaves, we get

$$D(T_m) = (D(T_i) + i) + (D(T_{m-i}) + m - i) = D(T_i) + D(T_{m-i}) + m. \quad (10.6)$$

The formula can be verified for each of the trees with $m > 1$ of Figure 10.5.

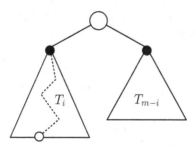

Figure 10.6. Recursive evaluation of the sum of the depths of the leaves.

We would like to infer from (10.6) a formula for d. Since the passage from D to d is by applying a minimum function, a first thought could lead to

$$d(m) = d(i) + d(m - i) + m, \qquad (10.7)$$

but this formula does not make any sense: the left-hand side depends only on m, whereas the right-hand side has an additional parameter i. The reason is that the i in eq. (10.6) is not really a parameter – it is the number of leaves in the left subtree and therefore induced by T_m. Formally, we should have written $i(T_m)$ instead of just i to make this dependency explicit. It turns out that the correct form of the attempt in (10.7) is rather

Claim 10.1. $d(m) = \min_{1 \leq i < m} \big(d(i) + d(m - i) + m \big). \qquad (10.8)$

Equation (10.8) may be mathematically sound as the free parameter i is now bound by the additional minimum, acting like a quantifier, but the correctness of the expression for $d(m)$ is surely not self-evident and needs to be shown.

Proof We show that there are inequalities in both directions. Let i be an index between 1 and $m - 1$. A tree T with m leaves for which $D(T) = d(m)$ will be called a *minimal* tree. Let $\hat{T}_i$ and $\hat{T}_{m-i}$ be minimal trees with i and $m - i$ leaves, respectively, and define $\hat{T}_m$ as the binary tree which has $\hat{T}_i$ as its left and $\hat{T}_{m-i}$ as its right subtrees. The tree $\hat{T}_m$ is not necessarily minimal, but $d(m)$ cannot be larger than $D(\hat{T}_m)$, which yields

$$d(m) \leq D(\hat{T}_m) = D(\hat{T}_i) + D(\hat{T}_{m-i}) + m = d(i) + d(m - i) + m$$

for the specific i we have chosen. But since this is true for any i in the given range, it follows that

$$d(m) \leq \min_{1 \leq i < m} \big(d(i) + d(m - i) + m \big).$$

The proof for the complementing inequality is not symmetric. Let $\tilde{T}_m$ be a minimal tree with m leaves. Denote the number of leaves of the left subtree of $\tilde{T}_m$ by j and use the notation $\tilde{T}_j$ and $\tilde{T}_{m-j}$ for the left and right subtrees of $\tilde{T}_m$. The subtrees are not necessarily minimal. We therefore have

$$d(m) = D(\tilde{T}_m) = D(\tilde{T}_j) + D(\tilde{T}_{m-j}) + m \geq d(j) + d(m - j) + m,$$

again just for the specific j mentioned. This is not true for all indices j, but since there exists a j for which it is true, it follows that

$$d(m) \geq \min_{1 \leq i < m} \big(d(i) + d(m - i) + m \big),$$

and hence there must be equality.   ∎

The formula can now be used to discover new values of $d(m)$, for example,

$$d(5) = \min \left\{ \begin{array}{l} d(1) + d(4) + 5 = 0 + 8 + 5 = 13 \\ d(2) + d(3) + 5 = 2 + 5 + 5 = 12 \end{array} \right\} = 12$$

$$d(6) = \min \left\{ \begin{array}{l} d(1) + d(5) + 6 = 0 + 12 + 6 = 18 \\ d(2) + d(4) + 6 = 2 + 8 + 6 = 16 \\ d(3) + d(3) + 6 = 5 + 5 + 6 = 16 \end{array} \right\} = 16,$$

but it would be more convenient to get a closed formula for $d(m)$, and not a recursive one. The following bound can be shown:

Claim 10.2. $\qquad\qquad\qquad d(m) \geq m \log_2 m.$

Proof by induction on m. For $m = 1$, indeed

$$d(1) \geq 1 \log_2 1 = 0.$$

Suppose then that the claim is true for $1 \leq i < m$, and let us show it also for $i = m$:

$$d(m) = \min_{1 \leq i < m} \left(d(i) + d(m - i) + m \right)$$

$$\geq \min_{1 \leq i < m} \left(i \log_2 i + (m - i) \log_2 (m - i) + m \right).$$

To find the minimum, define the function $f(x) = x \log_2 x + (m - x) \log_2 (m - x) + m$ on all the reals $1 \leq x \leq m$. The function $f(x)$ is differentiable and its derivative is

$$f'(x) = \frac{1}{\ln 2} \left(\frac{x}{x} + \ln x - \frac{m - x}{m - x} - \ln(m - x) \right).$$

Setting this to zero implies $\ln x = \ln(m - x)$ and thus $x = m - x$, that is, $x = \frac{m}{2}$. The second derivative of $f(x)$ at $x = \frac{m}{2}$ is $f''(\frac{m}{2}) = \frac{4}{m \ln 2} > 0$, so this is a minimum. Plugging the index at which the minimum is reached into the formula, one gets

$$d(m) \geq \left(\frac{m}{2} \log_2 \frac{m}{2} + \frac{m}{2} \log_2 \frac{m}{2} + m \right) = m \log_2 \frac{m}{2} + m = m \log_2 m. \quad \blacksquare$$

We can now return to the problem of finding a lower bound to the average complexity of a comparison based sorting algorithm. The quantity we wish to evaluate is $\frac{1}{n!} D(\mathcal{T})$, where $\mathcal{T}$ is the decision tree of a given sorting algorithm. The difficulty was that $D(\mathcal{T})$ depends on the shape of the tree, which is unknown, so the evaluation has to be based on the only information we have about the decision tree, namely, the number of its leaves, $n!$. The conclusion is

$$\begin{array}{l}\text{average number of}\\ \text{comparisons for sorting}\end{array} = \frac{1}{n!}D(\mathcal{T}) \geq \frac{1}{n!}d(n!) \geq \frac{1}{n!}n!\log_2 n!$$

$$= \log_2 n! = \theta(n\log n).$$

Interestingly, the lower bound on the average case is the same as for the worst case! It also implies that the average case complexity for methods that are optimal from the worst case point of view, like **Mergesort** or **Heapsort**, must also be $\theta(n\log n)$.

10.4 Quicksort

This section presents yet another example of the Divide and Conquer family of algorithms, a sorting technique known by its somewhat pretentious name **Quicksort**, especially in view of its very slow worst case performance. The method and some of its variants are nonetheless important enough to deserve their own section.

Given is an array $A[1]\cdots A[n]$ of n numbers, and we shall again assume that they are all different, to facilitate the discussion. **Quicksort** starts by picking one of the elements, K, and using it to partition the array into three subsets, which can be performed in a single linear scan of the set:

$S_1 = \{x \in A \mid x < K\}$ the elements of A that are smaller than K,

$\{K\}$ the singleton containing only K,

$S_2 = \{x \in A \mid x > K\}$ the elements of A that are larger than K.

The elements are then rearranged in-place in the original array, with S_1 on the left and S_2 on the right, as depicted schematically in Figure 10.7. The sets S_1 and S_2 are not sorted themselves, but K is already at its intended location in the final sorting order. All that remains to be done is thus to sort each of the subsets S_1 and S_2, which can be done recursively. The formal algorithm, in which $A[x : y]$ denotes the elements of A with indices between x and y, inclusive, is given in Figure 10.8.

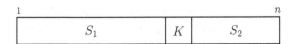

Figure 10.7. Partition of the array into three subsets.

Quicksort(A)
>   if $|A| > 1$ then
> $j \longleftarrow$ Partition(A)
> $S_1 \longleftarrow A[1 : j - 1]$ Quicksort(S_1)
> $S_2 \longleftarrow A[j + 1 : n]$ Quicksort(S_2)

Figure 10.8. Quicksort.

Quicksort does not specify which element K should be used for the partition step, and therefore programmers often pick the easiest choice, which is to use the first element $A[1]$ of the input array. The partition can then be done by initializing two pointers i and j, the former to the beginning and the latter to the end of the remaining array. We wish to have the elements of S_1 toward the left end of the array, and those of S_2 at the right end. This can be achieved by comparing the element i points to, with K. If it is smaller, it is already in the proper area, so we can increment i and check the next element, until an element that is larger than K is found. At this point, we start a similar process from the end, pointed to by j. If $A[j]$ is larger than K, we can step backward, until an element is found that is smaller. All one has to do to rectify the order is then to swap the elements $A[i]$ and $A[j]$, and to repeat the whole process until the pointers meet. Figure 10.9 is a schematic of one iteration of this process, where the $<$ and $>$ signs indicate whether the element is smaller or larger than K; the next iteration will start at the positions indicated by the broken line arrows.

At the end of this process, the indices i and j will have switched places, as can be seen in Figure 10.10(a), which corresponds to the general case. Figure 10.10(b) is the special case in which K is the largest element, so to stop the loop on i, it is convenient to use the first element *after* the array, $A[n + 1]$, as a sentinel element, a technique we have seen in Chapter 2. The other extreme case, when K is the smallest element, is shown in Figure 10.10(c). Now it is the loop of j that processes the entire array, but here, no sentinel element is needed, since $A[1]$ contains K, which will stop the iteration. Thus in all three cases, at the end of the main loop, we have $j = i - 1$, and the number of comparisons

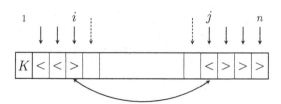

Figure 10.9. Schematic of the partition step.

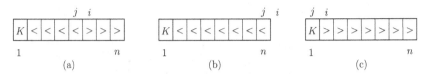

Figure 10.10. At the end of the partition step.

performed is $n + 1$: each of the $n - 1$ elements $A[2] \cdots A[n]$ is compared once, plus an additional comparison for each of the two elements pointed to by i and j at the end of the main loop. The index j points then to the rightmost of the elements that are smaller than K, or to K itself, if no such smaller elements exist; to finalize the partition into the form depicted in Figure 10.7, what remains to be done is to swap the elements K and $A[j]$. The partition algorithm returns the index j of the partition element K at the end of this step, and is given in Figure 10.11.

10.4.1 Worst Case

The worst case will occur when the partition element is repeatedly one of the extreme elements of the array. In that case, one of the sets S_1 or S_2 is empty and there is only one recursive call, but it is with a set of size $n - 1$. If $T(n)$ denotes the worst case number of comparisons used by Quicksort on an input of size n, one has

$$T(n) = n + T(n-1) = \sum_{i=1}^{n} i = \theta(n^2).$$

It is quite embarrassing that for the earlier choice of the partition element, the worst case is attained, among others, for an input which is already sorted, whereas in this case one would expect only very little work to be done. In addition, such an input is not unrealistic, as the input of a sorting procedure is often the output of some preprocessing that might already have produced some

```
Partition(A)
    K ⟵ A[1]
    A[n + 1] ⟵ ∞        // sentinel element
    i ⟵ 2      j ⟵ n
    while i < j do
        while A[i] < K do i++
        while A[j] > K do j--
        if i < j swap(A[i], A[j])
        i++      j--
    swap(A[1], A[j])
    return j
```

Figure 10.11. Partition step used in Quicksort.

order. To remedy this behavior, some heuristics suggest choosing the partition element differently, as we shall see in the following section, but the worst case will still be $\theta(n^2)$.

10.4.2 Average Case

For the average case, let us redefine $T(n)$ to stand for the average number of comparisons required by Quicksort to sort n elements, assuming a uniform distribution on the input permutations. As boundary condition, we have $T(1) = 0$. The number of comparisons in the partition part is $n + 1$, independently of the choice of K. The recursive steps, however, are influenced by K, since its relative position, as depicted in Figure 10.7, determines the sizes of the subsets S_1 and S_2. Assuming a uniform distribution implies that in each iteration, K has an equal chance to end up in one of the possible positions. For the first iteration this means that the probability of K being in position i, for $1 \leq i \leq n$, is $\frac{1}{n}$; the corresponding sizes of S_1 and S_2 are $i - 1$ and $n - i$, respectively. This can be summarized by the formula

$$T(n) = n + 1 + \frac{1}{n} \sum_{i=1}^{n} \left(T(i-1) + T(n-i) \right) = n + 1 + \frac{2}{n} \sum_{i=0}^{n-1} T(i). \quad (10.9)$$

To solve this recursion, it will be helpful to get rid of the fractional part, so that only integers are manipulated. Multiplying both sides of (10.9) by n, one gets

$$nT(n) = n(n+1) + 2 \sum_{i=0}^{n-1} T(i). \quad (10.10)$$

We handled recursions already, but this one is different in that $T(n)$ does not just depend on $T(n-1)$ or $T\left(\frac{n}{2}\right)$, but rather on all of its previous values. This should remind us the summation technique studied in Section 9.4.1: introduce an additional equation, which is similar to, but different from, eq. (10.10). Since the formula is true for every n, let us rewrite it for $n - 1$:

$$(n-1)T(n-1) = (n-1)n + 2 \sum_{i=0}^{n-2} T(i). \quad (10.11)$$

Subtracting (10.11) from (10.10) then yields

$$nT(n) - (n-1)T(n-1) = 2n + 2T(n-1), \quad (10.12)$$

in which most elements of the summation have been canceled. Rearranging the terms, we get

$$nT(n) = 2n + (n+1)T(n-1), \quad (10.13)$$

in which the $(n+1)$ is annoying, because if we had $(n-1)$ instead, we could have defined $G(n) = nT(n)$ and rewrite (10.13) as $G(n) = 2n + G(n-1)$, which is already easy to solve. To still enable a substitution, we divide the two sides of (10.13) by both n and $n + 1$:

$$\frac{T(n)}{n+1} = \frac{2}{n+1} + \frac{T(n-1)}{n}, \tag{10.14}$$

suggesting to define $G(n) = \frac{T(n)}{n+1}$, which transforms (10.14) into

$$G(n) = \frac{2}{n+1} + G(n-1)$$

$$= \frac{2}{n+1} + \frac{2}{n} + G(n-2)$$

$$\vdots$$

$$= \frac{2}{n+1} + \frac{2}{n} + \cdots + \frac{2}{k+2} + G(k) \qquad \text{for all } k < n.$$

The boundary condition for T implies $G(1) = 0$, so we get

$$G(n) = \sum_{i=3}^{n+1} \frac{1}{i} \simeq \ln n,$$

as this is the harmonic sum we have seen in the analysis of uniform hashing in Section 9.4. Returning to the function T, the conclusion is

$$T(n) = (n+1)G(n) \in \theta(n \log n).$$

Incidentally, the average case complexity of Quicksort can be used to prove the divergence of the harmonic series: if it converges, then $G(n)$ would be bounded by a constant, implying that $T(n) \in O(n)$, but this contradicts the lower bound on the average for sorting.

In spite of its bad worst case, the average complexity of Quicksort is the best one could expect, which is why the method is still popular. Another reason for the importance of Quicksort is that it is the basis for the linear time select algorithm to be studied in the following section.

10.5 Finding the kth Largest Element

The average of a set of numbers is a widely used statistical tool, but it should not always be applied, because it may be biased by extreme values. For instance, if a billionaire joins a group of 99 people who earn very little, the average wealth in the group may be more than 10 million! A more adequate measure in this and many other cases would be the median, rather than the average. The *median* of a set of different numbers is the element m that splits the set into equal halves, that is, (about) half of the elements are smaller, and half of the elements are larger than m. The average is better known, probably because it is easier to evaluate.

A first attempt for finding the median of a set could be based on sorting the set beforehand; the median is then stored in the middle element of the sorted array, so there are $O(n \log n)$ algorithms for finding the median. But are $\Omega(n \log n)$ comparisons really necessary? Sorting seems to be an overkill, since it would yield not just the median, but also any other percentile, so maybe if we are willing to settle for getting only the median, the complexity could be lowered?

This leads to the idea of using just a *partial* sort, though there are many possible interpretations for this partiality. For **Bubblesort** and **Heapsort**, for instance, the last k elements are already in order after k iterations. This means that to find the median, one could exit the sorting procedure after $\frac{n}{2}$ iterations. But for **Bubblesort**, this would still require $\sum_{i=n/2}^{n} i = \Omega(n^2)$ comparisons, and for **Heapsort**, $n + \sum_{i=n/2}^{n} \log i = \Omega(n \log n)$, so not much has been gained.

Quicksort seems to be a better choice in this context, because the partition step in itself is already a kind of partial sort. Refer to Figure 10.7 describing the order of the elements after the partition step. To complete the sorting, both S_1 and S_2 need to be sorted, but for finding the median, it is sufficient to sort only one of the sets, the one containing the element indexed $\frac{n}{2}$. This means that one of the recursive calls in the algorithm in Figure 10.8 could be saved in each iteration.

A new problem, however, arises. A recursive program is based on the assumption that the subproblem to be solved by a recursive call is identical to the original problem, just applied to a smaller input. For example, the first action of **Mergesort** is to sort, recursively, half of the original input array. But this assumption does not hold for the present problem. In our attempt to adapt **Quicksort** to find the median, the recursive call will be either with S_1 or S_2, unless, of course, their sizes are equal in which case the median is K. Yet it is not the *median* of S_1 or S_2 we are looking for, but the element in position $\frac{n}{2}$. An example will illustrate this difficulty. Suppose the set A in Figure 10.7 is of size 101, and that $|S_1|$, the size of S_1, is 69, so that K is stored at index 70. The median of A is the element that should be at position 50, and therefore belongs to S_1, but this is not the median of S_1; the latter should be at index 35, not at index 50.

This is one of the cases in which a more general, and thus supposedly, more difficult, problem will actually turn out to be easier to solve. Instead of writing an algorithm that returns the median of a set, we generalize the problem by adding an additional parameter, and look for an algorithm **Select**(A, k) which, given a set A of size n and an index k, with $1 \le k \le n$, returns the kth largest

Select1(A, k)

  $j \longleftarrow$ Partition(A)
  if $k = j$ then return $A[j]$
  else
        $S_1 \longleftarrow A[1 : j - 1]$
        $S_2 \longleftarrow A[j + 1 : n]$
        if $k < j$ then   Select1(S_1, k)
        else   // here $k > j$
                             Select1$(S_2, k - j)$

Figure 10.12. Select1(A, k) – find the kth largest element of A, first version.

element of A. Clearly,

$$\text{Median}(A) \;=\; \text{Select}\!\left(A, \frac{n}{2}\right),$$

so an algorithm for Select will in particular also solve the median problem, and in fact also any percentile.

Why is it easier to solve the more general problem? Because the addition of a parameter gives us the flexibility to use different parameters in different calls, which enables the use of recursion where it could not be applied before.

To find the kth largest element, we start with a partition step just as for Quicksort. Suppose the partition element was placed at index j. Then if $k = j$, we were very lucky: the partition element, that has been chosen independently of the input parameter k, just happened to be exactly the sought element! If k is smaller than j, then the element must be in S_1, and it is the kth largest element of S_1. The third case is when $k > j$; then the element is in S_2, but it is not the kth largest there. We know that there are j elements in A that are smaller than any element in S_2: all the elements of S_1 and the partition element K. Therefore the kth largest element of A will be the $(k - j)$th largest element of S_2. This is summarized in the algorithm of Figure 10.12, which assumes $|A| > 1$ and $1 \leq k \leq |A| = n$. We call it Select1 because this is only a first sketch that will be improved later.

The Select1 algorithm of Figure 10.12 might look better than Quicksort of Figure 10.8, because there is only a single recursive call, but remember that in the worst case of Quicksort, when the partition element fell always at the left or right end of the array, there was also only one recursive call. In fact, the worst case remains the same for Select1 as for Quicksort and will take time $\Omega(n^2)$.

It is the fact that there are no restrictions on the choice of the partition element which is to blame for this bad performance. If we could force it to fall always in the middle of the array, the sizes of S_1 and S_2 would be at most $\frac{n}{2}$, and the worst case complexity $T(n)$ of Select1 would satisfy the recurrence

$$T(n) = n + T\!\left(\frac{n}{2}\right) = n + \frac{n}{2} + \frac{n}{4} + \cdots = O(n). \tag{10.15}$$

But this means that we would like to choose K as the median of the set, which is exactly the problem we started with in the first place! We circumvent this complication by relaxing the requirement on K to be not necessarily *equal* to the median, but just *close to* it, where the exact meaning of this closeness will be defined later.

Instead of choosing K simply as $A[1]$, the first element of the array, in the Partition procedure, this command will be replaced in the improved version called Select by the following curious steps:

(i) Choose a small, odd integer b as parameter – its value will be fixed after the analysis.
(ii) Consider the array A as a sequence of $\frac{n}{b}$ disjoint subsets of size b:
$A[1 : b], A[b + 1 : 2b], \ldots$
(iii) Sort each of the b-tuples.
(iv) Define C as the set of the medians of the sorted b-tuples.
(v) Define K as the median of the set C of medians.

The parameter b should be small, so that the time for sorting a b-tuple may be considered as constant; it should be odd to facilitate the extraction of the median of each b-tuple. The size of the set C is $\frac{n}{b}$, thus the command in step 5 can be performed by a recursive call:

$$K \longleftarrow \text{Select}\!\left(C, \frac{n}{2b}\right).$$

To understand why this strange sequence of commands is helpful, consider the schematic of the n elements into a $b \times \frac{n}{b}$ matrix shown in Figure 10.13. Each column represents one of the b-tuples, which we assume here already sorted in increasing order bottom to top. The set C of the medians are the darker circles. We further assume that the columns are arranged so that the column containing K, the median of the medians which appears here in black, is in the center, and that the columns in the left part have their gray median elements smaller than K, and the columns in the right part being those with their gray median elements larger than K.

Pick one of the (white) elements in the lower left part of the matrix, that is, within the area surrounded by the solid black polygon. The element is smaller than the (gray) median above it, belonging to the same column, which in turn is smaller than the (black) partition element K. Since this is true for all the elements in this area, we know that all these elements are smaller than K, and thus belong to S_1. It follows that there are at least $\frac{n}{4}$ elements in S_1, so that S_2 cannot be larger than $\frac{3}{4}n$. A symmetric argument shows that all the elements in the upper right quarter, surrounded by the broken line, are larger than K and thus in S_2. Therefore $|S_2| \geq \frac{n}{4}$, implying that $|S_1| \leq \frac{3}{4}n$.

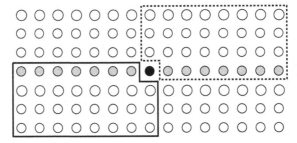

Figure 10.13. Schematic of the set A as a matrix of size $b \times \frac{n}{b}$.

We now understand that the ultimate goal of the complicated choice procedure for the partition element was to distance it from the extremities, and to force it to be close to the middle in the sense that its index should be in the range $\left[\frac{n}{4}, \frac{3n}{4}\right]$. This yields an upper bound on the size of the input set in the recursive call of at most $\frac{3}{4}$ of the size in the calling routine. Figure 10.14 summarizes the Select algorithm.

Line 1 deals with the boundary condition to exit the recursion. It obviously makes not much sense to apply the partition into b-tuples on very small input sets, and the size of 50 elements has been set empirically and does not influence the order of magnitude of the complexity. Smaller sets are just sorted by any method, and the kth largest element can then be found by direct access. Lines 3–5 are the definition of the partition element according to the steps we saw earlier, and the rest of the algorithm is just adapted from Select1.

Denote the number of comparisons made by Select on an input of size n by $T(n)$. Remark that though Select has also another parameter k, we seek a

Select(A, k)

```
1      if |A| < 50 then sort(A) and return k-th element
2      else
3          sort b-tuples A[rb + 1 : (r + 1)b] for 0 ≤ r < n/b
4          C ⟵ medians of b-tuples
5          K ⟵ Select(C, n/2b)
6          S₁ ⟵ {x ∈ A | x < K}
7          S₂ ⟵ {x ∈ A | x > K}
8          if k = |S₁| + 1 then return K
9          else    if k < |S₁| + 1 then      Select(S₁, k)
10                 else                       Select(S₂, k − |S₁| − 1)
```

Figure 10.14. Select(A, k) – find the kth largest element of A, with better worst case.

bound on $T(n)$ that is independent of k. If $n < 50$, then $T(n) < n \log_2 n < 6n$, according to line 1. Otherwise the following apply:

(i) Each b-tuple in line 3 can be sorted in $O(b^2)$ steps and there are $\frac{n}{b}$ such tuples, so the entire step requires at most bn comparisons.

(ii) There are no comparisons in line 4.

(iii) Line 5 is a recursive call with a set C of size $\frac{n}{b}$, which can be done in time $T\left(\frac{n}{b}\right)$.

(iv) Lines 6-7 are the partition, performed by a linear scan, that is, in $O(n)$.

(v) In the worst case, there is one more recursive call, either with S_1 or with S_2; in any case, the time will be bounded by $T\left(\frac{3n}{4}\right)$.

Collecting all the terms, we get

$$T(n) \leq \begin{cases} 6n & \text{if } n < 50 \\ T\left(\frac{n}{b}\right) + T\left(\frac{3n}{4}\right) + cn, & \text{if } n \geq 50 \end{cases} \tag{10.16}$$

for some constant $c > 1$. This recurrence is a bit different from those we have seen so far.

Background Concept: Recurrence Relations

Many programs are based on recursive algorithms and, consequently, the analysis of these algorithms contains recurrence relations, of which (10.16) is a typical example. The general solution of such relations is a subject for an entire course and is beyond the scope of this book. We shall just give here some useful rules of thumb.

If the function T we wish to evaluate recurs only once on the right-hand side, like, for example, in (10.15), we might be able to get a closed formula for $T(n)$ by repeatedly substituting the formula until a boundary condition is reached. But if there are multiple occurrences of T on the right-hand side, as in (10.16), substitution may not help, and the formula can get longer and increasingly complicated. It then often helps to guess the order of magnitude of $T(n)$, and to try to prove it by induction on n. The problem is, of course, to know what to guess.

For recursion to work properly, the recursive call must be with an input that is strictly smaller, in some sense, than the original one. Usually it is with an input set that is a strict subset of the input dealt with by the calling function. Suppose then that the recurrence relation for the given algorithm is of the form

$$T(n) \leq T(\alpha_1 n) + T(\alpha_2 n) + \cdots + T(\alpha_s n) + cn,$$

where all α_i are smaller than 1 and c is some constant. Then

(i) if $\alpha_1 + \alpha_2 + \cdots + \alpha_s < 1$, then one may guess that $T(n) \in O(n)$;
(ii) if $\alpha_1 + \alpha_2 + \cdots + \alpha_s = 1$, then one may guess that $T(n) \in \theta(n \log n)$;
(iii) if $\alpha_1 + \alpha_2 + \cdots + \alpha_s > 1$, then one may guess that $T(n) \in \Omega(n^d)$, for some constant $d > 1$.

No proof will be given here as this is just a suggestion for an educated guess. In any case, the actual formula has to be shown by induction.

Before solving the recurrence (10.16), recall that we still have the freedom of choosing the parameter b. The formula in (10.16) corresponds to $\alpha_1 = \frac{1}{b}$ and $\alpha_2 = \frac{3}{4}$. To get a linear behavior, we would like to have $\alpha_1 + \alpha_2 < 1$, thus $b = 3$ is not adequate. The smallest value for b is therefore $b = 5$. This means that we use quintuples in the first partition, each of which can be sorted in 7 comparisons as mentioned earlier. The recurrence becomes

$$T(n) \leq \begin{cases} 6n & \text{if } n < 50 \\ T\left(\frac{n}{5}\right) + T\left(\frac{3n}{4}\right) + cn, & \text{if } n \geq 50. \end{cases} \tag{10.17}$$

Claim 10.3. $\qquad\qquad\qquad T(n) \leq 20\,c\,n.$

Proof by induction on n. The inequality holds trivially for $n < 50$. Suppose then that it is true for all values up to $n - 1$, and let us show it for n, where $n \geq 50$:

$$T(n) \leq T\left(\frac{n}{5}\right) + T\left(\frac{3n}{4}\right) + cn$$

$$\leq 4\,c\,n + 15\,c\,n + c\,n = 20\,c\,n,$$

where we have used the inductive assumption on $\frac{n}{5}$ and on $\frac{3n}{4}$, which are both strictly smaller than n. This may sound trivial, but it is not: the size of a set has to be rounded to be an integer, and, for instance for $n = 2$, $\lceil \frac{3n}{4} \rceil = \lceil 1.5 \rceil = 2$, so it is *not* smaller than n. This is an additional reason for choosing the boundary condition not at $n = 1$ or 2, but high enough so that $\lceil \frac{3n}{4} \rceil < n$. ∎

We conclude that the kth largest element of an unordered set in general, and its median in particular, can be found in time that is linear in the size of the set, thus without sorting it. This fact has a multitude of applications, and has been used to improve the complexity of many algorithms.

Exercises

10.1 Show how to sort 5 elements in 7 comparisons.

10.2 You are given 12 balls that seem to be identical, but the weight of one of the balls is different. The problem is to find this ball and to decide if it is lighter or heavier by means of a two sided weighing scale.

   (a) Give a lower bound ℓ on the number of necessary weighings.
   (b) Show how to solve the problem in ℓ weighings.
   (c) Change the number of balls to 13 and derive the corresponding lower bound.
   (d) Show that the problem with 13 balls cannot be solved in 3 weighings.

10.3 Give a sorting algorithm and a probability distribution of the possible input permutations for which the average time complexity is $O(n)$.

10.4 Assuming a uniform distribution, the average time of any sorting algorithm has been shown in eq. (10.5) to be $\frac{1}{n!}D(T)$, where T is the corresponding decision tree. For the particular case of Quicksort, we saw another formula in eq. (10.9), which had only n in the denominator, not $n!$. Explain this presumed discrepancy.

10.5 You are given an unsorted array A of n numbers. Show that the task of building a search tree for the n elements of A requires at least $\Omega(n \log n)$ comparisons.

10.6 An additional possibility for a definition of a partial sort is to partition a given set of n different numbers into K subsets $S_1, \ldots, S_K$, each of size $\frac{n}{K}$, where K is an integer $K \geq 2$, such that each element in S_i is smaller than any element in S_{i+1}, for $1 \leq i < K$. The sets S_i themselves are not sorted. Show how to perform this partial sort in time $O(n \log K)$. **Hint:** Start with assuming that K is a power of 2, then show how to generalize to any K.

10.7 Instead of using the median of the medians of 5-tuples as partition element K in Select, could we not simply choose K as the median of some subset of A, for example, by

$$K \longleftarrow \text{Select}\left(A[1 : \tfrac{n}{2}], \tfrac{n}{4}\right),$$

as this would also imply an upper bound of $\frac{3}{4}n$ on the sizes of both S_1 and S_2? So what is wrong with this choice, which seems to be much easier to implement?

11

Codes

11.1 Representing the Data

You have reached the last chapter and it deals with *codes*, which share some common properties with data structures as auxiliary tools in many algorithms and programs. Studying these codes will also give an opportunity to conclude this work by reviewing some of the data structures introduced in previous chapters.

The purpose of codes is to bridge the communication gap between humans and machines. Our civilization has generated over the years some quite sophisticated natural languages, yet our computers insist on talking only binary, forcing us to translate whatever information we wish to share with a computer, be it a command or a piece of data, into some binary equivalent. This translation is often called an *encoding*, the translated elements are *code words* and their set form a *code*.

In the simplest scenario, the elements to be encoded are just the letters of some alphabet, like {a, b, c, . . . , y, z}, but one may need to encode also infinite sets as the integers {0, 1, 2, . . .}, or letter pairs {aa, ab, . . .}, or sets of words {the, of, which, . . .}. Ultimately, the set A to be encoded may be of any nature, as long as there is a well defined way to break a given file into a sequence of elements of A. We shall refer to A as an *alphabet* and call its elements *letters* or *characters*, even in the more involved cases, so these terms should not be understood in their restrictive sense.

The choice of a code will be guided by the intended application and expected properties. In many situations, it will be the simplicity of the processing of the code that will be considered as its main advantage, leading to the usage of some standard *fixed length* code, for which all the code words consist of the same number of bits. One of the popular such codes is the American Standard

Code for Information Interchange (ASCII), for which each code word is eight bits long, providing for the encoding of $2^8 = 256$ different elements.

The encoding and decoding processes for fixed length codes are straightforward: to encode, just concatenate the code words corresponding to the letters of the message, to decode, break the encoded string into blocks of the given size, and then use a decoding table to translate the code words back into the letters they represent. For example, the ASCII representation of the word ascii is

$$01100001011100110110001101101001011101001,$$

which can be broken into

$$01100001 \mid 01110011 \mid 01100011 \mid 01101001 \mid 01101001.$$

However, it is not always possible to use a fixed length encoding, for example, when the set $\mathcal{A}$ of elements is potentially infinite, and even when it is possible, it may be wasteful, for example when we aim for storage savings via data compression.

Of the many possible applications, we shall briefly address only on the following topics.

(i) **Compression codes:** trying to reduce the number of necessary bits to encode the data without losing a single bit of information
(ii) **Universal codes:** efficiently encoding the integers or other infinite alphabets
(iii) **Error-correcting codes:** recovering the original data even in the presence of erroneous bits
(iv) **Cryptographic codes:** dealing with the possibility of two parties to exchange messages, while hiding their contents from others, even if the encoded messages are accessible to all

This list is far from covering all the possible applications of codes, and even for those mentioned, it is just the tip of an iceberg: each of the preceding topics is on its own the subject of many books and entire courses.

11.2 Compression Codes

The frequencies of the characters in a typical text written in some natural language are not uniformly distributed, as can be seen in Table 11.1, showing the probabilities, in percent, of some of the characters for English, French and German. The order from left to right is by decreasing frequency in English.

Table 11.1. *Distribution of characters in natural languages*

	E	T	A	O	...	J	X	Q	Z
English	12.7	9.1	8.2	7.5		0.2	0.2	0.1	0.1
French	14.7	7.2	7.6	5.4		0.5	0.4	1.4	0.1
German	17.4	6.2	6.5	2.5		0.3	0.03	0.02	1.1

It therefore does not seem economical to allot the same number of bits to each of the characters. If one is willing to trade the convenience of working with a fixed length code for getting a representation that is more space efficient but harder to process, one could use *variable length* codes. One can then assign shorter code words to the more frequent characters, even at the price of encoding the rare characters by longer strings, as long as the *average* code word length is reduced. Encoding is just as simple as with fixed length codes and still consists in concatenating the code word strings. There are however a few technical problems concerning the decoding that have to be dealt with.

Not every set of binary strings can be considered as a useful code. Consider, for example, the five code words in column (a) of Figure 11.1. A string of 0s is easily recognized as a sequence of As, and the string 11001100 can only be parsed as BABA. However, the string 01001110 has two possible interpretations:

$$0 \mid 1001 \mid 110 = \text{ADB} \qquad \text{or} \qquad 010 \mid 0 \mid 1110 = \text{CAE}.$$

The existence of such a string disqualifies the given code, because it violates a basic property without which the code is useless, namely that the encoding should be reversible. We shall thus restrict attention to codes for which *every* binary string obtained by concatenating code words can be parsed only into the original sequence of code words. Such codes are called *uniquely decipherable* (UD).

A 0	A 11	A 11	A 1
B 110	B 110	B 011	B 00
C 010	C 1100	C 0011	C 011
D 1001	D 1101	D 1011	D 0101
E 1110	E 11000	E 00011	E 0100

	UD	prefix	complete
Non-UD	non-prefix	non-complete	
(a)	(b)	(c)	(d)

Figure 11.1. Examples of codes.

There are efficient algorithms to check the unique decipherability of a given code, even though infinitely many potential concatenations have to be considered a priori. A necessary condition for a code to be UD is that its code words should not be too short, and more precisely, any binary UD code with code word lengths $\{\ell_1, \ldots, \ell_n\}$ satisfies

$$\sum_{i=1}^{n} 2^{-\ell_i} \leq 1. \tag{11.1}$$

For example, the sums for the codes (a) to (d) of Figure 11.1 are 0.875, 0.53125, 0.53125 and 1, respectively. Case (a) is also an example showing that the condition in eq. (11.1) is not sufficient for a code to be UD.

On the other hand, it is not always obvious how to decode, even if the given code is UD. The code in column (b) of Figure 11.1 is UD, but consider the encoded string 11011111110: a first attempt to parse it as

$$110 \mid 11 \mid 11 \mid 11 \mid 10 = \text{BAAA10} \tag{11.2}$$

would fail, because the tail 10 is not the prefix of any code word; hence only when trying to decode the fifth code word do we realize that the first one is not correct, and that the parsing should rather be

$$1101 \mid 11 \mid 11 \mid 110 = \text{DAAB}. \tag{11.3}$$

11.2.1 Prefix Codes

Unlike in the example of eq. (11.3), we should be able to recognize a code word as soon as all its bits are processed, that is, without any delay; such codes are called *instantaneous*. Instantaneous codes have the *prefix property*, and are hence also called *prefix codes*. A code is said to have the prefix property if none of its code words is a prefix of any other. For example, the code in Figure 11.1(a) is not prefix because the code word for A (0) is a prefix of the code word for C (010). Similarly, the code in (b) is not prefix, since all the code words start with 11, which is the code word for A. On the other hand, codes (c) and (d) are prefix.

The equivalence between instantaneous and prefix codes is easy to see. Suppose a prefix code is given and that a code word x is detected during the decoding of a given string. There can be no ambiguity in this case as we had in the decoding attempt in eq. (11.2), because if there were another possible interpretation y which can be detected later, like in eq. (11.3), it would imply that x is a prefix of y, contradicting the prefix property. Conversely, if a code is instantaneous and a code word x is detected, then x cannot be the prefix of any other code word.

The conclusion is that the prefix property is a sufficient, albeit not necessary, condition for a code to be UD, and we shall henceforth concentrate on prefix codes. In fact, no loss is incurred by this restriction: it can be shown that given any UD code with code word lengths $\{\ell_1, \ldots, \ell_n\}$, one can construct a prefix code with the same set of code word lengths. As example, note that the prefix code (c) of Figure 11.1 has the same code word lengths as code (b). In this special case, the code words of code (c) are obtained from those of code (b) by reversing the strings; now every code word terminates in 11, and the substring 11 occurs only as suffix of any code word, thus no code word can be the proper prefix of any other. Incidently, this also shows that code (b), which is not prefix, is nevertheless UD. We shall return to this example in Section 11.3.2.

A connecting link between this chapter on codes and Chapter 4, which dealt with trees, is the following natural one-to-one correspondence between binary prefix codes and binary trees. We assign labels to both edges and vertices of a binary tree in the following way:

(i) Every edge pointing to a left child is assigned the label 0, and every edge pointing to a right child is assigned the label 1.
(ii) The root of the tree is assigned the empty string.
(iii) Every vertex v of the tree below the root is assigned a binary string which is obtained by concatenating the labels on the edges of the path leading from the root to vertex v.

It follows from the construction that the string associated with vertex v is a prefix of the string associated with vertex w if and only if v is on the path from the root to w. Thus the set of strings associated with the *leaves* of any binary tree satisfies the prefix property and may be considered as a prefix code. Conversely, given any prefix code, one can easily construct the corresponding binary tree. For example, the tree corresponding to the code $\{11, 001, 0100, 0101\}$ is depicted in Figure 11.2, in which the leaves labeled by the code words have been emphasized.

Based on this bijection between general binary trees and prefix codes, we can consider their sets as equivalent. In particular, we might be interested in the subset of codes corresponding to *complete* binary trees, see their definition and properties in Section 4.3. There are good reasons to consider complete trees: if not all the internal nodes of the tree have two children, like certain nodes in Figure 11.2, one could replace certain code words by shorter ones, without violating the prefix property, i.e., build another UD code with strictly smaller

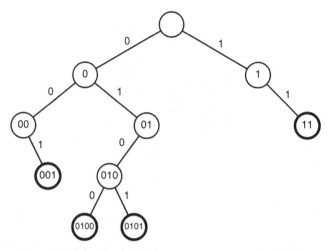

Figure 11.2. Tree corresponding to the code $\{11, 001, 0100, 0101\}$.

average code word length. For example, the nodes labeled 1 and 00 have only a right child, so the code words 11 and 001 could be replaced by 1 and 00, respectively; similarly, the vertex labeled 01 has only a left child, so the code words 0100 and 0101 could be transformed by deleting their third bit from the left, yielding 010 and 011, respectively.

As alternative, instead of replacing code words by shorter ones, one could add more code words to the code: if 0100 and 0101 remain in the tree, one could add, for instance, 011. After these amendments, the tree of Figure 11.2 is transformed into a complete one corresponding to the code in Figure 11.1(d), which is, accordingly, called a *complete code*. A code is complete if and only if the lengths $\{\ell_i\}$ of its code words satisfy eq. (11.1) with equality, i.e., $\sum_{i=1}^{n} 2^{-\ell_i} = 1$. This has been shown in Theorem 4.1. An equivalent definition is that a complete binary prefix code is a set C of binary code words which is a binary prefix code, but the addition of any binary string x turns the set into a code $C \cup \{x\}$ which is not UD.

11.2.2 Huffman Coding

Figure 11.3 summarizes schematically how the class of codes under consideration has been restricted in several steps. Starting with a restriction to general UD codes, passing to instantaneous, or equivalently, prefix codes, and finally to complete prefix codes, since we are interested in good compression performance. Even this last set of complete codes is large enough to focus further,

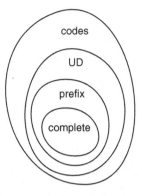

Figure 11.3. Progressively restricting the set of codes.

aiming for adapting an *optimal* code to a given distribution of the character frequencies.

The general problem can thus be stated as follows: we are given a set of n nonnegative weights $\{w_1, \ldots, w_n\}$, which are the frequencies of occurrence of the letters of some alphabet. The problem is to generate a complete binary variable-length prefix code, consisting of code words with lengths ℓ_i bits, $1 \leq i \leq n$, with optimal compression capabilities, i.e., such that the *total length* of the encoded text

$$\sum_{i=1}^{n} w_i \ell_i \qquad (11.4)$$

is minimized.

If one forgets about the interpretation of the ℓ_i as code word lengths, and tries to solve the minimization problem analytically without restricting the ℓ_i to be integers, but still keeping the constraint that they must satisfy the equality $\sum_{i=1}^{n} 2^{-\ell_i} = 1$, one gets

$$\ell_i = -\log_2\left(\frac{w_i}{W}\right) = -\log_2 p_i,$$

where $W = \sum_{i=1}^{n} w_i$ is the sum of the frequencies and thus the total length of the file, and $p_i = w_i/W$ is the relative frequency or probability of the ith letter. This quantity is known as *the information content* of a symbol with probability p_i, and it represents the exact number of bits in which the symbol should ideally be encoded. Note that this number is not necessarily an integer. Returning to the sum in (11.4), we may therefore conclude that the lower limit of the total size of the encoded file is given by

$$-\sum_{i=1}^{n} w_i \log_2 p_i = W\left(-\sum_{i=1}^{n} p_i \log_2 p_i\right).$$

The quantity $H = -\sum_{i=1}^{n} p_i \log_2 p_i$, which is the weighted average of the information contents, has been defined by C. E. Shannon as the *entropy* of the probability distribution $\{p_1, \ldots, p_n\}$, and it gives a lower bound on the average code word length.

Returning to our problem, the lower bound does not really help, because we have to satisfy the additional constraint that the code word lengths have to be integers. In 1952, D. Huffman proposed the following algorithm which solves the problem in an optimal way.

(i) If $n = 1$, the code word corresponding to the only weight is the null-string.
(ii) Let w_1 and w_2, without loss of generality, be the two smallest weights.
(iii) Solve the problem recursively for the $n - 1$ weights $w_1 + w_2$, $w_3, \ldots, w_n$; let α be the code word assigned to the weight $w_1 + w_2$.
(iv) The code for the n weights is obtained from the code for $n - 1$ weights generated in point 3 by replacing α by the two code words $\alpha 0$ and $\alpha 1$.

In the obvious implementation of the code construction, the weights are first sorted and then every weight obtained by combining the two which are currently the smallest, is inserted in its proper place in the sequence so as to maintain order. This yields an $O(n^2)$ time complexity. One can reduce the time complexity to $O(n \log n)$ by using two queues, as we saw in Section 2.2.1. As alternative, the weights could be used to build a min-heap in time $O(n)$ (see Chapter 7). Each iteration consists then of two min-extractions and one insertion, all of which can be done in $O(\log n)$, for a total of $O(n \log n)$.

As example, suppose we wish to build a Huffman code for certain countries according to the number of their Nobel laureates. The ordered frequencies are given in Figure 11.4 next to the name of the countries. In each iteration, the two smallest numbers are removed from the list, and their sum is inserted in the proper position, until only two frequencies remain. If 437 is assigned the code word $\alpha = 0$, then the code words for 241 and 196 are 00 and 01, and the other code words are derived similarly in a backward scan of the columns. The final code appears in the leftmost column of Figure 11.4, and the corresponding Huffman tree, showing the frequencies in its nodes, is in Figure 11.5.

1	USA	353	353	353	353	353	353	353	353	437
000	UK	125	125	125	125	125	125	196	241	353
010	Germany	105	105	105	105	105	116	125	196	
0010	France	61	61	61	61	91	105	116		
00110	Sweden	30	44	47	55	61	91			
00111	Switzerland	25	30	44	47	55				
01100	Japan	24	25	30	44					
01101	Canada	23	24	25						
01110	Russia	23	23							
01111	Austria	21								

Figure 11.4. Huffman code on Nobel laureates distribution.

The decompression of a Huffman encoded string, or actually of any binary string S, which is the encoding of some text according to a prefix code C, can be conveniently performed by repeatedly scanning the tree T corresponding to C. As initialization, a pointer p points to the root of T and an index i is used to identify the currently scanned bit of the encoded string. We assume that the leaves of the tree store the corresponding characters in their *value* fields. In the tree of Figure 11.5, the "characters" are country names and appear underneath the corresponding leaves. For example, the encoding of the countries of the Nobel Prize laureates in Chemistry and Physics for 2015 would be 000110110001101,

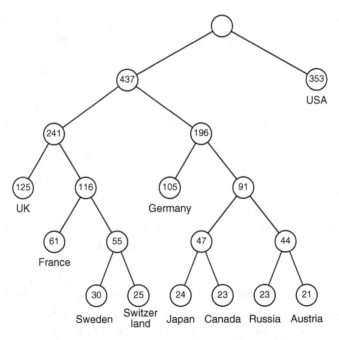

Figure 11.5. Huffman tree of the code of Figure 11.4.

```
Decode(S, T)
    p ⟵ root(T)
    for i ⟵ 1 to |S|
        if S[i] = 0 then
                    p ⟵ left(p)
        else    p ⟵ right(p)
        if p is a leaf then
                    output value(p)
                    p ⟵ root(T)
```

Figure 11.6. Decoding a string S using the tree T of the corresponding code.

to be decoded as **UK, USA, USA, Japan, Canada**. The formal decoding, with parameters S and T, is given in Figure 11.6.

The fact that Huffman's construction yields an optimal tree is far from being obvious. The proof is based on the following claims concerning optimal trees in general. Let T_1 be an optimal tree for a set of $n \geq 2$ weights $\{w_1, \ldots, w_n\}$. To simplify the description, we shall refer to the w_i as probabilities, but the claims are true for any set of weights. Denote the average code word length by $M_1 = \sum_{i=1}^{n} w_i l_i$, where l_i is the length of the code word assigned to weight w_i.

Claim 11.1. There are at least two elements on the lowest level of T_1.

Proof Suppose there is only one such element and let $\gamma = a_1 \cdots a_m$ be the corresponding binary code word. Then by replacing γ by $a_1 \cdots a_{m-1}$ (i.e., dropping the last bit) the resulting code would still be prefix, and the average code word length would be smaller, in contradiction with T_1s optimality. ∎

Claim 11.2. The code words c_1 and c_2 corresponding to the smallest weights w_1 and w_2 have maximal length (the nodes are on the lowest level in T_1).

Proof Suppose the element with weight w_2 is on level m, which is not the lowest level ℓ. Then there is an element with weight $w_x > w_2$ at level ℓ. Thus the tree obtained by switching w_x with w_2 has an average code word length of

$$M_1 - w_x \ell - w_2 m + w_x m + w_2 \ell = M_1 - (\ell - m)(w_x - w_2) < M_1,$$

which is impossible since T_1 is optimal. ∎

Claim 11.3. Without loss of generality one can assume that the smallest weights w_1 and w_2 correspond to sibling nodes in T_1.

Proof Otherwise one could switch elements without changing the average code word length. ∎

Theorem 11.1. Huffman's algorithm yields an optimal code.

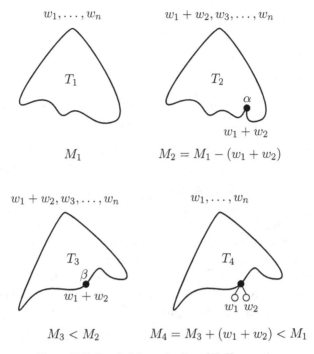

Figure 11.7. Proof of the optimality of Huffman codes.

Proof By induction on the number of elements n. For $n = 2$, there is only one complete binary prefix code, which therefore is optimal, namely $\{0, 1\}$; this is also a Huffman code, regardless of the weights w_1 and w_2.

Assume the truth of the theorem for $n - 1$. Let T_1 be an optimal tree for the weights $\{w_1, \ldots, w_n\}$ as the tree mentioned in the earlier claims. We shall show that a Huffman tree built for the same set of weights yields the same average code word length M_1, which shows that it is optimal.

It will be convenient to follow the description of the following various trees referring to their schematic in Figure 11.7. The weights appear above the trees, and the average code word length below them.

Consider the tree T_2 obtained from T_1 by replacing the sibling nodes corresponding to w_1 and w_2 by their common parent node α, indicated by the black dot in Figure 11.7, to which the weight $w_1 + w_2$ is assigned. Thus the average code word length for T_2 is $M_2 = M_1 - (w_1 + w_2)$. There is no reason to believe that T_2 should be optimal for the weights $(w_1 + w_2), w_3, \ldots, w_n$. We started from an optimal tree T_1, made some very local transformation on its structure, affecting only a few nodes, and assigned, seemingly arbitrarily, $n - 1$

new weights to the $n-1$ leaves of T_2. Why should such a minor modification of the tree keep the optimality of the tree we started with?

Nonetheless, we shall prove that this is precisely the case.

Claim 11.4. T_2 is optimal for the weights $(w_1 + w_2), w_3, \ldots, w_n$.

Proof If not, let T_3 be a better tree with average code word length $M_3 < M_2$. Note that while T_2 is almost identical to T_1, the shape of T_3 can be entirely different from that of T_2 and thus also from that of T_1, as shown in Figure 11.7. Let β be the leaf in T_3 corresponding to the weight $(w_1 + w_2)$. Consider the tree T_4 obtained from T_3 by adding children to β, thereby transforming it into an internal node, and assigning the weight w_1 to β's left child and w_2 to its right child. Then the average code word length for T_4 is

$$M_4 = M_3 + (w_1 + w_2) < M_2 + (w_1 + w_2) = M_1,$$

but this is impossible, since T_4 is a tree for n elements with weights $w_1, \ldots, w_n$ and T_1 is optimal among all those trees, so T_4 cannot have a smaller average code word length. ∎

We may now return to the proof of the theorem. Using the inductive assumption, the tree T_2, which is optimal for $n-1$ elements, has the same average code word length as the Huffman tree for these weights. However, the Huffman tree for $w_1, \ldots, w_n$ is obtained from the Huffman tree for $(w_1 + w_2), w_3, \ldots, w_n$ in the same way as T_1 is obtained from T_2. Thus the Huffman tree for the n elements has the same average code word length as T_1, hence it is optimal. ∎

11.3 Universal Codes

Huffman's solution is not always applicable, for example, when the set to be encoded is the set of the integers. Of course, the specific set we deal with will always be finite, however, we may sometimes wish to prepare a fixed code for all the possible elements, so the set for which code words have to be generated may not be bounded. In that case, using the standard binary representation of an integer is not possible: the number 13 can be represented as 1101 in binary, but we have to decide if to use 1101 as a code word, or maybe rather 01101 or 0001101. The set of the code words without leading zeros $\{1, 10, 11, 100, 101, \ldots\}$ is not a prefix code and is not even UD! It can be turned into a UD code by adding leading zeros to form a fixed length code, but how many bits should then be used?

Let us reconsider the problem of encoding a string by means of a dictionary we studied in Section 3.4.2. Given is a text T and a dictionary D, and the problem is to parse T into a sequence of elements of D, so that T can be replaced by the correspondent sequence of pointers to D. We mentioned that the problem of finding a good dictionary D is difficult, but J. Ziv and A. Lempel suggested that T itself could be used as the dictionary! All one needs to do is to replace substrings s of T by pointers to earlier occurrences of s in T. The form of these pointers will be pairs (off, len), where off gives the offset of the occurrence, that is, how many characters do we have to search backward, and len is the number of characters to be copied. Here is an example, due to F. Schiller:

```
von-der-Stirne-heiß-rinnen-muß-der-Schweiß- ···
```

could be replaced by

```
von-der-Stirne-heiß-rin(11,2)(23,2)mu(11,2)(27,5)chw(23,4) ···
```

The question is how to encode the numbers off and len, since they could, theoretically, be as large as the length of the text up to that point. One usually sets some upper bound on off, which effectively means that we are looking for previous occurrences only within some fixed sized window preceding the current position. This size might be, say, 16K, so that $\log_2 16K = 14$ bits suffice to encode any offset. Similarly, one could impose an upper limit on len, of, say, 256 characters, so that it can be encoded in 8 bits. But most of the copied items will be shorter, thus using always the maximum is wasteful. Moreover, a longer copy item is not unrealistic, because overlaps are allowed. For instance, a string of k identical characters ccc$\cdots$c (often 0s or blanks) can be encoded by $c(1, k-1)$.

The solution we seek should thus be able of encoding any integer in some systematic way. A simple way could be a *unary* encoding, using the code words

$$1, 01, 001, 0001, 00001, 000001, \ldots, \qquad (11.5)$$

that is, the length of the nth code word will be n, which is not reasonable for most applications. We shall rather aim at getting a code word of length $O(\log n)$ to represent n. Infinite code word sets with such a property have been defined by P. Elias as being *universal* codes.

11.3.1 Elias Codes

The two best known codes devised by Elias have been called γ and δ. To build the code word for an integer $n \geq 1$ in Elias's γ code, start by using its standard binary representation without leading zeros, $B(n)$. The length of $B(n)$ is $\lfloor \log_2 n \rfloor + 1$ bits. Consider $B(n)$ without its leading 1-bit, and precede this string by an encoding of its length, using the unary encoding of eq. (11.5). For example, $B(100) = 1100100$, so the encoding of (decimal) 100 will be the suffix of length 6 of $B(100)$, preceded by six zeros and a 1-bit: 0000001100100. $B(1) = 1$, hence the suffix is empty and the string to be pre-pended is 1, thus the γ code word for 1 is 1 itself.

For decoding, the code word is scanned from its left end up to the first occurrence of a 1. If m zeros have been read, we know that the length of the code word is $2m + 1$, of which the rightmost $m + 1$ are the standard binary representation of the sought integer. Some sample code words of Elias's γ code appear in the second column of Table 11.2.

Because of the unary encoding of the length, the γ code is wasteful for large integers, which led to the definition of the δ code. We again start, as for γ, with $B(n)$ without its leading 1-bit, but instead of using a unary code for the length part, the length will be encoded using the γ code. This time, it will be the length of $B(n)$ including the leading 1-bit, because otherwise, the length to be encoded for the integer 1 would be zero, and the γ and δ codes are only defined for $n > 0$. Taking the same example as before, the suffix of length 6 of $B(100) = 1100100$ will be preceded by the γ code word for $|B(100)| = 7$, which is 00111, thus the δ code word for 100 is 00111100100.

Decoding the δ code word of some integer x is done in two stages. First a γ code word is detected. Since γ is a prefix code, this can be done, e.g., by some tree traversal, and no separating bit is needed. If this code word represents the integer m, then $m - 1$ more bits $b_1 b_2 \cdots b_{m-1}$ have to be read, and x is the integer such that $B(x) = 1 b_1 b_2 \cdots b_{m-1}$. For example, if the given code word is 0001010111101000, its only prefix representing a γ code word is 0001010, which is the γ encoding of the integer ten. We then read the next 9 bits, precede them by a leading 1-bits, and get 1111101000, which is the binary representation of (decimal) 1000. Sample code words of Elias's δ code appear in the third column of Table 11.2.

The length of the δ code word for n, $2\lfloor \log_2(\lfloor \log_2 n \rfloor + 1) \rfloor + 1 + \lfloor \log_2 n \rfloor$, is therefore asymptotically smaller than that of the corresponding γ code word, which is $2\lfloor \log_2 n \rfloor + 1$, but that does not mean that δ codes are always preferable to γ codes. The integers to be encoded do generally not appear with a uniform distribution, and it will often happen that the smaller values are much more frequent than larger ones. Yet, it is precisely for these small values that γ has shorter code words than δ, and there are probability distributions on the integers for which the *average* code word length will be shorter for γ than for δ.

Table 11.2. *Elias's γ, Elias's δ, and Fibonacci codes*

Index	Elias's γ	Elias's δ	Fibonacci
1	1	1	11
2	010	0100	011
3	011	0101	0011
4	00100	01100	1011
5	00101	01101	00011
6	00110	01110	10011
7	00111	01111	01011
8	0001000	00100000	000011
9	0001001	00100001	100011
15	0001111	00100111	0100011
16	000010000	001010000	0010011
17	000010001	001010001	1010011
100	0000001100100	00111100100	00101000011
128	000000010000000	00010000000000	00010001011
1000	00000000011111101000	0001010111101000	0000010000000011

It should also be mentioned that encoding the integers is not restricted to numerical applications only. Consider a large corpus of textual data written in some natural language. A popular way to encode it is by generating a code for all the different *words*, rather than just for the different characters. This extended "alphabet" may consist of hundreds of thousands of different terms, and using Huffman coding according to their probabilities of occurrence in the text yields quite good compression performance. The advantage of using this particular dictionary is that large texts are often the heart of some *Information Retrieval* system, as those mentioned in Section 8.1.1. Such systems need the list of the different terms anyway in their inverted files, so there is no additional overhead in using the list also for compression.

It will often be convenient not to generate a new optimal Huffman code after each update of the text, but to use a code that is fixed in advance. The encoding algorithm would then be as follows:

(i) Sort the different terms by nonincreasing frequency.
(ii) Assign the ith code word of some universal code, which is the encoding of the integer i, to the ith term of the sorted list.

For example, the most frequent words are, in order,

for English: the, be, to, of, and, a, in, that, have, I, ...
for French: le, de, un, être, et, à, il, avoir, ne, je, ...
for German: der, die, und, in, den, von, zu, das, mit, sich, ...

The first terms in English, the, be, and to, could then be encoded with a γ code by $1, 010$, and 011, respectively.

11.3.2 Fibonacci Codes

An alternative to Elias codes with interesting features is to base the code on the Fibonacci numbers we have seen when studying the depth of AVL trees in Section 5.2. The standard representation of an integer as a binary string is based on a numeration system whose basis elements are the powers of 2. If the number B is represented by the k-bit string $b_{k-1}b_{k-2}\cdots b_1 b_0$, then

$$B = \sum_{i=0}^{k-1} b_i 2^i.$$

But many other possible binary representations do exist, and let us consider those using the Fibonacci sequence as basis elements. Recall that we have defined the Fibonacci sequence in eq. (5.7) as

$$\{F(0), F(1), F(2), F(3), \ldots\} = \{0, 1, 1, 2, \ldots\},$$

but the sequence of basis elements should be $\{1, 2, 3, 5, \ldots\}$, thus it should start with index 2.

Any integer B can be represented by a binary string of length $r - 1$, $c_r c_{r-1} \cdots c_2$, such that

$$B = \sum_{i=2}^{r} c_i F(i).$$

The representation will be unique if one uses the following procedure to produce it: given the integer B, find the largest Fibonacci number $F(r)$ smaller or equal to B; then continue recursively with $B - F(r)$. For example, $31 = 21 + 8 + 2$, so its binary Fibonacci representation would be 1010010. As a result of this encoding procedure, there are never consecutive Fibonacci numbers in any of these sums, implying that in the corresponding binary representation, there are no adjacent 1s.

This property can be exploited to devise an infinite code whose set of code words consists of the Fibonacci representations of the integers: to assure the code being UD, each code word is prefixed by a single 1-bit, which acts like a comma and permits to identify the boundaries between the code words. The first few elements of this code would thus be

$$\{u_1, u_2, \ldots\} = \{11, 110, 1100, 1101, 11000, 11001, \ldots\},$$

where the separating 1 is put in boldface for visibility. A typical compressed text could be 1**1**001110011011111101, which is easily parsed as $u_6 u_3 u_4 u_1 u_4$. Though being UD, this is not a prefix code, in fact, this is the code in the example in Figure 11.1(b). In particular, the first code word 11, which is the only one containing no zeros, complicates the decoding, because if a run of several such code words appears, the correct decoding of the code word preceding the run depends on the parity of the length of the run, as we have seen in eqs. (11.2) and (11.3).

To overcome this problem, the example in Figure 11.1(c) suggests to reverse all the code words, yielding the set

$$\{v_1, v_2, \ldots\} = \{11, 011, 0011, 1011, 00011, 10011, \ldots\},$$

which is a prefix code, since all code words are terminated by 11 and this substring does not appear anywhere in any code word, except at its suffix. This code is known as *Fibonacci code* and a sample of its code words appears in the last column of Table 11.2.

One of the advantages of a Fibonacci code is its robustness against errors. If a bit gets lost, or an erroneous bit is picked up, or some bit value is swapped, the error will not propagate as it might for other variable or even fixed length codes. For Fibonacci, at most three code words can be affected, and mostly only one or two. For example, if the emphasized, third bit of $v_3 v_1 v_2 = 00\mathbf{1}1\text{-}11\text{-}011$ is turned into a zero, the string would be interpreted as $00011\text{-}1011 = v_5 v_4$.

The length of a Fibonacci code word is related to the fact that $F(i) \simeq \phi^i / \sqrt{5}$, where $\phi = 1.618$ is the golden ratio, see eq. (5.9). It follows that the number of bits needed to represent an integer n using the Fibonacci code is $1.4404 \log_2 n$, similarly to the formula for the depth of an AVL tree we saw in eq. (5.2). The Fibonacci code word for n is thus about 44% longer than the minimal $\log_2 n$ bits needed for the standard binary representation using only the significant bits, but it is shorter than the $2 \log_2 n$ bits needed for the corresponding Elias γ code word. On the other hand, even though the number of bits is increased, the number of 1-bits is smaller on the average: while in a standard binary representation, about half of the bits are 1s, it can be shown that the probability of a 1-bit in the Fibonacci code words is only about $\frac{1}{2}\left(1 - \frac{1}{\sqrt{5}}\right) = 0.2764$, so even when multiplied by 1.44, this gives an expected number of only $0.398 \log_2 n$ 1-bits, rather than about $0.5 \log_2 n$. This property has many applications.

11.4 Error Correcting Codes

Our next topic considers a different application of codes: if the previous two sections focused on producing an encoding that is inexpensive in the number of necessary bits, we now concentrate rather on the correctness of the data. The assumption is that for some reason, the decoder might get an erroneous string, which is not identical to the one produced by the encoder. We still wish to be able to recover the original message, if possible. For simplicity, we assume that there is only a *single* wrong bit, which corresponds to a scenario of a so low probability p for an error, that the possibility of two or more errors might be neglected.

Often the knowledge about the occurrence of an error, rather than its exact location, is sufficient. This can be achieved by adjoining a single bit, often called *parity bit*, consisting of the XOR, or equivalently, the sum modulo 2, of the given n data bits. For example, if we wish to encode the number 1618, its 11-bit standard binary representation would be 11001010010, but we would add as the twelfth bit the XOR of these bits, which is 1, getting

$$1618 \quad \longrightarrow \quad 110010100101,$$

where the parity bit has been emphasized. To decode such an *Error detection code*, we again apply XOR, but on all the bits, including the parity bit. We should get 0. If not, one of the bits has been changed, possibly the parity bit itself. There is no way to know which one of the bits is in error, but the very fact that we know that some error has occurred is enough for the decoder to ask the encoder to resend the data.

11.4.1 A Sequence of Error Correcting Codes

A simple way to enable even correction, not only detection, is to transmit every bit three times. The original data can then be recovered, even if there is a single error, by using the majority rule for every bit-triple. But one can do better than adding $2n$ check-bits to n data bits.

Organize the n data bits into a square with side length $\sqrt{n}$ bits, and add a parity bit for each column and each row. A single error in any of the n data bits can then be located by intersecting the row and the column corresponding to the only affected parity bits. We thus got error correction at the price of additional $2\sqrt{n}$ bits.

A further step would then be to rearrange the data into a cube of side length $\sqrt[3]{n}$. Three vectors of parity bits are then needed, each of length $\sqrt[3]{n}$ and each corresponding to a partition of the cube into planes according to another dimension. Each parity bit will now be the XOR of one of the 2-dimensional planes, that is, of $\sqrt[3]{n^2}$ bits. A single error in one of the data bits will affect exactly three of the parity bits, and the location of the erroneous bit is at the intersection of

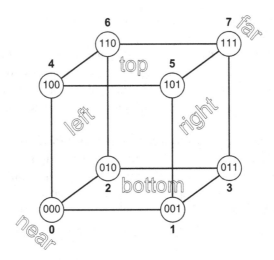

Figure 11.8. Layout of eight data bits in a three-dimensional hypercube with six parity bits.

the three corresponding planes. With such a layout, only $3\sqrt[3]{n}$ additional bits are needed.

For the general case, the data bits are arranged into a k-dimensional hyper-cube with side length $n^{1/k}$. The number of vectors of parity bits will be k, and each bit will be the xoring of all the data bits of a $(k-1)$-dimensional hyper-plane, all the bits of the same vector corresponding to the $n^{1/k}$ disjoint $(k-1)$-dimensional hyperplanes forming the original hypercube, and each of the k vectors corresponding to such a partition in a different dimension. The number of parity bits is $kn^{1/k}$. Figure 11.8 shows a 3-dimensional hypercube with side length 2, and its partition into two 2-dimensional planes in each of the three dimensions: left–right, near–far, top–bottom.

What value should be chosen for k? Note that this is almost an identical derivation to the one in Section 10.1, leading from a simple selection sort to heapsort. The same function $kn^{1/k}$ had to be optimized, and the solution was to use $k = \log_2 n$. This corresponds to a $\log_2 n$-dimensional cube of side length 2 bits, which is the smallest possible side length. The number of parity bits should thus be $2\log_2 n$.

Figure 11.8 is the hypercube corresponding to $n = 8$, each vertex corre-sponding to one of the n data bits and being labeled by the 3-bit binary rep-resentation of its index i, $0 \le i < 2^3$; vertices are connected by edges if and only if they correspond to numbers differing exactly by a single bit in their binary representations.

For the parity bits, the left–right dimension corresponds to the first (right-most) bit in the binary representation, that is, left is the xoring of all the data bits having a 0 in the first bit of the binary representation of their index, and right is the xoring of the complementing set of those with 1 in the first bit. Similarly, the near–far dimension corresponds to the second bit, so near is the xoring of the bits indexed 0, 1, 4, and 5 (0 in the second bit), and far is the xoring of the complementing set. Finally, the top–bottom dimension corresponds to the third (leftmost) bit. Summarizing, each of the $2 \log_2 n = 6$ parity bits is obtained by xoring a subset of $\frac{n}{2}$ bits, as follows:

left	0,2,4,6	right	1,3,5,7
near	0,1,4,5	far	2,3,6,7
bottom	0,1,2,3	top	4,5,6,7.

Here is an example of how the parity bits can be used to correct a single error. Suppose the data bit indexed 6 is flipped. This will have an effect on all the parity bits that include 6 in their lists: left, far, and top. Rearranging the bits from left to right and reconverting to the corresponding 0 and 1 values, one gets: top, far, left = 110, which is the binary representation of 6, the index of the wrong bit.

If the side of the hypercube is longer than 2 bits, we need to know the index of the projection of the erroneous bit on each of the dimensions. But if the side length is just 2, we are left with a binary choice, as the possible indices in each dimension are just 0 or 1. Therefore, it suffices to keep only the parity bits corresponding to 1 values, that is right, far, and top. This corresponds to indicating only the 1-bits of the index of the wrong bit, which is enough to recover it, unless its index is 0 and thus has no 1-bits. In addition, one also needs to deal with the case in which no error has occurred. To solve both problems, one might reduce the set of data bits and index them only by the nonzero values. This method of adding $\log_2 n$ parity bits defined according to the binary representation of the indices of the n data bits is known as *Hamming code*. R. Hamming also suggested to store the parity bits interleaved with the data bits at the positions whose indices are powers of 2.

11.4.2 Hamming Code

Here is a more standard definition of the Hamming code. Given are $n = 2^m - 1$ bits of data, for some $m \geq 2$. According to Hamming's scheme, they are indexed from 1 to n, and the bits at positions with indices that are powers of 2 serve as parity bits, so that in fact only $n - m$ bits carry data. The ith parity bit, which will be stored at position 2^{i-1} for $i = 1, 2, \ldots, m$, will be set so that the

XOR of some selected bits will be zero. For the parity bit at 2^{i-1}, the selected bits are those whose indices, when written in standard binary notation, have a 1-bit in their ith bit from the right. That is, the parity bit stored in position $2^0 = 1$ is the XOR of the bits in positions $3, 5, 7, \ldots$, the parity bit stored in position $2^1 = 2$ is the XOR of the bits in positions $3, 6, 7, 10, 11, \ldots$, and so on.

An easy way to remember this procedure is by adding a fictitious first 0-bit, indexed 0, and then scanning the resulting binary string as follows. To get the first parity bit, the one stored in position $2^0 = 1$, compute the XOR of the sequence of bits obtained by repeatedly skipping one bit and taking one bit. This effectively considers all the bits with odd indices (the first of which, with index 1, is the parity bit itself). In general, to get the second, third,. . ., ith parity bit, the one stored in position 2^{i-1}, for $i = 1, 2, \ldots, m$, compute the XOR of the sequence of bits obtained by repeatedly skipping 2^{i-1} bits and taking 2^{i-1} bits.

Continuing our earlier example, consider $n = 15 = 2^4 - 1$ bits, of which only $15 - 4 = 11$ contain data, and assume the data is the standard 11-bit binary representation of 1618, namely 11001010010. This will first be stored as a string in which the bit positions indexed by powers of 2 are set to 0 and the 11 information bits are filled, from left to right, in the remaining positions. Adding the 0-bit at position 0 yields

$$_0\mathbf{0}\,0\,1\,\mathbf{0}\,1\,0\,0\,\mathbf{0}\,1\,0\,1\,0\,0\,1\,0, \qquad (11.6)$$

where the zeros in the positions reserved for the parity bits have been emphasized, and the leftmost 0 is smaller to recall that this bit does not carry information. The parity bits in positions 1, 2, 4 and 8 are then calculated, in order, by XORing the underlined bits in the following lines:

$$_0\underline{0}\,0\,1\,\underline{0}\,1\,0\,\underline{0}\,0\,1\,\underline{0}\,1\,\underline{0}\,0\,1\,\underline{0}\,,$$

$$_0\,0\,\underline{0}\,1\,0\,1\,\underline{0}\,0\,0\,1\,0\,\underline{1}\,0\,\underline{0}\,1\,\underline{0}\,,$$

$$_0\,0\,0\,1\,\underline{0}\,1\,0\,0\,0\,1\,0\,1\,0\,\underline{0}\,1\,0\,,$$

$$_0\,0\,0\,1\,0\,1\,0\,0\,\underline{0}\,1\,0\,1\,0\,0\,1\,0\,,$$

which yields, respectively, the bits 0, 1, 0, 1. The final Hamming code word is therefore

$$_0\mathbf{0}\,1\,1\,\mathbf{0}\,1\,0\,0\,1\,1\,0\,1\,0\,0\,1\,0. \qquad (11.7)$$

Figure 11.9 is an example of how the Hamming code is able to recover from a single bit-flip. Suppose the data is the 11-bit representation of 1618, as given, with the 4 parity bits, in eq. (11.7), and suppose there is an error at bit

	0	1	2	3	4	5	6	7	8	9	10	11	12	13	14	15		
index	0	0	1	1	0	1	0	0	1	1	0	1	0	**1**	1	0	number	bit
1																	5	**1**
2																	4	**0**
4																	3	**1**
8																	5	**1**

Figure 11.9. Example of correcting a single bit error in position 13.

position 13, that is, the 0-bit there has turned into a 1-bit. The bits appear in the upper line of the body of the table, while the indices appear in the header line. The leftmost column is the index of the given parity bit, and for each of these, the underlined bits are those taken into account when calculating the parity bit. The column headed number gives the number of 1-bits in the set of underlined bits, and the last column is their parity (1 if odd, 0 if even).

The bits in the last column, read bottom up to correspond to the bits indexed 8421, are 1101, which is the standard binary representation of the number 13, the index of the error. We thus know that this bit is wrong, can correct it, and end up with the original data, as requested. If there is no error, all the calculated parity bits would be 0, yielding 0000 in the last column – an indication that the correct data has been received.

11.5 Cryptographic Codes

Cryptography is a fascinating field of research and has undergone radical changes in the past few decades. It is beyond the scope of this book, and we shall just give very simple and historical examples to show the existence of cryptographic codes. It should be mentioned that many of the modern cryptographic methods are based on advanced mathematical tools, and in particular on prime numbers, which we have seen in Chapter 7 in the context of hashing. The relevant prime numbers are huge, using hundreds of bits, like, for example, $2^{393} - 93$, for which sophisticated programs are needed to even know that they are really prime.

Methods for encoding information so that its true content can be understood only by an intended partner, but remains hidden to any occasional or malicious eavesdropper, have been used for thousands of years. Their usefulness and even necessity are obvious, not only to keep military secrets, but modern life, and in particular commerce and banking related transactions we wish to perform from our wireless phones, would be jeopardized if it were not possible to keep the data confidential.

The general paradigm is to be given two complementing encoding and decoding functions $\mathcal{E}$ and $\mathcal{D}$, both depending on some key K that is supposed to be kept secret. A message M, called the *cleartext* in the particular jargon of the cryptographers, is encrypted by applying

$$C = \mathcal{E}_K(M),$$

thereby producing the *ciphertext C*, which, in itself, should look like some random bunch of symbols and, at least apparently, not convey any information. Nonetheless, whoever is in possession of the secret key K may apply the inverse function for decoding, and get

$$\mathcal{D}_K(C) = \mathcal{D}_K(\mathcal{E}_K(M)) = M,$$

that is, reproduce the original message M.

The challenge is to find appropriate pairs of functions $\mathcal{E}$ and $\mathcal{D}$. Modern cryptography even considers *public key* encryption, in which the encoding function $\mathcal{E}$ is not hidden, but known to everybody, and yet its corresponding inverse function $\mathcal{D}$ can only be derived by somebody who knows the secret key K. These keys are chosen long enough, say of 1000 bits, so that an attempt to try all the possible variants, 2^{1000} in our example, may safely be ruled out.

Before the advent of the modern methods, that are often based on the difficulty to solve certain computationally hard problems, the encoding and decoding functions were much simpler. One of the oldest examples is a so-called *Caesar's code*: indexing the alphabet $\{A, B, C, \ldots, Z\}$ by $\{0, 1, 2, \ldots, 25\}$, the secret key K is just one of these numbers, and

$$\mathcal{E}_K(x) = (x + K) \bmod 26,$$

that is, in the encoding, each character is shifted cyclically K positions forward in the alphabet. For example, if $K = 5$ is chosen, then the encoding of the cleartext

SECRETKEY

would be the ciphertext

XJHWJYPJD.   (11.8)

If it is known that a Caesar's code is used, an enemy could try all the possible shifts, since there are only 26 possibilities, until a reasonable cleartext is obtained. Moreover, the enemy would then not only know the specific message at hand, but also the key K, which enables the decoding also of subsequent text enciphered in the same way. This action of revealing or guessing the secret key is called *breaking* the code, and it is one of the objectives of the enemy.

Caesar's code is a particular case of a more general class called a *substitution cipher*, in which a permutation of the alphabet is given, and each character is replaced by the one with the same index in this permutation. In this case, the secret key is the used permutation or its index, and it cannot be found by exhaustive search, since the number of possibilities is $26! \simeq 4 \cdot 10^{26}$. Nevertheless, a substitution cipher is not really secure, because if a long enough text is given, one could analyze the frequency patterns of the occurrences of the characters, and compare it with the known probabilities in the given language. For example, even for a short text like that displayed in eq. (11.8), the most frequent character is J, which we would guess to be a substitute for the most frequent character in English, which is E.

The idea of Caesar's code has been taken one step further by B. Vigenère, who suggested using a different shift for every character of the text, according to the key K which is now chosen as some secret string. So if the secret key is SECRETKEY, the first nine characters will be shifted cyclically by 18, 4, 2, 17, 4, 19, 10, 4, and 24 positions, respectively. The shifts for the subsequent characters of the cleartext are obtained by repeating this sequence as often as necessary. In the resulting ciphertext, the same letter can represent different cleartext characters, depending on their position, so that a frequency analysis is not possible. However, other attempts to break the code may be successful in what is called a *cryptographic attack*.

An example of encoding using a Vigenère cipher is given in Table 11.3. The chosen cleartext encodes the fact that we are at the end of this book. In the spirit of enciphering the information, let us first translate this idea into French, using the string

C'est fini.

It is common practice to translate everything to upper case and to remove blanks and punctuation signs. We then have to choose a key K. This is very similar to an almost daily request we are confronted with, namely of choosing a *password* for the numerous applications on our computers and cellular phones. Most of these passwords are somehow related to our names, birth dates or telephone numbers, which is why hackers can so easily break into our digital accounts. Many applications therefore urge us to use "stronger" passwords, and often even suggest some randomly generated ones, which, in principle, are impossible to guess. So let us use here also such a random string, for example, RKAOGWOS. The resulting ciphertext appears in the last line of the table, and should be void of any meaning (is it?).

Table 11.3. *Example of a Vigenère encoding*

Cleartext	C	E	S	T	F	I	N	I
Secret key	R	K	A	O	G	W	O	S
Ciphertext	T	O	S	H	L	E	B	A

Exercises

11.1 For each of the codes Elias-γ, Elias-δ, and Fibonacci,

(a) derive a formula for the number n_j of code words of length j, for all possible values of j;

(b) use n_j to prove that the codes are complete by showing that

$$\sum_{i=1}^{\infty} 2^{-\ell_i} = \sum_{j=1}^{\infty} n_j 2^{-j} = 1,$$

where ℓ_i is the length in bits of the ith code word, as used in eq. (11.1).

11.2 Show that the average code word length L for a Huffman code built for the set of probabilities $\{p_1, p_2, \ldots, p_n\}$ satisfies

$$H \leq L \leq H + 1,$$

where $H = -\sum_{i=1}^{n} p_i \log_2 p_i$ is the entropy as defined in Section 11.2.2.

11.3 In a prefix code no code word is the prefix of any other, and one could similarly define a suffix code in which no code word is the suffix of any other. The set of reversed code words of any prefix code is thus a suffix code. A code that has both the prefix and the suffix properties is called an *affix* code, in particular, every fixed length code is an affix code.

(a) Give an example of a variable length affix code. Note that it might not be possible to find an affix code if the alphabet is too small. **Hint:** Try a code with nine code words.

(b) Show that the number of different variable length affix codes is infinite.

(c) Affix codes are called *never-self-synchronizing* codes. Show why.

11.4 Suppose that instead of using a binary alphabet $\{0, 1\}$ to encode a message, one could use some alphabet $\{\alpha_1, \alpha_2, \ldots, \alpha_r\}$ with r symbols, for $r > 2$.

(a) Extend Huffman's algorithm to produce an optimal r-ary code for a given set of probabilities $\{p_1, p_2, \ldots, p_n\}$, by working with r-ary trees in which every node can have up to r children.

(b) Consider the following algorithm. Given a set of probabilities $\{p_1, p_2, \ldots, p_n\}$, produce first an optimal 4-ary code, then replace, in each code word, the four symbols $\{\alpha_1, \ldots, \alpha_4\}$ by $\{00, 01, 10, 11\}$, respectively. Show that the resulting binary code is not always optimal, and formulate a condition on the distribution for which this algorithm does produce an optimal code.

11.5 Show how, by the addition of a single bit, one can turn a Hamming code from an error-correcting code for a single error into a code capable to correct a single error and to detect a double error.

11.6 What is the shape of the Huffman tree if the weights of the characters are the first n nonzero Fibonacci numbers $1, 1, 2, \ldots, F(n)$?

11.7 This extends exercise 4.4 of the chapter on trees. Given are n ordered integer sequences $A_1, \ldots, A_n$, of lengths $\ell_1, \ldots, \ell_n$, respectively. We wish to merge all the sequences into a single ordered sequence, but without constraints on adjacency, so that at each stage, any pair of sequences may be merged. The number of steps needed to merge a elements with b elements is $a + b$. Find an optimal way to merge the n sets, that is, such that the number of comparisons is minimized.

Appendix

Solutions to Selected Exercises

1.2

j	1	2	3	4	5	6	7	8	9	10	11
$S[j]$	A	B	R	A	C	A	D	A	B	R	A
$\Delta_2[j]$	17	16	15	14	13	12	11	13	12	4	1

j	1	2	3	4	5	6	7	8	9	10	11	12
$S[j]$	A	A	B	A	A	A	B	A	A	B	A	A
$\Delta_2[j]$	18	17	16	15	14	13	8	14	13	8	2	2

1.3 The last k entries of the Δ_2 array of S all contain the value k.

1.4 Text: AAAAAAAAABBC, Pattern: BCBCBC

1.6 Define an array B and store in $B[i]$ the sum of the first i elements of A. Formally: $B[0] = 0$, and

$$B[i] = B[i-1] + A[i] \qquad \text{for } 1 \le i \le n.$$

Each element of the array B can thus be evaluated in $O(1)$, and we have

$$sum(i, j) = B[j] - B[i-1].$$

1.7

	V_1	V_2	V_3	V_4
A_1	yes	no	yes	yes
A_2	no	yes	no	no
A_3	no	no	no	no
A_4	no	no	no	no

2.1 The idea is to scan the list with two pointers, one advancing at twice or three times the pace of the other. Formally:

```
p ← head     q ← head
while next(q) ≠ NIL
    p ← next(p)
    q ← next(next(next(p)))
q ← p
while next(q) ≠ NIL
    print value(p)
    p ← next(p)
    q ← next(next(p))
```

Using the same technique, there is a cycle in the list if and only if p and q will point to the same element in some iteration.

2.3(a) Use binary search.
   (b) Use, alternatingly, one step of binary search, and one step of a linear search from the beginning of the array.
   (c) Search from the beginning in exponentially increasing steps, that is, check at indices $1, 2, 4, \ldots, 2^i$ until an index i is found for which $A[2^i]$ is positive but $A[\min(n, 2^{i+1})]$ is negative. Then use binary search on the range $[2^i, \min(n, 2^{i+1})]$.

2.4 The parking lot is in fact a stack. If the input order is 1, 3, 2, this cannot be rectified by the use of a stack. Indeed, the cars 3 and 2 have to enter the stack, since car 1 has to be the first to get on the highway. But then car 3 will precede car 2.

2.8(b) $f(n) = 2^{\sqrt{\log n}}$
   (c) $T(n) = \log^* n$ (see Section 8.2.3).

3.1 The following figure gives a counter example. There are two paths from s to t in the graph G: the upper path has weight 10, and the lower path weight 11. Adding 10 to the weight of each edge yields the graph G' on the right side. Now it is the lower path that has the smaller weight. The shortest paths are emphasized. The reason for the failure of this procedure is that not all the paths consist of the same number of edges, so adding a constant weight to each edge does not have the same effect on all the paths. For instance, the total weight of the upper path was increased by 30, and that of the lower path only by 20.

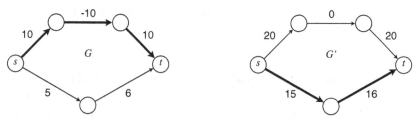

Counterexample for Exercise 3.1.

3.2 (a) Set the weight of all edges touching vertex T to infinity.

(b) Let ε be the smallest difference between different weights (if all weights are integers, then $\varepsilon = 1$), and decrease the weights of all the edges corresponding to airline X by $\frac{\varepsilon}{n}$, where n is the number of vertices. There are at most $n - 1$ edges in a path, so the choice of the shortest paths is not affected by this amendment, but it gives priority to the edges with reduced weights.

(c) Give the same weight to all edges.

(d) There is an edge (fr_a, to_a) with weight 0 for every flight a, where fr_a and to_a are vertices corresponding to airports. For each airport, there is an edge (to_a, fr_b) from every incoming flight a to every outgoing flight b. If a and b are operated by the same airline, the weight of the edge is 0, otherwise 1.

(e) Use the same graph as in point (d), but change the weight of the edge (fr_a, to_a) to the length of the flight a, and the weight of (to_a, fr_a) to the waiting time at the airport for the connection between a and b.

3.3 Let $\mathcal{P}$ be the set of all the paths from s to t. We wish to maximize the probability of getting from s to t without corruption, that is, find

$$\max_{Q \in \mathcal{P}} \prod_{(a,b) \in Q} p(a, b).$$

Applying log and multiplying by -1, this maximization is equivalent to finding

$$\min_{Q \in \mathcal{P}} \sum_{(a,b) \in Q} - \log p(a, b).$$

Therefore, change the weight of the edge (a, b) to $- \log p(a, b)$; now the problem can be solved by applying algorithm A.

3.4 Define a graph $G = (V, E)$. The vertices correspond to countries, and there is an edge $(x, y) \in E$ if and only if x and y have a common border. The problem is to find a color assignment to the vertices, that is, a function $f : V \to \{1, 2, \ldots, k\}$, such that

$$(x, y) \in E \ \to \ f(x) \neq f(y).$$

It should be noted that while every map can thus be transformed into a graph, it is not true that every graph corresponds to a map. The subset of graphs corresponding to maps is called *planar graphs*. Such graphs can be drawn in a way that avoids the crossing of edges. For example, the full graph with four vertices is planar, but the full graph with five vertices is not. The four-color problem relates to planar graphs. For nonplanar graphs, the question whether the vertices can be colored by four colors is apparently also very difficult.

4.2 The following figure displays the only binary tree with the given traversals.

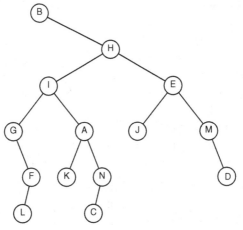

Tree with in-order traversal B G L F I K A C N H J E M D and post-order traversal L F G K C N A I J D M E H B.

It is not always possible to determine the tree on the basis of its **pre-order** and **post-order** traversals alone. The two trees in the following figure have both **A B** as **pre-order** and **B A** as **post-order** traversal.

4.5 Use in-order traversals of the trees to get the ordered lists of their elements. Then merge the lists and store the merged list, in order, in an array A at positions $A[1]$ to $A[m-1]$, where $m = 2^n = k + \ell + 1$. The full binary search tree storing the merged list has value $A[\frac{m}{2}]$ as its root, the two children of the root hold the elements with indices $\frac{m}{4}$ and $\frac{3m}{4}$, and in general, the 2^i elements on level i, for $i = 0, 1, \ldots, n-1$, are those with indices

$$2^{n-1-i} + j\, 2^{n-i} \qquad \text{for } 0 \le j < 2^i.$$

5.2 Note that we need a lower bound for $N(k)$:

$$N(k) = N(k-1) + N(k-2) + 1$$
$$> 2N(k-2) > 4N(k-4) > \cdots > 2^i N(k-2i)$$
$$= 2^{k/2} = \sqrt{2}^k = 1.414^k.$$

5.6 (a) $\binom{F_i}{F_{i-1}} = A^{i-1} \binom{F_1}{F_0}$.

  (b) $A^{16} = \left(A^8\right)^2$.

  (c) $A^8 = \left((A^2)^2\right)^2$.

  (d) $A^5 = A^4 \times A$. $A^{12} = A^8 \times A^4$. For general k, write k in its standard binary representation as a sum of powers of 2.

  (e) If k is a power of 2, one can evaluate A^k in $\log k$ steps. This is called *repeated squaring*. For general k, one first prepares $B[i] = A^{2^i}$ for $0 \le i < \log k$, using $B[i] = (B[i-1])^2$, and then multiplies the elements $B[i]$ with indices corresponding to the positions of the 1-bits in the binary representation of k, overall $O(\log k)$.

5.7 One such tree is given in the following figure. It is a minimal AVL tree of depth 4. Deleting the black node requires 2 rotations. In general, deleting one of the leaves of a minimal AVL tree of depth $k+2$ may lead to k rotations.

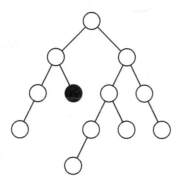

Minimal AVL tree requiring two rotations for deleting the black node.

6.1 (a) No. The insertion may imply a node split, but the deletion does not necessarily then imply a fusion: it might be possible to do a balancing step with the other sibling node (not the one created by the split, since it is also only about half filled).

   (b) No again. An element *x* which is not in one of the leaf nodes is replaced by its successor. Re-inserting *x* will place it in a leaf, and it might remain there if there are no splits.

6.2 First extract the maximal element of *A* or the minimal element of *B* and call it *s*; it will serve as a separator. Denote the root nodes by R_A and R_B, respectively.

   If *A* and *B* have the same height *h*, create a new root *R* containing only *s*, and let R_A and R_B be the children of *R*. Perform a balancing step with *R*, R_A and R_B (which, depending on the number of elements in the nodes, may lead to merging the 3 nodes into one new root).

   If the height *h′* of *B* is less than *h*, let *D* be the rightmost node of *A* on level *h* − *h′*, and let *E* be the parent node of *D*. Insert *s* as the rightmost element in *E* and add R_B as the rightmost child of *E*. Now perform a balancing step with *E*, *D* and R_B; this may involve adding elements to R_B, or splitting *E*, which in turn may trigger more updates.

6.3 (a)

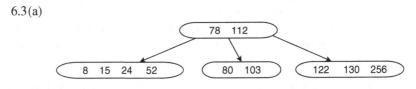

   (b)

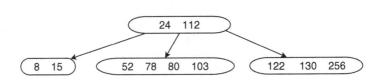

   (c)

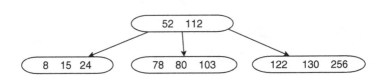

(d)

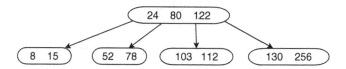

(e) If the order of the tree is 4, the deletion of 40 does not trigger any change in the structure, since the number of elements in a node should then be between 1 and 3.

7.1 (a) The depths of both A and B are $k - 1$.

(b) The depth of C will be k.

(c) Extract the last element of B (rightmost on lowest level) and call it x. Create a new binary tree with x as root and A and B as subtrees. Apply heapify on x. Complexity $O(k) = O(\log m)$.

7.2 (a) Correctness does not change, the $n/2$ first iterations are just redundant, so it is less efficient.

(b) Does not work. Counterexample: a vector with elements 5, 4, 3, 7.

7.4 (a) The search-min-heap is:

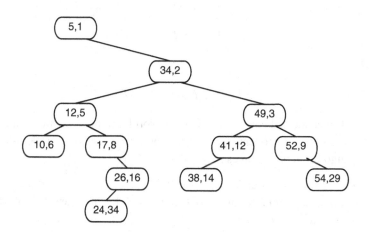

The search-max-heap is:

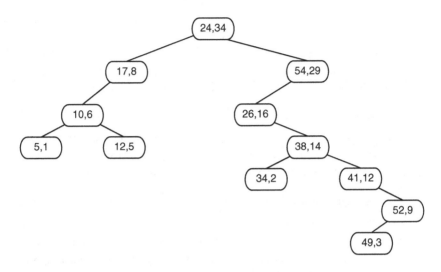

(b) and (c) For the search-min-heap: find the element (s_0, h_0) with minimal h-value and make it the root of the tree. Partition the rest of the set into L, those having smaller s values than s_0, and R, those with larger s values than s_0. These will be the left and right subtrees, which are constructed recursively.

8.2 Interestingly, the bound will still be logarithmic.

8.3(a) Sorting the edges, $E \log E$, applying BFS or DFS on a graph with at most V edges in each of the E iteration, for a total of

$$E \log E + EV = O(EV).$$

(b)

$$E \log E + E \log V = O(E \log E).$$

(c) The connected components in the Union-Find forest are trees and are the same components (contain the same nodes) as those in Kruskal's algorithm, but the trees may differ.

9.1 $h(X) = X \bmod 9$. Let $X = \sum_{i=0}^{r} d_i 10^i$, so that $d_r d_{r-1} \cdots d_2 d_1 d_0$ is the decimal representation of X. But $h(10^i) = 1$ for all i, and we get that $h(X) = h(\sum_{i=0}^{r} d_i 10^i) = h(\sum_{i=0}^{r} d_i)$ is just the sum of the digits.

9.4 No. The probability of choosing x in $[0, \frac{1}{2})$ is $\frac{1}{2}$, but then $x^2 \in [0, \frac{1}{4})$, so the lower quarter of the table has a higher chance of being chosen. The distribution is therefore not uniform, so the function is not suitable as a hash function.

10.1 Denote the elements by A, B, C, D, E. Compare A with B and C with D. Without loss of generality, $A > B$ and $C > D$. Compare A and C and assume $A > C$. Insert E into the sorted list $A > C > D$, using binary search. That is, compare E to C, and if it is smaller, compare with A, otherwise, compare with D. This takes 2 comparisons. This yields one of 4 possible orderings: $EACD, AECD, ACED$, or $ACDE$. We know already that B is smaller than A, so the sort is completed by inserting B in the correct place to the right of A for any of the preceding four orderings. That is, B has to be inserted into CD, ECD, CED, or CDE. This can again be done in two comparisons by binary search.

10.2 (a) Each weighing has three possible outcomes, the number of possible answers is 24 (12 balls times 2 possible choices for each), so the lower bound of comparisons is $\ell = \lceil \log_3 24 \rceil = 3$.

(b) (1) Compare 4 against 4 balls. (1a) If they are equal, we know that the different ball is in the remaining 4. (2) Compare 3 of the remaining with 3 good balls. (2a) If they are not equal we know already if the different ball is lighter or heavier, so (3) we choose 2 of them and compare them 1 to 1. (3a) If they are equal, the different ball is the remaining one, otherwise (3b) we see which one is the different one. (2b) If the second comparison gave equality, the different ball is the only one left out. So we use (3) one test to see if it is lighter or heavier.

(1b) If in the first comparison we got inequality, we know that the remaining 4 balls are good. Denote the 12 balls as 0000, LLLL, HHHH, according to whether we know if they are good, or possibly light or possibly heavy. (2) The second weighing will be LLLH against 000L, leaving HHH0 aside. (2a) If there is equality, the different ball is among HHH0, so it must be one of the HHH and it must be heavy. (3) Test H against H to find the different one, as earlier. (2b) If LLLH is lighter than 000L, the different ball is one of the 3 L balls on the left, so we need only one more test to find which. (2c) If LLLH is heavier than 000L, either the H on the left is heavier, or the L on the right is lighter. Compare one of them against a 0 ball.

(c) $\ell = \lceil \log_3 26 \rceil = 3$.

(d) If we start by weighing at most 4 against 4 and have equality, we are left with at least 5 balls, and thus 10 possibilities, which cannot be resolved in 2 weighings that have only 9 possible outcomes. If we start by weighing at least 5 against 5 and get inequality, we also have at least 10 possibilities.

10.3 Suppose the probability for getting an input that is already sorted is $1 - \frac{1}{n \log n}$. Then it is worth checking whether the input is sorted by a linear scan, and otherwise apply some other sort (e.g., mergesort). The expected complexity is then

$$\left(1 - \frac{1}{n \log n}\right) O(n) + \frac{1}{n \log n} O(n \log n) = O(n).$$

10.5 If a search tree can be built in less than order of $n \log n$, and in-order traversal of the tree, which can be performed in $O(n)$, would give the elements in sorted order in time less than $n \log n + n$, contradicting the lower bound $\Omega(n \log n)$ for comparison based sorting.

10.6 If $K = 2^m$, find the median and partition into two sets by comparing to the median, in time cn, for some constant $c > 1$. Then do the same for each half, in time $c\frac{n}{2} + c\frac{n}{2} = cn$ again. Then repeat for each quarter, etc., in $\log K$ iterations of $O(n)$ each.

If K is not a power of 2, let $L = 2^{\lceil \log K \rceil}$ be the next highest power of 2. Add $\left(\frac{L-K}{K}\right)n$ dummy elements of value ∞. Partitioning the $n + \left(\frac{L-K}{K}\right)n = \left(\frac{L}{K}\right)n$ elements into L subsets of equal size $\frac{n}{K}$ effectively partitions the n real elements into K subsets of equal size.

10.7 The recurrence for $T(n)$ would then be

$$T(n) \leq T\left(\frac{n}{2}\right) + T\left(\frac{3}{4}n\right) + cn$$

instead of eq. (10.17). This is the case $\alpha_1 + \alpha_2 = \frac{1}{2} + \frac{3}{4} > 1$, so $T(n)$ would not be linear in n.

11.1(a) For the Fibonacci code, the number n_j of code words of length j is $F(j-1)$, for $j \geq 2$.

(b) Denote the sum $\sum_{j=2}^{\infty} n_j 2^{-j} = \sum_{j=2}^{\infty} F(j-1)2^{-j}$ by A. We the can derive the following equation:

$$A = F(1)2^{-2} + \sum_{j=3}^{\infty} F(j-1)2^{-j}$$

$$= \frac{1}{4} + \sum_{j=3}^{\infty} \left(F(j-2) + F(j-3)\right)2^{-j}$$

$$= \frac{1}{4} + \sum_{j=2}^{\infty} \frac{1}{2}F(j-1)2^{-j} + \sum_{j=1}^{\infty} \frac{1}{4}F(j-1)2^{-j}$$

$$= \frac{1}{4} + \frac{1}{2}A + \frac{1}{4}A,$$

which implies $A = 1$.

11.3 (a) 10, 111, 011, 001, 000, 1101, 1100, 0101, 0100.

(b) The example shows that at least one such code exists. Let us show that for every given affix code, there is another affix code with a larger number of code words. Let $A = \{a_1, \ldots, a_n\}$ be an affix code. Consider the set $B = \{b_1, \ldots, b_{2n}\}$ defined by $b_{2i} = a_i 0, b_{2i-1} = a_i 1$ for $1 \leq i \leq n$. B is an affix code with a code word set twice as large as A.

11.5 Add the XOR of all the bits as additional parity bit X. Denote the vector of Hamming parity bits by B. If $X = 0$ and $B = 0$, then there is no error. If $X = 0$ and $B \neq 0$, there is a double error, which cannot be corrected. If $X = 1$, then there is a single error at address B.

11.7 The number of comparisons to merge the n sets is $\sum_{i=1}^{n} n_i \ell_i$, where n_i is the number of times the sequence A_i participates in a merge. This is exactly the same minimization problem as Huffman's. The optimal solution is therefore to repeatedly merge the two shortest sequences.

Index

Printed in the United States
by Baker & Taylor Publisher Services